A National Geogr

THE STORY OF AMERICA

...aphic Picture Atlas

By John Anthony Scott

Published by
The National
Geographic Society

Gilbert M. Grosvenor
President

Melvin M. Payne
Chairman of the Board

Owen R. Anderson
*Executive
Vice President*

Robert L. Breeden
*Vice President,
Publications and
Educational Media*

Prepared by
National Geographic
Book Service

Charles O. Hyman
Director

Ross S. Bennett
Managing Editor

Staff for this book

Elizabeth L. Newhouse
Editor

David M. Seager
Art Director

Linda B. Meyerriecks
Picture Editor

Anne Elizabeth Withers
Chief Researcher

Thomas K. Hamburger
Edward Lanouette
Paul Mathless
David F. Robinson
Shirley L. Scott
Editor-Writers

Margaret Sedeen
Consulting Editor

Jennifer G. Ackerman
Paulette L. Claus
Mariana Tait Durbin
Melanie A. Patt-Corner
Penelope A. Timbers
L. Madison Washburn
Jayne Wise
Editorial Researchers

Greta Arnold
Illustrations Research

Andrew J. Swithinbank
Map Coordinator

Charlotte Golin
Design Assistant

Diana E. McFadden
Jane S. Offen
Illustrations Assistants

John Frith
Production Manager

Karen F. Edwards
Richard S. Wain
*Assistant Production
Managers*

Georgina L. McCormack
Teresita Cóquia Sison
Editorial Assistants

John T. Dunn
Ronald E. Williamson
Engraving and Printing

Richard L. Watson, Jr.
Duke University
Chief Consultant

Judith M. Hobart
Educational Consultant

Biographies by
Thomas B. Allen
Jean Fritz
Lillie G. Patterson

Maps by
John D. Garst, Jr.
Judith Bell Siegel
Gary M. Johnson
Peter J. Balch
Susan M. Johnston
John G. Leocha
Robert W. Northrop
Hildegard G. Schantz
Mark Seidler

Paintings by
John Berkey
Tony Chen
Michael A. Hampshire
Vladimir Kordic
Wayne McLoughlin
Patricia A. Topper

*Cover and chapter
titles by*
Gerard Huerta

Contributions by
William P. Beaman
Deborah Berger
LaVerle Berry
Judith Gersten
Caroline Hottenstein
Kathleen M. Kiely
Anne Leighton
Robert Menaker
Amanda Parsons
Marguerite Suarez
Elizabeth C. Wagner

Teresa S. Purvis
Charles M. Israel
Index

490 illustrations
First edition: 225,000 copies

Library of Congress
CIP data page 324

Bicentennial celebration, Washington, D. C., July 4, 1976

Contents

Foreword

By Alistair Cooke

The Statue of Liberty

A German philosopher once wrote, "History is something that never happened, written by a man who wasn't there." A lot of famous people have held an equally low opinion of history, mainly, I think, because it often doesn't support their pet theories and political prejudices. But history is not a theory or a political platform. Studying it is a continuous attempt to find out what happened, how, and why.

There used to be a law professor at Columbia University who was well known for his course on "Evidence." One day, while he was lecturing to a class of new students, three people—two men and a woman—dashed into the classroom. One of them fired a gun at the ceiling. The three of them then rushed from the room.

As you might guess, the class was in an uproar until the professor quieted them. He then revealed that he had arranged the whole incident. "Imagine yourselves," he said, "in a court of law. You are called on as a witness. You must tell exactly what you saw."

He called on a dozen students whose versions of the incident were wildly different. Some said there had been two women and one man. Some said there were three men, that two people had fired guns, that there had been three shots or four. Some said the shots had been fired at the professor or at the windows. And so on. This lively incident was meant to teach the students not to trust too much the testimony of eyewitnesses.

In one of the most famous incidents in American history, scores of bystanders dictated to lawyers what they swore had happened on a snowy March day in 1770, when the Boston Customs House was guarded by a single British sentry. Somehow, a gun went off. The onlookers panicked. More soldiers came running, and some people were killed. The incident became known as the Boston Massacre. A highly imaginative engraving of the incident, made by a man who had not been there, provoked indignation from Massachusetts to South Carolina. And the Revolutionary War was not far off. You might like to look sometime at some of these eyewitness accounts and guess what the outcome might have been if a different story of the incident had been circulated.

To me, the main fascination of history is the fun of playing detective. Nobody has ever defined the historian's job better than an old Greek, Polybius, who wrote, more than 2,000 years ago, "It is natural for a good man to love his country and his friends, and to hate the enemies of both. But when he writes history he must abandon such feelings and be prepared to praise enemies who deserve it and to censure the dearest and most intimate friends."

As an amateur historian for more than 50 years, let me tell you that history is a very exciting hobby.

Nomads, Explorers, and Settlers

Beginnings to 1630

eople have been living on earth for a long time—hundreds of thousands of years—but they have lived in the Western Hemisphere only a short time. The first immigrants arrived in North America from Asia as long ago as 40,000 years—during the last Ice Age, when glaciers blanketed much of the Northern Hemisphere.

As glaciers formed on land, ocean levels dropped, uncovering part of the ocean floor. The dry land eventually formed a grassy, treeless plain connecting Alaska and Siberia. The lush grasses of this plain lured animals: caribou, giant bison, woolly mammoth. The animals lured humans.

We call these first immigrants to America Paleo-Indians. They traveled in family bands and spent their lives as nomads, or wanderers, in search of prey. They followed the animals they needed to live. Meat and bone marrow provided most of their nourishment. Animal skins and furs protected them from cold. They chipped their tools and weapons from stone or carved them from bone.

A notched caribou leg bone unearthed in the Canadian Yukon may be evidence of these first Americans. Archaeologists think the bone was used 27,000 years ago to scrape animal hide. By studying prehistoric sites in Colorado and New Mexico and the hunting methods of primitive tribes, archaeologists have been able to put together the following picture of a hunt 12,000 years ago.

For big hunts, family bands of Paleo-Indians united and chose a skilled chief. Imagine such a group moving silently through the woods toward a herd of bison grazing on a winter prairie. At a signal from their leader, the group runs toward the bison from three sides, waving skins and shouting. They chase the herd to a snowy streambed banked with steep, icy slopes the hunters had packed and smoothed in advance. The terrified bison pile into each other as they slide into the slippery trap. They bellow in pain and fear as a score of waiting men attack with spears. The hunt chief, wrapped in ceremonial furs and wearing a headdress, surveys the killing from a treetop post over the streambed.

When the last bison is stilled, the hunters wade into the pile of bleeding beasts and carve them with sharp stone blades. The hunters cut tongues and livers from several of the animals and immediately eat the still warm flesh. Then, using stone and bone tools, they butcher the bison and stack the bones.

These hunters, the ancestors of present-day Indians, were the first people to explore the continent. Eventually they spread from the Arctic to the southernmost tip of South America. Over thousands of years, descendants of these hunter-explorers stopped wandering and settled down. By the time Europeans arrived in North America, many Indians had become skilled farmers and had built rich and complex civilizations.

For the Paleo-Indian hunter the world began to change some 10,000 years ago. The earth warmed, and the ice that had covered much of the continent gradually retreated toward the Poles. West of the Rocky Mountains, deserts took over much of the land. As climate and plant life changed, many of the beasts that had run wild

A caribou runs across an Alaskan meadow. Hunters from Asia followed herds of migrating caribou and other animals into North America during the last Ice Age. The hunters lived off the meat, dressed in hides, and made tools from the bones and antlers. The hunters killed their prey with sharp stone points (left) attached to wooden spear shafts.

9

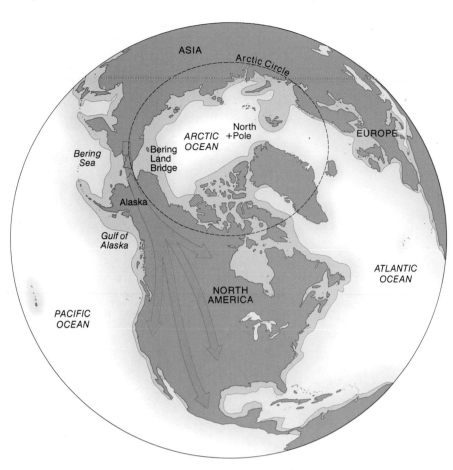

died out. The Paleo-Indians could no longer count on mammoth, sloth, or abundant bison. Unless the human hunters could adapt, they too would face extinction.

With less big game, these early Americans began to depend more on foraging for food. Men and women chased small animals; they caught fish and snared birds; they dug up roots and tubers and gathered wild fruits, vegetables, seeds, and nuts. During this period people moved with the seasons, taking from the wilderness whatever the wilderness offered.

In the desert, life depended mostly on finding vegetables. But in the forests of the eastern United States, game abounded and hunters became adept at trapping otter, beaver, opossums, squirrels, rabbits, and turkeys. Eventually these nomadic hunters and gatherers set up camps or villages where they lived for part of each year. At Koster, in the Illinois River Valley, people built America's first known permanent houses about 7,000 years ago.

Farming Begins in North America

Around 300 or 400 B.C. a revolutionary change took place. People began to come north from what is now Mexico bringing the knowledge of planting and harvesting. Farming transformed North America's primitive societies by freeing people from lives entirely occupied by hunting and gathering. This freedom led to a more settled existence, the development of new skills, and, eventually, to the emergence of North America's great early civilizations.

Instead of roaming the forests in search of food, the Paleo-Indians learned to domesticate wild plants and roots; that is, to plant the seeds so they sprouted and bloomed. They learned to sow only the seeds of plants that gave the best crops. Native Americans tried out this domestication process with dozens of wild grasses, shrubs, and roots. A complete list of their contributions to the world's great food crops would be a long one. It would include corn, potatoes, tomatoes, squash, peanuts, avocados, and many types of beans. Corn, more than any other plant, made possible the cultures that began to flourish in the southwest desert.

The first known agricultural community in North America grew up along the Gila and Salt Rivers in the desert of present-day Arizona. There, about 300 B.C., a culture known today as Hohokam began to emerge. Using pointed sticks and flat stones, the Hohokam people built America's first known irrigation canal—a three-mile channel connecting cornfields with the Gila River. Hohokam women produced some of North America's first pottery.

As knowledge of agriculture spread, groups of farmers clustered around the fertile areas where their crops would thrive. Over time, as greater numbers of people gathered together, they built cities, developed elaborate religions, and improved their irrigation and agricultural techniques.

One group to reach a high level of civilization was the Anasazi, a corn-growing people of the southwest. Centuries before

With an agonized shriek and a swing of its tusks, a wounded mammoth struggles against a band of Ice Age hunters and their dogs on the Bering land bridge. The hunters hurl and jab sharpened sticks, tormenting the elephant-like beast as it slowly dies in a boggy watering hole. Women and older men approach carrying stone knives and hand axes that will be used to carve the tons of meat. The band will eat their fill, then build crude shelters and stay until the food supply is gone. When hunger prods them, they will move on in search of more big game.

Bering Land Bridge

■ Present-day land
□ Additional land which existed 18,000 years ago
➡ Possible migration routes

Between 40,000 and 10,000 years ago, ancestors of today's American Indians trekked across the thousand-mile-wide Bering land bridge that once linked Asia and North America. The map shows the way the continents might have been linked before melting glaciers raised sea levels that covered the bridge. Although glaciers had spread over much of North America, the early migrants found ice-free passages and moved southward in search of food. Over the next several thousand years, humans fanned out to nearly every habitable place in the hemisphere.

Europeans arrived in America, the Anasazi built apartment houses, solar observatories, and water systems. Without the aid of beasts of burden or knowledge of the wheel, they constructed hundreds of miles of roads and built extensive irrigation projects. In underground ceremonial chambers called kivas, Anasazi men performed ceremonies to coax rain and mark the seasons.

By the 14th century the Anasazi had deserted their settlements. Archaeologists think an extended drought dispersed the ancient society. Today some of the Anasazi's customs are continued by their descendants, the Pueblo Indians.

Corn, and the vital resource needed to grow it—water—figure heavily in the religion of the southwestern peoples. According to the legend of one Pueblo tribe, the Zuni, corn came as a gift from the gods; indeed it was the greatest of all life's gifts. The legend says that the first people were born following the union of Sky, the father, and Earth, the mother. In the legend Earth-mother speaks to her mate.

(Continued on page 16)

Hunters pursue game into the Americas, 10,000 to 40,000 years ago.

First crops cultivated, 5,000 years ago.

Hunter-gatherers build first permanent houses, 7,000 years ago.

Ice Age ends, big game declines, 10,000 years ago.

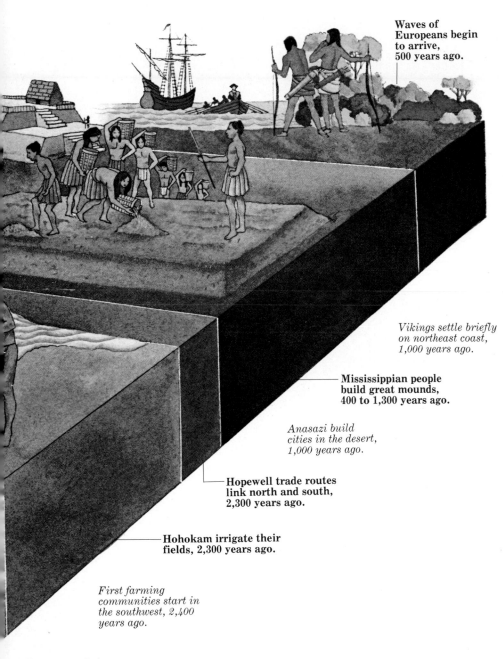

Waves of Europeans begin to arrive, 500 years ago.

Vikings settle briefly on northeast coast, 1,000 years ago.

Mississippian people build great mounds, 400 to 1,300 years ago.

Anasazi build cities in the desert, 1,000 years ago.

Hopewell trade routes link north and south, 2,300 years ago.

Hohokam irrigate their fields, 2,300 years ago.

First farming communities start in the southwest, 2,400 years ago.

Pottery made in the southeast, 4,000 years ago.

As the time line at left shows, North America's native peoples moved through several stages of development before the Europeans arrived. When the big game declined in numbers at the end of the Ice Age, people foraged for food, and many eventually learned to farm. Farming peoples gathered in fertile areas, irrigated their fields, and often took up trading. Some built towering temple mounds and great cities.

Major Settlements Before Columbus

- Paleo-Indian and Paleo-Eskimo (to 8000 B.C.)
- Eskimo (after 5000 B.C.)
- Archaic (8000-1000 B.C.)
- Woodland (1000 B.C.-A.D. 500)
- Mississippian (after A.D. 700)
- Anasazi and Hohokam (after A.D. 500)

The map above shows where prehistoric people left their mark on North America. The stone points of spears 11,000 years old have been found across the continent. Centuries-old earth mounds still dot the Midwest and Southeast, and the ruins of once grand cities still stand in the Southwest.

An air of activity marks a 12th-century festival at Pueblo Bonito, the Anasazi civilization's major city in Chaco Canyon. Men in the plaza inspect colorful capes brought by traders from the south. Others prepare for a ceremony in one of the circular pits called kivas, perhaps to encourage rain. In the foreground women wearing woven cotton dresses cook a special meal that's likely to include elk or mountain sheep.

Today the ruins of Pueblo Bonito bake in the New Mexico desert. The D-shaped city served as an Anasazi center of trade and religion. In the 12th century irrigation systems watered fields to feed Chaco Canyon's population of 7,000. Highways linked canyon villages to civilizations beyond. By the 14th century the Anasazi had abandoned the canyon, probably driven away by drought.

"Soon," she tells Sky-father, "I shall bring forth children from my womb. They shall live in the hollow places of my lap with mountains circling each hollow. My warm breath will drift across the mountains; as it meets your cold sky-wind, the rain will fall in a fine mist. This falling water will give life to my children forever."

Sky-father doesn't want to leave all the work to Earth-mother. He will provide food—grains of corn that are as endless as the stars that litter the skies. "I too will be of help," says the Sky-father. "See!" On the outstretched palm of his hand, the seven stars of the Big Dipper gleam like golden grains of corn. "These," he says, "shall hang forever in the sky to guide our sons and daughters as they wander. And when the rain falls, seed grains like these stars, but numberless, shall spring from your bosom to nourish them."

From the southwestern desert, the knowledge of farming spread slowly eastward. Among the early easterners to grow corn were the Adena people who lived in the Ohio River Valley since about 800 B.C. The Adena and the people who followed them in the valley, the Hopewell, built enormous mounds of earth, some of which can still be seen today. The mounds are shaped like birds, snakes, or men, but their contours are so large they can only be recognized from the air. Excavations of these mounds show that many of them were used to bury people. They often contained obsidian from the Rocky Mountains, shells from the Gulf of Mexico, mica from the Appalachians, and other exotic materials—proof that these easterners traveled widely.

From water travel to making dinner, Indians of the northeastern woodlands (above) depended on trees. The Indians shaped birch-bark canoes on cedar frames. They sewed the canoes with spruce roots and caulked them with pine gum. They made wigwams with bark and ground corn in mortars made out of hollow logs.

Pulling, pushing, biting—anything went in the Indian game of stickball, North America's oldest sport. In this 19th-century painting (left), rival teams strain to reach a leather ball they hope to carry over a goal line. French settlers named the game "lacrosse" and later eliminated much of the violence. In the Indians' version the quest for victory sometimes led to broken bones, bloodshed—and even death.

About A.D. 700 a corn-growing culture known today as "Mississippian" began to flourish along the Mississippi River. The Mississippians built large mounds with flat tops. Thousands of laborers worked on the Mississippian mounds. They shaped them into giant platforms—sometimes a hundred feet high—on which they built temples or houses for their leaders.

When Europeans came to America almost 500 years ago, they found remnants of the advanced Mississippian society and of a great variety of other cultures. Some native peoples lived in great farming communities in the southwest. Others still followed the ways of their ancestors: foraging and fishing for food in what is today California, harpooning whales and spearing salmon in the Pacific northwest, chasing buffalo across the endless plains that stretched eastward from the Rockies.

In the northeast and in the western Great Lakes region, explorers found Indians who combined agriculture, hunting, and fishing as a way of life. These were the Algonquians. In most Algonquian settlements—as in other Indian settlements in the east and on the prairies—women did most of the farming and often owned the fields, while men did most of the hunting.

The Algonquians taught the Europeans how to plant corn and squash. Dozens of everyday English words—like moccasin, moose, tomahawk, and hominy—are derived from their language. Today American cities and states bear Algonquian names: Chicago, Milwaukee, Massachusetts, Wisconsin, Michigan, and many others.

In the eastern Great Lakes region European explorers found the Mohawk, Seneca, Oneida, Onondaga, and Cayuga Indians. These tribes made up the Iroquois nation, or league. The Iroquois' strong political system and skill in warfare enabled them to continue living in eastern North America longer than other tribes. But eventually they too would be pushed out of their homes by the growing number of white settlers in America.

The First Europeans in America

The first known contact with Europeans took place about a thousand years ago when Vikings from Greenland settled very briefly on an island off the North American coast, later named Newfoundland. Were the Vikings the first white people to visit America before Columbus? It is possible that other such visitors came, but so far there is no proof of that.

To Europeans the year 1492 marks the start of a new era of growth and exploration. To the rich cultures of the native Americans, it marks the beginning of a steep decline.

In that year Christopher Columbus, a tall, red-haired Italian sea captain in the service of the king and queen of Spain, sailed westward in search of Asian riches. Columbus badly underestimated the distance between Europe and Asia, but his mistake led to the discovery of a new world. He reached the Caribbean islands after 33 days at sea and landed on a number of them, including Cuba, Haiti, and San Salvador. He found these islands tree-covered and beautiful, with large flocks of parrots that "obscured the sun." Most of the people who lived in this tropical paradise were friendly and peaceful. Columbus thought he had reached a group of islands off the coast of China and Japan. Because that area of Asia was known as the Indies, he called the people he met Indians.

On an island in the West Indies that he named San Salvador, Columbus was especially delighted with the gentle Taino people who came to the shore to greet him. "They are so ingenuous and free with all they have," wrote Columbus in his journal, "that no one would believe it who has not seen it; of anything that they possess, if it be asked of them, they never say no; on the contrary, they invite you to share it. . . ."

The Europeans who landed in the New World did not come to share; they came to take. Their urge for conquest, their firearms, and their diseases—measles, smallpox, influenza, and typhus—never before seen in the New World, proved disastrous for North America's native people.

Boatloads of European soldiers came armed with swords, guns, and knives. Some imagined finding silks and spices that would bring a fortune at home. Some hoped to find a water route through or around America that would take them to Asia and its fabled riches. Some dreamed of great estates with slaves to serve their every need. All were lured by reports of gold, silver, pearls, and rubies. The hundred years that followed Columbus's first voyage in 1492 might be called the first modern gold rush.

Totem poles tell a story, display a family crest, or mark a grave. The middle figure with two front teeth and a cross-hatched tail is a beaver. Beavers on some Alaskan poles represent a mythical beaver who killed an Indian chief, then destroyed his village by tunneling beneath it.

Totem pole from the Alaskan coast

Indians of North America
Thinking they had reached land near India, 15th-century Europeans called the many diverse peoples of America by one name: "Indian." In the southwest, the Hopi Indians (1) built adobe cities and farmed nearby fields. Other Indians—like the Paiute (2) of the Great Basin—roamed the desert in search of food, as their ancestors had for thousands of years.

In the Subarctic, Cree Indians (3) hunted, fished, and gathered berries. On the northwest coast the Kwakiutl (4) caught salmon, performed elaborate winter rituals, and carved totem poles. On the Plateau, the Flathead Indians (5) customarily tied boards to the heads of newborns to shape their profiles. In what is now southern California, the Pomo Indians (6) developed basket making to an art. Male Cheyenne Indians (7) of the Great Plains hunted buffalo on foot. (They had no horses until the Spanish brought them.)

In the northeast, Iroquois Indian women (8) farmed and ruled the bark-covered longhouses. The Cherokee (9), who spoke an Iroquoian language, inhabited much of the southeast. Far to the north, Eskimos (10) hunted in kayaks; their settlements spanned the Arctic. The disunity and isolation of the Indians made it easy for Europeans to conquer a land they called the "New World."

10 Eskimo

Aleut

Tlingit

4 Kwakiutl

Eskimo

Eskimo

3 Cree

Montagnais-Naskapi

Nootka

Blackfoot

Cree

5 Flathead

Ojibwa

Algonquin

Nez Perce

Huron

Crow

7 Cheyenne

Mohawk

6 Pomo

Dakota

2 Paiute

Arapaho

Ute

8 Iroquois

Navajo

Powhatan

1 Hopi

Zuni

Comanche

9 Cherokee

Apache

Natchez

Seminole

The Vikings Settle in America

The first European to see North America may have been a tenth-century seafaring Scandinavian—or Viking—named Bjarni Herjulfsson. He never became famous. But if Viking sagas and archaeological evidence are to be believed, Bjarni, or one of his fellow Vikings, deserves some credit. According to one saga, Bjarni was on his way from Iceland to Greenland in A.D. 986 when a storm blew his small ship off course. When the sun finally shone, Bjarni looked out at an unfamiliar, wooded coast. Quite by accident, Bjarni had discovered America—500 years before Christopher Columbus.

A strong wind eventually landed Bjarni in Greenland, and his reports inspired "a big strapping fellow," Leif Ericsson, to explore. Leif sailed for Bjarni's new land about A.D. 1000 in Bjarni's ship on the theory that ships, like horses, can retrace their routes. Leif and his men called the new country Vinland because of its many grapevines, and they stayed for a few months. "Nature was so generous here," the sagas say, "that . . . no cattle would need any winter fodder, but could graze outdoors."

A few years later, a friend of Leif's decided to start a colony in Vinland. Thorfinn Karlsefni brought his wife and about 160 others, the sagas report. They raised livestock, caught fish, and built houses. Thorfinn and his wife, Gudrid, had a son, Snorri— the first European child we know

A Viking family at L'Anse aux Meadows, Newfoundland

22

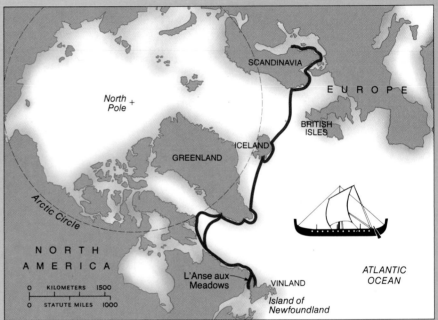

of to be born in America. For years scholars debated whether the sagas were history or legend. Then in the 1960s archaeologists uncovered foundations of Viking houses, workshops, and a smithy at a place called L'Anse aux Meadows in Newfoundland. These may be the remains of Thorfinn Karlsefni's settlement.

What happened to these first European immigrants? The sagas say Newfoundland natives attacked them after being scared by a bellowing Viking bull.

Outnumbered, the Vikings soon fled back to Greenland. Vikings never settled permanently in America but their Scandinavian descendants did—after landing in New York in the 17th century.

Routes of the Vikings
Westward came the Vikings—fierce Norse seafarers who roamed far from their Scandinavian homes. In the ninth century they sailed to Iceland. In the tenth they settled a barren land and named it Greenland in hope of luring other colonists. About the year A.D. 1000, Vikings stumbled onto a new, fertile land. They called it Vinland, the sagas say. Archaeological evidence indicates it was the Island of Newfoundland.

"Land! Land!" After nearly five weeks at sea, Christopher Columbus and his homesick, anxious crew row to a Caribbean island on October 12, 1492. When they reached the shimmering white beach, a report of the voyage says, they knelt on the ground "embracing it with tears of joy for the immeasurable mercy of having reached it." Columbus then stood and gave the island its name, "San Salvador"—Holy Savior.

Offering a crucifix on a chain, French explorer Jacques Cartier befriends an Iroquois Indian in 1534 near present-day Quebec. When the French approached, Cartier wrote, the Indians "all came after our long boat, dancing and showing many signs of joy, and of their desire to be friends." The French gave trinkets and offered hard biscuits and wine—causing the Indians to believe that the French ate wood and drank blood.

Columbus's explorations opened up a world richer than anything Europeans dreamed existed. Spain, France, England, and Holland began to claim huge territories. These overseas possessions, or empires, lay close to the shores of the oceans or were easy to reach by great American rivers like the Rio Grande, the Hudson, and the Mississippi, on which oceangoing vessels could sail.

Since Europeans had become masters of seafaring, the waters that once separated the Old and New Worlds now linked them. The sea captain commanded the new age: He was an explorer, soldier, merchant, pirate, and ruler of empire all rolled into one.

The Race to Claim Land

The Spanish began the first serious exploration of the New World. In 1540 Francisco Coronado led an expedition halfway across North America. One of his lieutenants discovered the Grand Canyon. Coronado himself marched through what is now Texas and Oklahoma to Kansas. The expedition was grueling—Coronado and his men battled Indians and endured heat so intense it killed many of their horses.

In two years of wandering Coronado learned much about America, but he found nothing to make him rich. His men bitterly complained that they had not found gold, nor had they discovered the paradise they imagined.

Other countries raced with Spain to claim New World lands. John Cabot, an Italian sea captain sailing for the English king, had crossed the North Atlantic in 1497 to the land where the Vikings had once been. The king named it Newfoundland. Jacques Cartier, a French sea captain, made three round trips across the Atlantic between 1534 and 1542, discovering the St. Lawrence River and the Indian village of Hochelaga, a place now called Montreal. In 1576, Martin Frobisher, an English sea captain, sailed in a northwesterly direction far along the Canadian shore, looking for a northwest passage through the continent that would take him to China.

Explorations such as these began to revolutionize European knowledge of the globe. The earth was much bigger than Europeans had ever thought. The New World began to take shape on 16th- and 17th-century maps as an immense land barrier extending almost from pole to pole.

In the last half of the 16th century, the Spanish, French, English, and Dutch began the first attempts to establish permanent settlements. In 1599, Spanish colonists pushed up the broad valley of the Rio Grande, bringing some of the first horses and cattle to the North American mainland. They started a settlement at San Gabriel. In 1608, Samuel de Champlain, one of France's greatest soldiers and sea captains, founded the first French outpost at Quebec.

Sir Walter Raleigh, an explorer, writer, pirate, and favorite of Queen Elizabeth I of England, organized the first British colonial expeditions to America. The queen was intrigued with the idea that colonies might provide gold, a passage to Asia, and a chance to challenge Spain in the New World. In 1584 she gave Raleigh a

European Explorers of North America

Five years after Columbus landed on San Salvador in the Caribbean Sea, the English hired John Cabot (1) to "seek out . . . regions . . . of the heathen." Cabot landed briefly on the Island of Newfoundland and claimed it for England.

Although Cabot reached the North American Continent first, Spaniards led its exploration. Juan Ponce de Leon (2) sailed from Puerto Rico to the mainland in 1513 and named it "Florida," Spanish for "flowery." Other Spaniards, like Francisco Coronado (3) and Hernando de Soto (4), explored the interior of the continent. De Soto, described as "fond of this sport of killing Indians," led 570 men from Florida to the Mississippi in search of gold. Coronado's men never found the gold they sought, but they did discover the Grand Canyon.

In 1524 the French sent Italian explorer Giovanni da Verrazano (5) to find a passage to Asia. He didn't get beyond the harbor of what is now New York. A decade later, French explorer Jacques Cartier (6) sailed up the St. Lawrence to the site of present-day Montreal.

But no explorer won the recognition of Amerigo Vespucci. In 1507 a French mapmaker, impressed by Vespucci's account of his voyage to the New World, labeled the new land "America."

charter—a document permitting him to explore the eastern coast of North America and the "remote, heathen and barbarous lands" that lay beyond it.

Charters enabled explorers to take land in the name of the crown. They gave the holders the power to recruit settlers, to transport them across the ocean, and to establish and run settlements. English charters gave settlers certain protections that French and Spanish colonists did not have. They guaranteed colonists all rights and privileges of Englishmen back home: representative government, trial by jury, and the right to own personal property.

Raleigh quickly dispatched two captains—Philip Amadas and Arthur Barlow—to explore the coast and claim land on which to start a colony. Amadas and Barlow came ashore on Roanoke Island in Pamlico Sound off North Carolina and brought back glowing accounts. The seashores, they said, were "sandy and low toward the water's edge, and so overgrown with grapes that the surging waves flowed over them." The Indians planted corn, fished, and hunted in the forests. They were, Amadas and Barlow reported, "most gentle, loving and faithful, void of all guile and treason. . . ."

Impressed with the report, Raleigh named this claim Virginia, in honor of Elizabeth, the Virgin Queen. Since mapmakers had little knowledge of America, Virginia had no precise boundaries; it included all the land that Raleigh's men could seize and hold.

England's First Colony

In 1585, Raleigh's first party of colonists—about a hundred men and boys—arrived by ship and spent a terrible winter on Roanoke Island. They hunted for gold and demanded corn from the Indians. The colony didn't survive for long. The Indians, resentful of constant demands for food and labor, stopped being "gentle and loving." They fought with the settlers and planned an attack to wipe out the English colony. Before the attack took place, British ships arrived and hauled the beleaguered survivors home.

Raleigh refused to give up his dream of establishing permanent settlements in America. In 1587 he dispatched a group of about 120 people, including 17 women and 11 children, to Virginia under the leadership of John White. After a month in America, White's daughter, Eleanor Dare, gave birth to the first English child born on American soil, Virginia Dare.

White helped the colonists build a fort and settle in. He then sailed to England for supplies. Just as he planned to return, war broke out between England and Spain. It was two years before White could cross the Atlantic to his friends and family in the New World. When he did, he could find no trace of the settlers.

White found the fort deserted and overgrown with weeds. White's sea chests had been broken open, his precious books and maps ruined. "My books," he wrote, "were torn from their covers, the frames of my maps and pictures were rotted and broken by rain, and my armor was almost eaten through with rust." The word "Croatoan" carved on a post provided a clue: The colonists might

Land Claims 1620
- ■ British
- ▨ British and French
- ▨ Spanish
- ▨ British and Spanish
- ▢ Unclaimed

European nations competed for land in the New World even before they knew the extent of the continent. Spanish claims spanned the south from coast to coast. The French and British only explored the east—but extended their claims into the unknown west. The nations didn't always agree on what land belonged to whom.

Castillo de San Marcos stands guard at St. Augustine, Florida, as it has since the late 17th century when the Spanish built it to protect their empire's northernmost point. Greed for gold drove many Spaniards to the New World, but a search for the fabled Fountain of Youth lured Ponce de Leon to Florida, which he claimed for Spain in 1513. Other Spaniards settled St. Augustine about 50 years later. They built the fort to guard against attacks by rival English and French forces. Its jagged, sturdy walls—made of cemented seashells—frustrated the English sea raiders who regularly attacked the Spanish colony. Although Spanish explorers claimed a large part of North America, Spain's only permanent settlements here were in the southeast and west.

Algonquian-speaking Indians greeted the first French and English settlers to the east coast of North America. John White, an artist who came with Raleigh's first colonists, painted this view of the Indian settlement of Pomeiooc near Roanoke Island. Tortoises found on the east coast "look very ugly," one colonist wrote. "Nevertheless, they are very good to eat, as are their eggs."

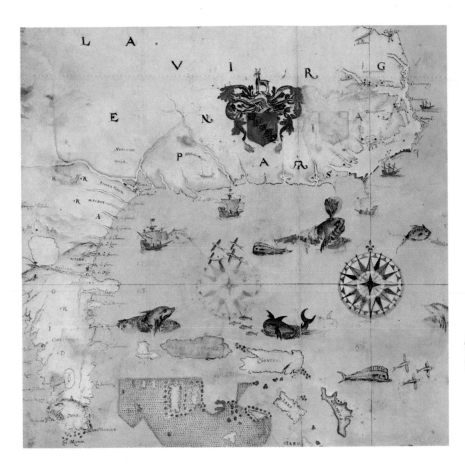

A 16th-century map (left) bearing Sir Walter Raleigh's crest shows English ships making their way to the coast of North America amid whales, dolphins, and flying fish. Queen Elizabeth gave Raleigh a charter to seize all the land he could. He claimed most of the continent between the Chesapeake Bay and Florida and named it Virginia after Elizabeth, the Virgin Queen.

In this painting by John White the daughter of an Algonquian chief holds a doll dressed in English court costume, and her mother carries "a gourd full of some kind of pleasant liquor." Indian children, an English settler noted, "are greatly delighted with puppets and babes ... brought out of England."

have fled to a nearby island by that name. However, no trace of the colonists was ever found. What happened to them? Did they die of starvation, wander off into the wilderness, or get killed by Indians? No one knows.

Seventeen years passed before the English tried again to establish a colony in the New World. Sir Walter Raleigh had lost all his influence at the royal court with the death of the queen in 1603. Now a group of wealthy gentlemen who called themselves the London Company put their money into a settlement project. The company obtained a charter like Raleigh's to settle part of the vast territory called Virginia, a land that now stretched between the central parts of present-day South Carolina and Maine. Companies like the London Company were the first English governments in America. Their agents, or "governors," passed and enforced laws in the name of the king.

The London Company's first three ships sailed for America in late 1606. The 104 settlers, all men, picked a spot on the sheltered waters of the James River and named it Jamestown. At first the London Company's settlers at Jamestown did not do much better than the Roanoke settlers had. They looked for gold, stole from the Indians, and starved by the dozens.

To encourage Englishmen to move to America and work for them, the London Company and other companies distributed brochures describing an American paradise where the sun always shines. The oranges, apples, lemons, and other fruit were "so

John Smith
1580-1631

John Smith's life was a long string of narrow escapes. Short, bushy-bearded, cocky, he was looking for adventure when he came to Jamestown in 1607. He hadn't expected to fall in love with the country, but he did. Determined that the colony should succeed, he traded, fought, explored, mapped, built—often single-handedly, for the settlers were such a lazy, quarrelsome lot, it was a wonder that the settlement survived its first two years.

Indeed, it was a wonder that John, himself, survived. Once, using his native guide as a shield, he kept 200 Indians at bay. Again threatened by warriors, he suggested a fistfight, then grabbed the chief by the hair. (The Indians were so shocked, they backed off, Smith reported.)

Sometimes John was just lucky. Once his head was already on the "block" when instead of being killed, he found himself adopted into the tribe. Once he was poisoned but threw up the poison. Once enemies among the settlers were about to execute him when in the nick of time, an English ship sailed up, and the captain saved him. Once, stung by a stingray, he was so sure he would die, he ordered his grave dug. Fortunately he didn't have to use it. But when a bag of gunpowder on his hip exploded, he was so badly burned, he went home to England to recover.

Later he sailed to New England and mapped it, but never again would anyone hire him to work in an American settlement. So he returned to London and wrote the first great book about America, *The Generall Historie of Virginia, New England, and the Summer Isles*. At 51 he died unadventurously in bed.

JEAN FRITZ

Pocahontas, an Indian princess, rescues Captain Smith from the "block."

delicious that whoever tastes them will despise the insipid watery taste of those we have in England." America, the brochures boasted, was a land where everybody stayed young, where game was plentiful, and life easy.

Those who braved the voyage soon discovered that the reality was much different. The swampland around Jamestown brought mosquitoes and malaria. The bad water spread dysentery. Indians attacked, and hunger was always present. By 1609 only a handful of the original Jamestown settlers remained. With supplies and morale low, their leader, the sea captain and explorer John Smith, ordered the settlers to prepare meals from whatever they could gather—acorns, wild fruit, sturgeon. Unless forced to gather food, Smith wrote, the demoralized colonists "would have all starved or have eaten one another."

Tobacco Brings Prosperity

Business went poorly for the London Company until about 1612 when a farmer named John Rolfe discovered a strain of tobacco that the English liked. Rolfe is most famous for falling in love with a woman of the Powhatan tribe, Pocahontas, and marrying her. Rolfe's tobacco discovery changed the fortunes of the English colonies in America forever. The tobacco that the Indians had been growing for centuries did not appeal to the Europeans. Rolfe's new strain was milder and had a more pleasing taste. It became an overnight sensation in Europe, creating a booming demand. Soon prosperous tobacco farms studded the James River area.

During these early years of tobacco growing, the London Company sent settlers streaming to the American colony. Englishmen, who once needed to be coaxed, now flocked to Virginia to make their fortunes. Between 1619 and 1624, some 5,000 English settlers came to Virginia. But sickness, starvation, and Indian attacks claimed most of the newcomers, and the population increased by only 200 during the period. Despite these problems, by 1630 English ships regularly crowded the James River, bringing more settlers and picking up tobacco to sell across the ocean.

Farther north, Holland laid its North American claim through the efforts of another English sea captain, Henry Hudson. In 1609, Hudson sailed 150 miles up the river that would be named for him looking for a passage through the continent to China. Hudson found no such thing, but he was amazed at what he saw: a beautiful valley filled with mountains, lakes, forests, and wildlife. The Indians of the valley, members of the Mahican and Wappinger tribes, raised corn and clothed themselves in skins of fur-bearing animals—beaver, otter, mink, wildcat, and bear.

Soon Henry Hudson's employers, merchants who called themselves the Dutch East India Company, organized settlements in the Hudson Valley like the London Company's outposts on the James River. While the English colonies prospered by growing tobacco, the Dutch made most of their money by exporting furs.

Jamestown's thatched houses (above), covered with a plaster made from mud and shells, protected settlers from rain, but not from bitter winters, malaria-carrying mosquitoes, and Indian attacks. The metal helmets (left), found near Jamestown, had been useful on open European battlefields but were of little value in the forests of the New World.

Residents of Martin's Hundred—a 17th-century settlement near Jamestown—clear the fields and forests, repair a thatched roof, and tend to livestock. The fort in the background was built as a refuge from Indian attacks, but a surprise raid killed dozens of settlers here in 1622. Disease and famine also took their toll: Between 1619 and 1621, about 70 percent of the 3,500 Virginia colonists perished.

In 1626 the Dutch bought Manhattan Island from friendly Indians for $24 worth of beads and trinkets. At the tip of the island and on the Hudson River near present-day Albany, they built forts as centers for their fur trade.

These forts also helped protect the settlers from Indian attacks. Constructed first of wood and then of stone, the forts were used to store guns and gunpowder and to house soldiers. Europeans built forts wherever they went. Along with iron axes and plows, guns, cannons, and knives, forts were part of the Europeans' superior technology that enabled them to move steadily inland and overcome Indian resistance.

The Dutch Encourage Farming

In 1629 another Dutch company, the Dutch West India Company, decided to bring in more people and increase the amount of land farmed in the colony. The company distributed large parcels of land along the Hudson River to wealthy Dutchmen to settle and farm. Each landholder, called a patroon, was responsible for bringing 50 adults over to work his land. The patroons ran their estates like feudal lords. They held court and gave their workers as few rights as serfs. The prospect of moving to a Dutch colony under these circumstances was not a welcome one for most people, so the colony grew slowly.

Unlike the owners of the London Company, the Dutch organized their colonial outposts carefully. Even before the patroon system was established, the Dutch selected farmers and craftsmen who brought over their families as well as the seeds, plows, and tools they would need in the New World. The Dutch company also saw that the settlers had all the animals they needed for farm and breeding purposes. In 1625 two shiploads of stallions, mares, bulls, cows, hogs, and sheep were sent across the Atlantic Ocean. On

Male passengers on the Mayflower *sign a compact promising to write and obey "just and equal laws . . . for the general good of the colony." Although women weren't allowed to sign, the compact brought an element of democracy to America. Whereas a king or his representative ruled other colonies, the adult male May-flower settlers began to elect their own leaders.*

Dampness, cold, overcrowding, and the threat of drowning faced passengers and crew aboard the Mayflower *as they made their way to the New World in the fall of 1620. Quarters (1) for the 102 passengers in the converted merchant ship offered little room for play or privacy—each person had about 18 square feet, the size of a single bed. In calm weather the crew cooked meals in the galley (2), but usually both crew and passengers ate "salt horse and hardtack"—cold salted meat or fish, and a biscuit. The provisions (3), piled above the rocks used for ballast, spoiled before the two-month journey ended. The sea posed a constant threat to life. One storm swept a man overboard, but he held on to some rigging and was rescued. Another storm cracked the main beam and sent water pouring into the passenger quarters. The beam was fixed, and the* Mayflower's *skilled captain, Christopher Jones (4), sailed on.*

In this painting an officer (5) on the quarterdeck relays Jones's instructions to a helmsman (6) who moves a whipstaff to control the rudder. Three sailors turn a capstan to hoist the sails (7), while another checks a windlass used to raise the anchor (8). Amazingly, only one person died on the storm-tossed voyage. The passengers shouted with joy when they sighted land, but their luck didn't hold. Only half lived through the first Cape Cod winter.

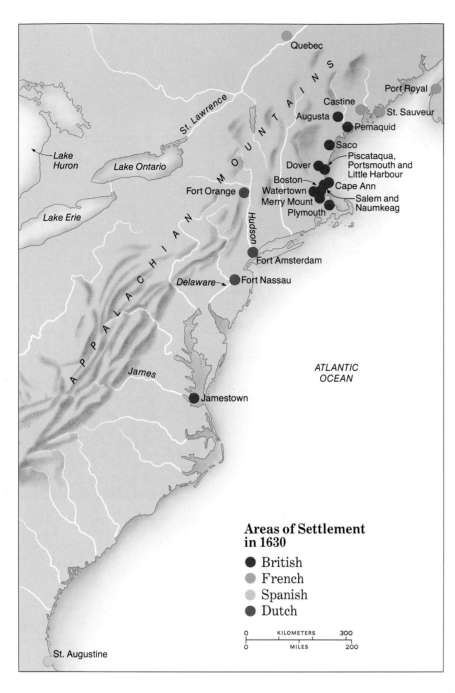

By 1630 tiny settlements dotted the Atlantic coast and the banks of the rivers that flowed into it (above). Spanish colonists had founded St. Augustine—America's oldest permanent settlement—in 1565. Tobacco trade helped the English colony of Jamestown flourish after a rough start in 1607, and New England grew rapidly after the Mayflower's landing. Trade in furs built French Quebec and the Dutch trading posts along the Hudson River.

Pilgrims from the Mayflower struggle against biting cold after debarking at Plymouth on December 18, 1620. The winter days became excruciating. At one point only 7 of the 102 who came could stay on their feet to bury the dead and care for the sick. Yet none of the survivors returned to England when the Mayflower set sail in spring. One Pilgrim wrote to England, "It is not with us as with other men, whom small things can discourage."

board ship each animal had plenty to eat, its own stall with a floor of sand three feet deep, and, we are told, "its respective servant who attends to it. . . ."

As the Jamestown and Hudson Valley settlers struggled for a toehold in the New World, another group of English colonists began a new outpost farther up the coast.

These settlers did not seek to get rich from selling luxuries like tobacco or furs. They were simple people who came in search of a place where they could live and worship as they pleased.

The first New England settlers came on the *Mayflower* in 1620. They were a band of 102 people, mostly English villagers—small farmers, farm workers, and village craftsmen. The ship was supposed to land near Jamestown but landed instead at Cape Cod, a sandy spit of land extending off Massachusetts into the Atlantic Ocean. The leaders of this group included William Brewster, a postmaster, and William Bradford, a weaver and merchant. They decided to stay.

There were very few wealthy people among these Pilgrims and only one professional soldier. Women and children outnumbered the men. Elizabeth Hopkins was pregnant when she boarded the *Mayflower* with her husband, Stephen, and their three children, Giles, Constanta, and Damaris. Her baby, born while the *Mayflower* crossed the Atlantic, was christened Oceanus.

The Pilgrims settled at the foot of Cape Cod in 1620 and built the village of Plymouth. When they wrote to their friends back home, they said nothing about gold or silver or how to get to China. They had found a place, as one settler wrote, where they "might live as contented . . . as in any part of the world. For fish and fowl, we have great abundance."

Even so, the New England colonists, like other early settlers, struggled with hunger, disease, and death, and tiny Plymouth remained a backwater in New England life.

New England Colonies Grow

Boston, the first major New England settlement, was started in 1630 by a group of well-to-do investors who also sought to live and worship in their own way. These settlers were called Puritans because they had wanted to purify the Church of England of what they considered extravagant frills, like colorful robes, prayer books, and stained glass windows.

The Puritans received a charter from King Charles to settle around Massachusetts Bay. Unlike other charters granted by the king, this one did not require the company's directors to live in England. That meant that the principal investors could cross the Atlantic Ocean themselves to share the hardships and the rewards of the enterprise. The Massachusetts Bay colonies prospered and grew. Soon tiny settlements dotted the area where the Charles River enters into Massachusetts Bay. In the years after 1630 the first trickle of immigrants to the Boston area would turn into a flood.

Pieces of Our Past
Beginnings to 1630

Indians and Pilgrims prepare America's first Thanksgiving feast in a modern painting. The 1621 event celebrated the settlers' first harvest, produced with Indian help. The Indian guests brought turkeys and venison. Colonists provided geese, ducks, and fish. President Lincoln declared Thanksgiving a national holiday in 1863.

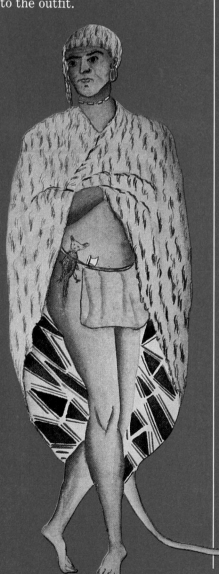

A cloak of bison skin (below) kept this Natchez Indian warm in winter. A painted design on the lining, a tail, and a mouse tucked in the waistband added glamour to the outfit.

A polished bison horn was used by Indians as a container for pigments. This horn held iron oxide, a red pigment. Indians used such colors to decorate their caves, their decoys—and themselves.

Snow goggles made of ivory protected Eskimos from "snow blindness" caused by bright sun reflected on snow. Eskimos today still use the ancient eyepieces, sometimes smearing soot inside to help absorb glare.

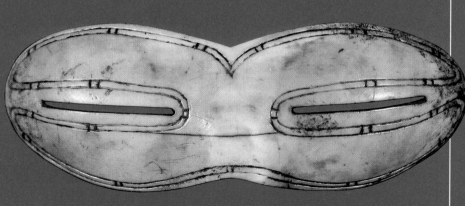

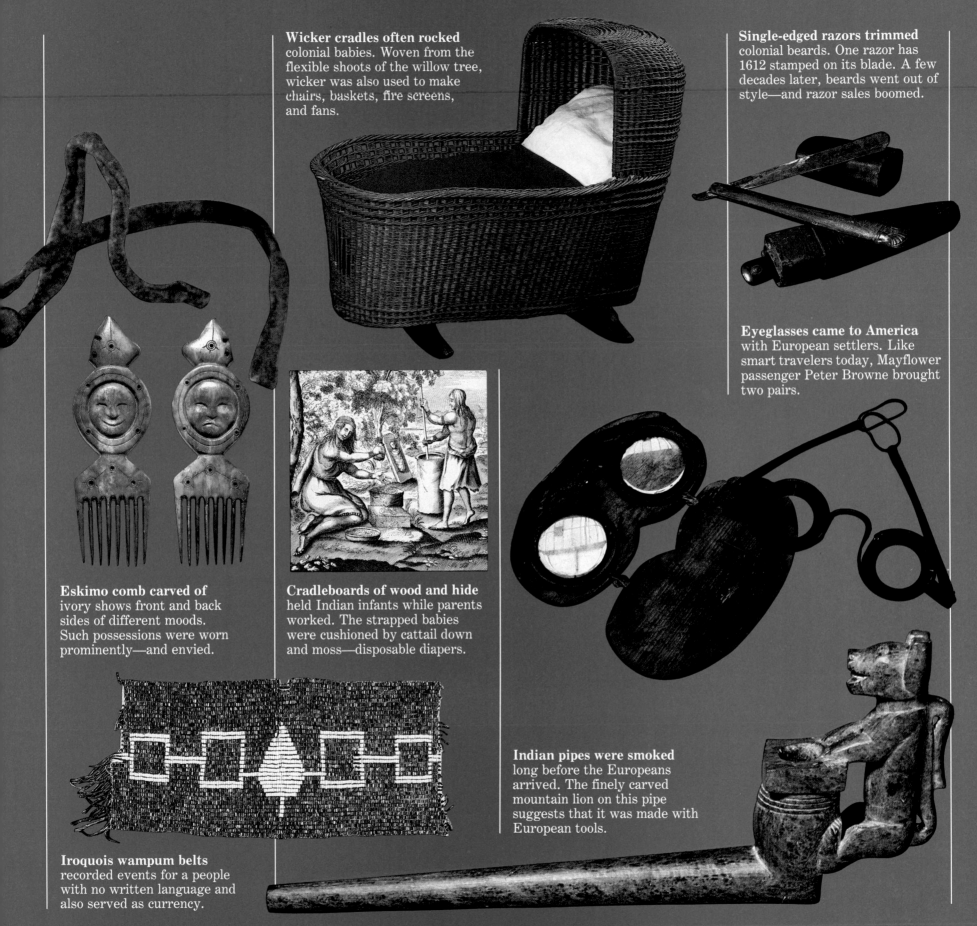

Wicker cradles often rocked colonial babies. Woven from the flexible shoots of the willow tree, wicker was also used to make chairs, baskets, fire screens, and fans.

Single-edged razors trimmed colonial beards. One razor has 1612 stamped on its blade. A few decades later, beards went out of style—and razor sales boomed.

Eyeglasses came to America with European settlers. Like smart travelers today, Mayflower passenger Peter Browne brought two pairs.

Eskimo comb carved of ivory shows front and back sides of different moods. Such possessions were worn prominently—and envied.

Cradleboards of wood and hide held Indian infants while parents worked. The strapped babies were cushioned by cattail down and moss—disposable diapers.

Indian pipes were smoked long before the Europeans arrived. The finely carved mountain lion on this pipe suggests that it was made with European tools.

Iroquois wampum belts recorded events for a people with no written language and also served as currency.

COLONIES
IN THE
WILDERNESS

Frontier, Farm, and City 1630-1763

Tens of thousands of English settlers arrived on the eastern shores of America during the 17th century. To New England came farmers, fishermen, craftsmen—people of no great wealth. They were, for the most part, Puritans who had left their homeland to escape political and religious persecution. Although still subjects of Charles I, King of England, they had been granted the freedom to make their own laws. They cleared the forests near sheltered harbors and set up townships like the English villages from which they had come. The townspeople divided the lands among themselves and started family farms, on which they planted wheat and corn and raised livestock for their own use. "The air of the country is sharp," said one Massachusetts woman, "the rocks many, the trees innumerable, the grass little, the winter cold." Because the cold winters and rocky soil made commercial farming unprofitable in New England, many colonists turned to fishing, shipbuilding, or trade for their livelihoods.

In contrast to New England, the middle colonies had a more temperate climate and richer soil. Charles II (who became king in 1660) granted vast tracts of land to individuals called proprietors. He made his brother James, Duke of York, proprietor of all the lands between the Connecticut and Delaware Rivers, including the territory that the English took from the Dutch in 1664. James renamed the Dutch lands New York. The proprietors sought to sell portions of their holdings by advertising the natural wealth of the valleys, rivers, fields, and forests. "There is so great an increase of grain," boasted one proprietor, "that within three years, some plantations have got 20 acres of corn, some 40, some 50. . . . There are also peaches, in great quantities." These advertising efforts attracted aristocrats, country gentlemen, and poor farmers from Europe. Large manors and small farms grew side by side in the Hudson and Delaware Valleys. The big landowners brought in servants and slaves to work their farms and made handsome profits by raising grain for export to the West Indies, New England, and parts of the South.

The warmer climate and fertile soil of the southern colonies also favored large-scale farming, once the wilderness had been cleared. In 1670 Virginia explorer John Lederer wrote that "the parts inhabited here are pleasant and fruitful . . . cleared of wood, and laid open to the sun." He noted many wild animals including a "rattlesnake of an extraordinary length and thickness. . . . I judged it two yards and a half or better from head to tail, and as big about as a man's arm." But in spite of snakes and other dangers and hardships, many Virginians had made their fortunes growing tobacco by the end of the 17th century. The back-breaking labor was

Early settlers chopped down trees to clear the land and to provide lumber for their houses. The Swedes and Finns introduced log cabins to Delaware in 1638, but the English preferred wooden clapboard houses, a great improvement over the wigwams, caves, and sod-covered holes in which they first took shelter. The hardships of frontier life took a heavy toll (left). Those who escaped attack by Indians faced epidemics of smallpox, diphtheria, and whooping cough, which sometimes wiped out entire families.

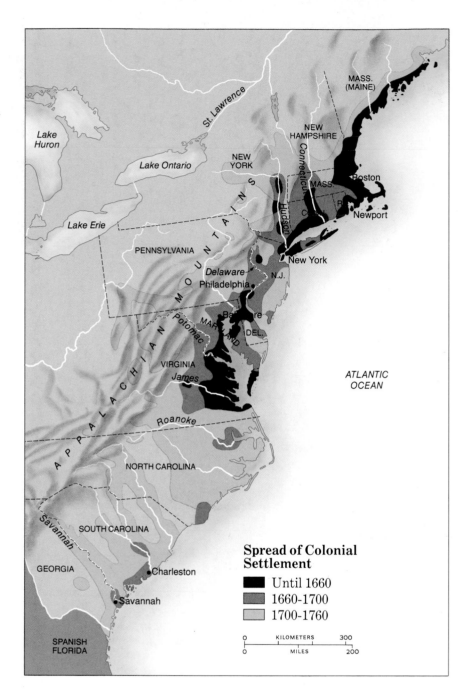

Spread of Colonial Settlement

- ■ Until 1660
- ■ 1660-1700
- □ 1700-1760

```
0    KILOMETERS    300
0       MILES      200
```

*"Whence came all these people?"
a New York farmer wondered in
late colonial times. By 1760 the
population was 20 times greater
than it had been a century before.
As more immigrants arrived,
fingers of settlement reached in
along rivers and spread into
fertile lowlands. The low broad
barrier of the Appalachian
Mountains slowed further
movement to the west.*

performed by African slaves, who were brought to the colony in large numbers to toil in the fields. Farther south, along South Carolina's coastal plain and many tidal rivers, planters raised rice on huge tracts of land also with the help of slave labor.

During the colonial period the British settlements in America grew so fast that by 1750 there were 13 separate colonies stretching in an almost unbroken band from the swampy shores of Georgia to the rocky coasts of Maine. The Indians, who had lived on this land for thousands of years, watched with angry eyes and despairing hearts as more and more settlers moved in with their axes, guns, and plows to clear the thickets, kill the animals, and push back the forest. Some Indians fled westward. Others, to save their homes, took the only remedy open to them—the warpath. Armed with tomahawk, bow and arrow, or gun, they swooped down to kill the European intruders or to drive them away. The longest and bloodiest encounter began in 1675 when several Indian tribes went on the warpath along much of the frontier, north and south.

On the Warpath

In New England a conflict called King Philip's War broke out between the New England settlers and several allied tribes, including the Wampanoags of Rhode Island under Philip, their chief. One well-recorded attack took place on February 10, 1676, when a band of Nipmuck Indians struck at the town of Lancaster, Massachusetts, killing nearly 50 villagers, and carrying off Mary Rowlandson, the minister's wife, as a hostage. She later wrote about her captivity.

That first night Mary and her little girl slept on the open ground. The child was delirious with fever and kept calling pitifully for a drink of water. "My sweet babe," Mary wrote a week later, "like a lamb departed this life on February 18, 1676. It being about six years, and five months old. It was nine days . . . in this miserable condition, without any refreshing of one nature or other, except a little cold water."

The Nipmucks and their prisoners moved northwest through the cold forest. They traveled with difficulty because, as Mrs. Rowlandson recounts, there were hundreds in the group. "Old and young, some sick, and some lame, many had papooses at their backs, the greatest number at this time with us, were squaws, and they travelled with all they had, bag and baggage." To cross rivers, they had to build rafts and then wait their turn to be shuttled across. In early March, New England militiamen came after them.

The Nipmucks now had two enemies to fight—the New England soldiers and starvation. Settlers destroyed the Indians' corn, hoping that starvation would force them to surrender. As the Indians fled through the forest with Mary Rowlandson, they ate anything they could find—"groundnuts . . . acorns, artichokes, lily roots . . . old bones . . . horses guts, . . . all sorts of wild birds which they could catch: also . . . beaver, tortoise, frogs, squirrels, dogs, skunks, rattlesnakes, yea the very bark of trees." Mrs. Rowlandson spent

New England fishermen found abundant cod from Cape Cod, Massachusetts, to the shores of Nova Scotia. On large wooden platforms called stages at the water's edge (left), they cleaned, salted, and dried most of the cod for export and pressed cod livers to extract the oil.

Joshua Winsor's fine house in Duxbury (above) reflected his prominence in the Massachusetts cod-fishing industry. In New England, stony soil and bitter winters forced many settlers to abandon efforts to farm for profit, but they learned to harvest the wealth of the sea. By the late 17th century, fishing had become the most important business in Massachusetts.

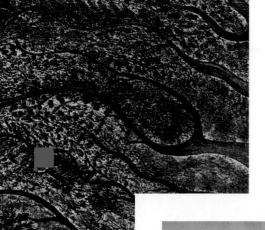

Southern tobacco plantations, often covering thousands of acres, supplied a market for the leaf in England. A large plantation was organized like a town. The owner's house overlooked buildings that lodged carpenters, blacksmiths, weavers, shoemakers, slaves, and sometimes a school for the owner's children. At the dock, ships picked up barrels of tobacco and delivered goods from London and other ports.

This Chesapeake Bay youth collects tobacco leaves on a pointed stick just as colonial boys did 300 years ago. The leaves will be carried to a curing barn and hung up to dry.

three months as a prisoner of the Nipmucks, sharing their hardships, before she was ransomed.

The Nipmucks, like other Indians of the east, were outnumbered. Many died in battle or were taken captive and enslaved. By the early 18th century the European settlers had driven the Indians from most of the land between the Atlantic Ocean and the Appalachian Mountains.

The settlers benefited from the many sheltered bays and fine harbors that jutted into the Atlantic coastline. Important seaports sprang up around these harbors, including Boston, Charleston, New York, Philadelphia, and Newport. There merchants grew rich by shipping fish, lumber, tobacco, rice, wheat, and indigo (a plant from which blue dye is made) to Europe and the West Indies and by bringing back slaves, wine, molasses, clothing, guns, and axes for sale to the colonists. Some 55,000 people, or about 4 percent of all the people in the Colonies, lived in these coastal cities. By 1750 some of the ports were serving as gateways through which tens of thousands of immigrants passed on their way inland. Not only were these ports shipping centers but also centers of communication with Europe. Wealthy and powerful leaders lived here, as did skilled craftsmen—printers, shipbuilders, sail makers, carriage makers, bricklayers, and rope makers. Information and ideas from the other colonies and from Europe entered through seaport towns and spread inland by means of books and newspapers.

One of the fastest growing cities was Philadelphia. In 1680 the city didn't exist. By 1750 it had risen to become America's biggest city and its cultural capital and center of trade.

Penn Founds Philadelphia

Philadelphia's founder, William Penn, was an English nobleman who belonged to a religious group in England known as the Society of Friends. When the Friends met together for prayer, they expressed their feelings. Because they wept, groaned, and trembled with joy or sorrow or fear, they came to be called Quakers—people who quake or tremble.

Many of the Friends were poor, and most suffered rough treatment in England because of their beliefs. The Friends thought that all people were equal in God's eyes, so they refused to "uncover," or take off their hats, when the king passed by in his coach. Their behavior was considered a terrible insult to His Majesty, and the Friends were often punished. Members of the Society spent a lot of time in the pillory, where passersby pelted them with rotten eggs, fruits, and vegetables. Because the Friends were determined to hold services in their own way, and not in accordance with the Church of England, they had to pay heavy fines. Between about 1650 and 1689, more than 4,000 went to jail, and nearly 500 died there. Ordinary citizens burned the Quakers' houses and barns, smashed their tools, and drove away their sheep and cattle.

William Penn dreamed of starting an American colony where the Friends could live and worship in peace. In 1681 he obtained a

Kidnapped by Indians: Mary Rowlandson's Ordeal

"They came and beset our house, and quickly it was the dolefulest day that ever mine eyes saw." Mary Rowlandson, frontier wife, thus described in her memoirs the Indian attack on Lancaster, Massachusetts, in the early morning of February 10, 1676.

Thirty-seven townspeople, including Mary and her three children, huddled in the Rowlandson house as the musket fire and war cries of hundreds of Nipmuck Indians drew near. "They shot against the house, so that the bullets seemed to fly like hail," Mary recounted. Then the Indians set fire to the wood-frame house and, as the occupants fled the blaze, war-painted braves set upon them, "gaping before us with their guns, spears and hatchets to devour us." Mary herself was wounded by a bullet that passed through the child she carried and into her side. The child later died.

The Nipmucks took Mary hostage and forced her to hike a winding route (on map, above) through the snowy wilderness. "My head was light and dizzy, my knees feeble, my body raw," she wrote. She earned her keep by making stockings and shirts for her captors. After 11 weeks and 5 days of captivity, the Indians freed Mary Rowlandson on May 2 for a ransom of 20 pounds.

charter from Charles II, giving him a piece of land between New York and Maryland, in payment of a debt owed his father by the crown. Penn built a town on an elbow of land where the Delaware and Schuylkill Rivers meet. He named his city Philadelphia, from the Greek words meaning "brotherly love." It was a good location, and the city prospered. To the west lay fertile and level lands that supported farmers and provided the city with food. Philadelphia was a great port—easily accessible to the ocean, yet far enough inland that it was well protected from Atlantic storms. Seagoing vessels could sail up the Delaware to the town docks. Philadelphia merchants bought up the produce of the rich farmlands around the town and sent it abroad in return for ironware, guns, clothing, fine furniture, and many other luxuries. City shipyards built the ships that made this trade possible.

By 1750 settlers of other nationalities and religious groups had joined the Quakers in Philadelphia. That year a ship named *Osgood* sailed up the Delaware River and docked at the town. The *Osgood* carried immigrants from Germany, among them a church organist and schoolteacher named Gottlieb Mittelberger. When Mittelberger went ashore, he was amazed at the town's wealth. Elegant houses built of brick or stone lined the broad streets. Women wore "fine white aprons, on their shoes generally large silver buckles, round their throats fine strings of beads, in their ears costly rings with fine stones, and on their heads fine white bonnets embroidered with flowers and trimmed with lace and streamers." When they went walking or out for a drive, Mittelberger said, "they wear blue or scarlet cloaks reaching down to the waist."

Luxurious goods were piled on the town's docks: "fruit, flour, corn, tobacco, honey, many varieties of hides . . . spices, sugar, tea, coffee, rice, rum, fine china vessels, Dutch and English cloth, leather . . . silks, damask, velvet, etc."

Mittelberger also noted eight churches, including "three German, one Swedish, and one belonging to the Quakers" and "a school where several languages are taught." Penn's colony was the first large community in modern history where settlers of different faiths and backgrounds lived side by side as equals.

A Horrible Crossing

Hundreds of poor people arrived with Mittelberger on the *Osgood*. Most of them would never live to have silver buckles on their shoes or wear a scarlet cloak. They had come to America to escape the poverty and misery of the Old World. They faced the hard work of clearing land for the well-to-do Pennsylvania farmers and laboring in the fields and on the docks. These people bore the dangers of the Atlantic because they had dreams of a better life in the New World for themselves and their children. The Atlantic crossing was more horrible than they could have imagined. Many who set sail from the Dutch port of Rotterdam fell ill, died, and had to be buried at sea. The water the immigrants were forced to drink during the long weeks of the crossing

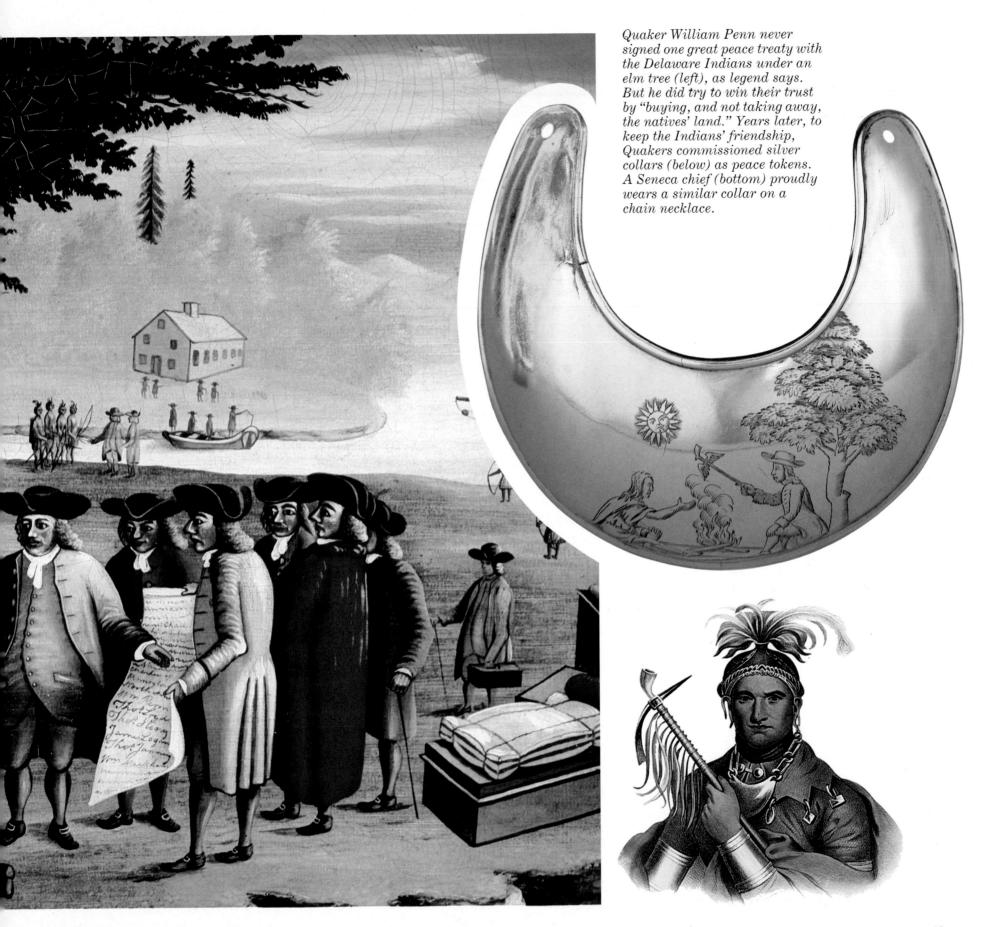

Quaker William Penn never signed one great peace treaty with the Delaware Indians under an elm tree (left), as legend says. But he did try to win their trust by "buying, and not taking away, the natives' land." Years later, to keep the Indians' friendship, Quakers commissioned silver collars (below) as peace tokens. A Seneca chief (bottom) proudly wears a similar collar on a chain necklace.

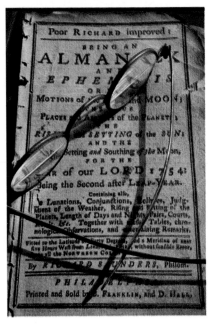

Philadelphia in 1752 (left) was a city of great cultural and religious diversity. The four large steeples, from left to right, mark the State House and the Christ, Presbyterian, and German Reformed Churches.

Benjamin Franklin examines a freshly printed page in a colonial print shop (above, right). A runaway printer's apprentice from Boston, he arrived in Philadelphia at age 17 with one Dutch dollar in his pocket and grew up to be the most prominent printer in the Colonies. Ben Franklin's mind was filled with ideas for improving the world around him. For 25 years he published the popular Poor Richard's Almanack, *which contained wise and witty rules for living. When he found that glasses "proper for reading" were "not the best for greater distances," he combined the two, inventing bifocals (above). His daring experiments with electricity made him a leading scientist of his day. But some of Franklin's later works were his greatest. As a contributor to both the Declaration of Independence and the Constitution, Benjamin Franklin helped shape the United States of America.*

was "often very black, thick with dirt, and full of worms," Mittelberger wrote. "Even when very thirsty, one is almost unable to drink it without loathing." There was little food. "We had to eat the ship's biscuit," he wrote, "full of red worms and spiders' nests. True, great hunger and thirst teach one to eat and drink everything—but many must forfeit their lives in the process."

For more than 150 years—from the very first settlements until the Revolution broke out in 1775—immigrants from Europe continued to arrive. Many were so poor that they had no money to pay the cost of the transatlantic trip. To obtain passage, these people signed a contract, or "indenture," which bound them into servitude for a period of four to seven years, depending on their age and health. Other immigrants started out with enough money to pay for the voyage, but by the time they reached America, they had lost it all. This happened because passenger ships often spent several weeks traveling from port to port picking up people and cargo before setting out to cross the Atlantic. The delays forced the passengers to spend all the money they had so carefully saved, just to stay alive. When the ships at last made the crossing, many immigrants found themselves deeply in debt to the captain or the merchant who owned the vessel. Under the law they could be sold for a term of service to any person who would come to the ship and pay the debt. Pennsylvania and Virginia farmers and planters, always eager for cheap labor, flocked to Philadelphia to buy white servants from the sea captains.

"Our Europeans who have been purchased," wrote Mittelberger, "must work hard all the time. For new fields are constantly being laid out; and thus they learn from experience that oak tree stumps are just as hard in America as they are in Germany." Indentured children were called "apprentices" and had to work until they reached their early 20s. When their terms were up, the servants took their "freedom dues"—a bag of corn, a suit of clothes—and headed for the backcountry of Pennsylvania, Maryland, Virginia, or the Carolinas to start their own life. The German immigrants who settled the backcountry were joined by other European settlers. Thousands of Scotch-Irish—so called because they descended from Scots who had colonized Northern Ireland—also learned to grow wheat in the hills of Pennsylvania and the red earth of Virginia and Maryland. These people were thrifty, hardworking, and self-sufficient.

Struggling to Survive

Up and down the frontier—the unsettled inland wilderness from Georgia to Maine—these backwoods people struggled for survival against winter cold, summer heat, hard work, loneliness, and disease. Charles Woodmason, a British clergyman visiting North and South Carolina during the 1760s, wrote that the cabins are "quite open and exposed. [They have] little or no bedding, or anything to cover them—not a drop of anything, save cold water, to drink—and all their clothing [is] a shirt and trousers, shift and petticoat . . . no shoes or stockings—children run half naked."

Most people who lived on the frontier, especially those far from overland trails or navigable rivers, had to raise their own food and make all their own clothes. Large families were a necessity. There was so much work to be done that a family could not survive without the help of many hands. Even small children had to work.

Parents worked side by side in the endless task of making a home. The woman's job was as heavy as the man's. She had to spin thread, weave cloth, and sew the cloth together, stitch by stitch, to make clothes. She had to dig and weed the garden, raise the vegetables, and store and dry them for winter use. She had to watch the hens and gather the eggs. She had to draw water from the well, haul it to the cabin, and heat it for washing or for cooking. To make a fire, she had to strike flint with steel to spark "tinder," or dry twigs. And she had to make soap to wash tub after tub of clothes.

A favorite song with frontier settlers tells the story of an old man who boasted that he could do more work in a day than his wife could do in three.

*"With all my heart!" the old woman said,
"But then you must allow
That you must do my work for a day,
And I'll go follow the plow."*

"There is hardly any trade in England but the same may be met with in Philadelphia," said an astonished visitor to the city in 1710. From the Arch Street wharf and other Philadelphia docks, merchants shipped Pennsylvania crops—flour and lumber, wool and meat—to southern colonies and Europe.

Sea captains navigated merchant ships along Atlantic trade routes with the help of this "backstaff"—an instrument used to measure altitudes at sea. Boston craftsman Thomas Greenough made it in 1760.

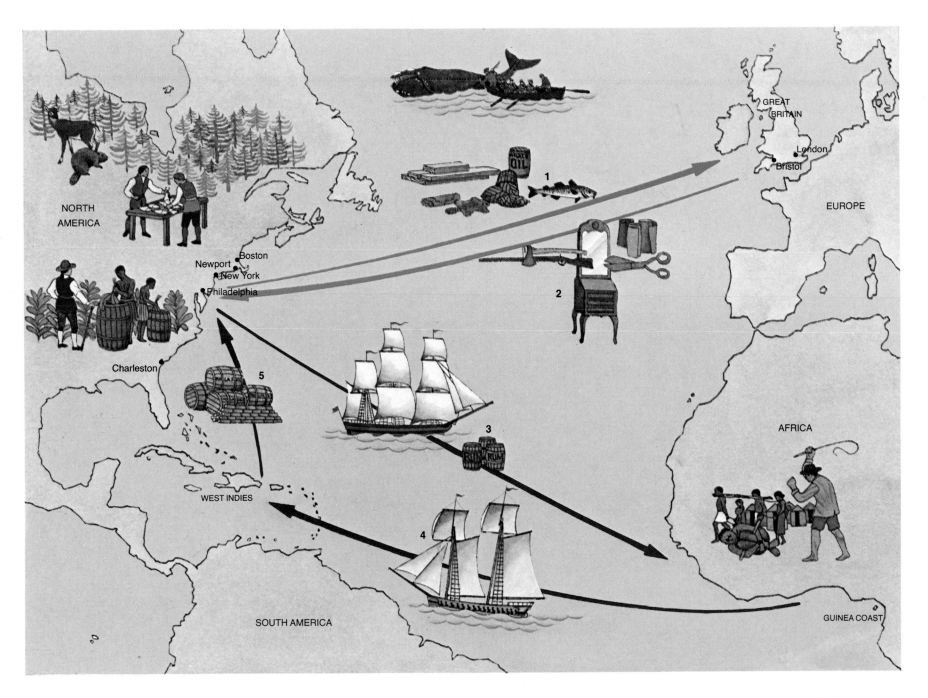

GREAT
BRITAIN

London

Bristol

EUROPE

NORTH
AMERICA

OIL

1

2

Newport   Boston
New York
Philadelphia

Charleston

5

3

AFRICA

4

WEST INDIES

SOUTH AMERICA

GUINEA COAST

Colonial Trade

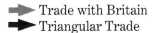

Trade with Britain
Triangular Trade

These merchants "try all ports" and "risk all freights to keep their ships in constant employ," wrote an observer of Massachusetts commerce in 1676. To Britain (1) colonial vessels carried the bounty of America's forests, fields, and waters—timber and tar, tobacco and rice, whale oil,

dried fish, animal pelts—and returned with goods made in Britain's workshops (2)—axes and muskets, cloth, tools, and fine furniture.

Other colonists built their fortunes sailing "rum-boats" in the triangular trade with Africa and the West Indies. In 1752 one skipper sailed the ship Sanderson *from Newport to Africa (3) with a cargo of 8,220 gallons of rum. Bartering the liquor for 56 slaves, he then crossed the ocean to the*

West Indies (4), with his cargo crammed below deck. On the island of Barbados he sold the slaves for molasses and sugar, which he carried home to New England (5)—where distillers made the molasses into rum.

Cowry shells (right), iron, and other goods bought slaves for the Colonies. Bound in groups called coffles (opposite), slaves were marched from inland jungles to coastal trading posts. There, traders bought and branded the healthy ones, then loaded them on ships. A broadside from Charleston, South Carolina (below), advertises the recent arrival of slaves.

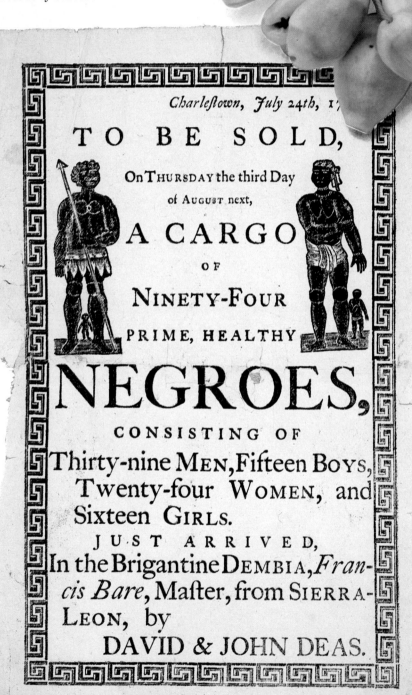

Charlestown, July 24th, 17

TO BE SOLD,

On THURSDAY the third Day

of AUGUST next,

A CARGO

OF

NINETY-FOUR

PRIME, HEALTHY

NEGROES,

CONSISTING OF

Thirty-nine MEN, Fifteen BOYS,
Twenty-four WOMEN, and
Sixteen GIRLS.

JUST ARRIVED,

In the Brigantine DEMBIA, Francis Bare, Master, from SIERRA-LEON, by

DAVID & JOHN DEAS.

So the old man set about performing the chores that fell to the woman on a pioneer farm. But after the cow had kicked him, the pig had pushed him in the mud, and he "quite forgot" to spin the daily spool of yarn, he realized the folly of his boast.

> *And when he saw how well she plowed,*
> *And ran the furrows even,*
> *He swore she could do more work in a day,*
> *Than he could do in seven.*

The frontier woman had to carry baby after baby and to act as midwife to other women when they gave birth. ("It would ease your pain, honey, if you lay on your side and hollered.") There were no doctors in the wilderness. If you became sick, the cure was simple. "There you must lie," Woodmason explained, "till nature gets the better of the disease, or death relieves you." Many babies died before their first birthday. Those who survived infancy often did not make it through their first five years. Diseases like diphtheria, scarlet fever, whooping cough, and smallpox claimed their lives. Cemeteries were filled with the tiny graves of children.

How Children Lived

There was little time for education on the frontier. Children grew wise in the ways of the forest and did well the tasks to which they were set. Girls spun wool and knitted. Boys watched the cattle and sheep. John and David Brainerd, raised on a Connecticut farm in the 1720s, wrote that a boy "must rise early and make himself useful. . . . His whole time out of school must be filled up with some service, such as bringing in fuel for the day, cutting potatoes for the sheep, feeding the swine, watering the horses, picking the berries, gathering the vegetables, spooling the yarn." A child's labor, then, was a large part of his life. Mothers even sang about work as they rocked their babies to sleep:

> *On the westward hill the sheep will stray.*
> *My child will watch them from break of day.*
> *Berry picking shall be his play.*
> *Sleep now, my darling, 'til break of day.*

It is likely that half of all the white people who came to America during colonial times came as indentured servants. William Penn valued these people because they were, as he put it, "the hands and feet of the rich." But there were never enough of them. After the middle of the 17th century, and especially in the South, employers began to seek another source of labor, the peoples of Africa.

The African slave trade in America started just after the New World was discovered. Spanish, French, Dutch, and English traders and sea captains bought or kidnapped Africans to toil on big sugar plantations in the Caribbean. American merchants, too,

54

56

"When our slaves are aboard we shackle the men two and two, while we lie in port, and in sight of their own country," wrote Thomas Phillips, commander of the English slave ship Hannibal in 1693, "for 'tis then they attempt to make their escape, and mutiny." Bound in iron cuffs at wrist and ankle, slaves were tightly packed below deck in tiers of platforms two to three feet high. The women and children remained unchained in separate compartments.

Many slaves, desperate at being torn from their homeland, friends, and families, tried to kill their keepers. Some committed suicide by starving themselves or jumping overboard.

Slaves were fed twice a day on meals of horsebeans, yams, and rice, and if they refused to eat, force-fed with a funnel. When the weather permitted, "we . . . let the slaves come up into the sun to air themselves," Phillips wrote, "and make them jump and dance for an hour or two . . ."—sometimes to the beat of an African drum. "If they go about it reluctantly. . . ," wrote an observer on one ship, "they are flogged . . . with a cat-o'-nine-tails."

An unbalanced diet, lack of fresh air for much of the voyage, and unsanitary conditions caused widespread diseases and epidemics. Scurvy, dysentery, malaria, measles, and smallpox killed slaves and crew alike. Even so, close to 9.5 million slaves survived the Atlantic journey between the 16th and 19th centuries.

Taproom at Buckman Tavern, Lexington, Massachusetts

mostly from Newport, Boston, and New York, hastened to profit from the sale of human beings. The first slaves on the American mainland were brought from the Caribbean, but beginning in the 1670s, merchants shipped them directly from Africa. By the early 18th century announcements like the following were common in the newspapers: "TO BE SOLD, A PARCEL OF NEGROES, JUST ARRIVED—MEN, WOMEN, BOYS AND GIRLS." These "parcels" were sometimes taken off the the slave ships, as one observer noted, "entirely naked . . . having only corals of different colors around their necks and arms."

Like the German immigrants who crossed with Mittelberger on the *Osgood*, many Africans did not survive the Atlantic trip. During the crossing they died of disease, despair, or the battering they took when crammed into the stinking holds of the slave ships. Some broke their chains, attacked the ship crews, and died fighting. Others, once they had revolted, refused to be captured alive. As one ship's officer wrote, they "leaped overboard and drowned themselves in the ocean with much resolution, showing no manner of concern for . . . life."

Buckman Tavern

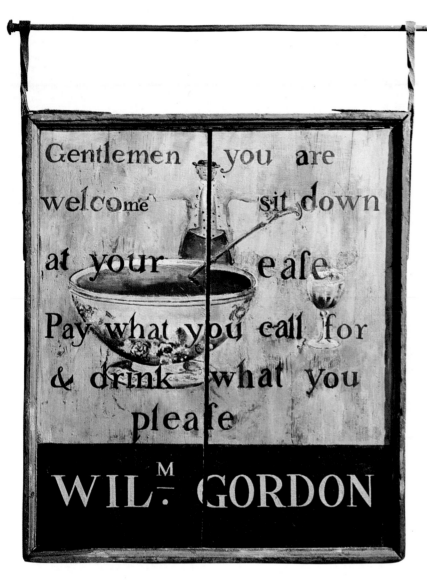

Colonial travelers exchanged news at America's many inns and taverns. Local people gathered there, sometimes to watch a play or bid at an auction. Early almanacs measured distances not from town to town, but from tavern to tavern. A signboard (above) beckoned folk to sample tavern fare: fowl and mutton, cabbage and hoecake, cider, rum, and brandy. At Buckman Tavern (opposite, lower) in Lexington, Massachusetts, townspeople met in the taproom (opposite, upper) to argue local politics, hear the latest news, or play a round of cards over quarts of beer that cost only a penny each.

By 1750 there were more than 235,000 African slaves throughout British America, doomed to work until they died for white masters and mistresses. Most slaves labored on the big tobacco, rice, and indigo plantations of the South. Thousands of others labored as seamen, craftsmen, dockworkers, house servants, coachmen, and farm laborers in the middle colonies as well as New England. Slavery was a condition that a person inherited. A child born of a slave was a slave from birth. Black mothers brought their babies into the world knowing that they would face the same lifetime of toil and torment that they themselves endured.

Hard Traveling

In 1750 most Americans lived in the countryside, scattered over a huge area. Getting from one colony to another was slow and difficult. Sailing along the coast was the easiest way to travel. There were no surfaced roads. On land you had to walk, ride horseback, or travel in a horse-drawn wagon along rough trails through the woods. No bridges spanned the wide rivers. When you came to a river you either had to ride your horse across, wade and swim, or be ferried across on a boat. When the waters were in flood, crossing a river was a hard and dangerous experience.

In 1672 an irregular mail service had been set up between Boston and New York. It lasted only a few months, but it improved communication between the colonies. The first mails were carried by "postriders," mailmen who rode horseback on trails that wound along rivers, over hills, and through forests. The earliest trail from New York to Boston ran through New Haven, Hartford, and Springfield and was called the Boston Post Road. In those days it took about two weeks to cover the more than 250 miles between Boston and New York. A modern automobile covers the same distance in about four hours.

The communities along the Boston Post Road, like most colonial communities, usually centered around a church or a meetinghouse. A church provided a place where people might come together to worship, to do business, to make laws, to learn the Bible. A minister cared for his people in health and in sickness, comforted them in trouble, and taught the children.

The church also prepared people for death. In the Colonies death lurked everywhere—in freezing winter storms, in summer fevers, in childbirth, in snakes' fangs and bears' claws, in falling trees, in flooding rivers, and in treacherous seas. The church taught that wickedness in this life, without God's forgiveness, would bring punishment forever in the burning fires of hell and that everyone needed the daily help of the church if they wished to overcome sin and reach heaven.

Jonathan Edwards, one of the most famous colonial preachers, expressed this belief with terrifying force in a sermon at Enfield, Connecticut, in 1741. "O sinner!" he warned, "consider the fearful danger you are in: it is a great furnace of wrath, a wide and bottomless pit. . . . You hang by a slender thread, with the flames of divine

Sarah Knight's Journey in 1704

"The roads all along this way are very bad, encumbered with rocks and mountainous passages," wrote Sarah Knight of her 270-mile journey from Boston to New York in October 1704. The widow was heading south on horseback to settle the estate of a rich relative (1).

She rode with a "postrider," a hard-riding horseman who carried mail between Boston, New York, and Philadelphia. In summer postriders averaged 30 to 50 miles a day on "post roads"—narrow paths that cut through the wilderness. The postriders doubled as guides for travelers, but Sarah's companion "put on very furiously," she wrote, "so that I could not keep up."

As darkness fell, and Sarah found herself alone in Indian country, "each lifeless trunk, with its shattered limbs, appeared an armed enemy," she recorded, "and every little stump like a ravenous devourer."

Sarah forded a stream "so very fierce a horse could sometimes hardly stem it" and crossed the swollen Pawtuxet River in a small, unsteady canoe (2). Frozen with fear, she sat not daring "to lodge my tongue a hair's breadth more to one side of my mouth than t'other."

New England inns and taverns (3), (4) served pickled mutton and pork to weary travelers like Sarah and offered them only "wretched" cornhusk mattresses, often in a room with two or three other persons.

Postriders left mail with innkeepers to pass along to townfolk who paid the postage.

Tottering timber bridges spanned Connecticut rivers and streams. At one, "under which the river run very swift," Sarah's horse stumbled and nearly slipped into the water (5). But she met with no harm and arrived in New Haven (6), six days and five nights from Boston.

Well rested after a two-month stay, Sarah set off again for New York, taking a ferry across the Housatonic River (7). Outside the city she marveled at bridges "of such a breadth that a cart might pass with safety," built, perhaps, with funds collected by a toll-keeper—"three pence for passing over with a horse" (8).

After a final sleepless night in a tavern's "little leanto chamber" with "covering as scanty as my bed was hard," Sarah reached New York (9).

Preferring rough roads to a cramped and dangerous winter sea trip, the widow returned home the way she had come. Thankfully, she wrote:

"Now I've returned to Sarah Knight's
Thro' many toils and many frights
Over great rocks and many stones
God has presarv'd from fracter'd bones."

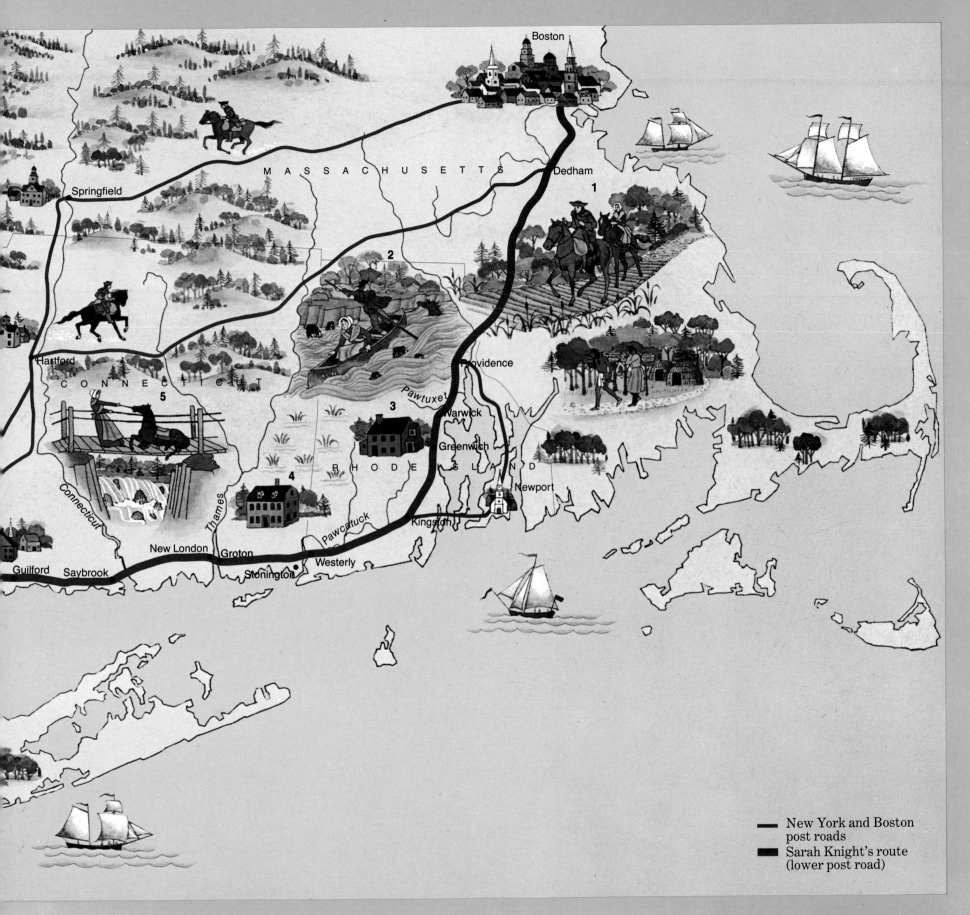

Boston

Dedham

MASSACHUSETTS

1

Springfield

2

Hartford

CONNECTICUT

Pawtuxet

Providence

Warwick

5

3

Greenwich

RHODE ISLAND

4

Newport

Connecticut

Thames

Pawcatuck

Kingston

New London

Groton

Westerly

Guilford   Saybrook

Stonington

New York and Boston
post roads

Sarah Knight's route
(lower post road)

Colonial churches, like the Old Ship Meeting House in Hingham, Massachusetts, helped early Americans face life and death in a dangerous new world. Englishman George Whitefield (below) was the most popular traveling evangelist during a religious movement called the Great Awakening. His stormy sermons drew crowds of 30,000 souls, who sobbed and trembled as his ringing voice painted pictures of a burning hell.

wrath flashing about it . . . and you have . . . nothing to lay hold of to save yourself." Many colonists believed deeply that they were in constant danger, that they needed the church as much as they needed food, clothing, and shelter.

But as the years passed and settlements multiplied, the church could not keep pace with them. More and more people found themselves living miles away from an organized congregation. Their need to be part of a church community found expression in a series of religious revivals that swept the country from time to time. The greatest of these movements was called the Great Awakening. It began in the mid-1730s and lasted until the end of the 1740s. Ministers called "itinerants," or wanderers, traveled throughout the Colonies to talk about God and the church wherever they could find an audience—in meetinghouses, on village greens, at campsites, in forest clearings, on city streets.

An Exciting Event

I t was a great event in a colonial community when word got around that a minister was soon to arrive. Nathan Cole, a Connecticut farmer, told about the excitement that gripped people in the year 1740 with news that George Whitefield, one of the greatest of the itinerant preachers, was coming to preach in Middletown. Middletown lies on the edge of the broad Connecticut River as it sweeps southward to Long Island Sound. "When we got to Middletown old meeting house," wrote Cole, "there was a great multitude . . . of people, assembled together. . . . I turned and looked towards the Great River and saw the ferry boats running swift backward and forward bringing over loads of people, and the oars rowed nimble and quick. . . . The land and banks over the river looked black with people and horses. . . . I saw no man at work in his field, but all seemed to be gone." When Whitefield came to Middletown, he was in the second year of a tour that had begun in Georgia and had taken him from one end of the country to the other. Nathan Cole described him as looking "almost angelical" when he stood up to speak "before some thousands of people with . . . [an] undaunted countenance."

Men like Whitefield brought the promise of salvation. People at these meetings prayed, sang, shouted, clapped their hands, wept, and fainted. They then set about organizing churches, building meetinghouses, and sending for ministers to lead them in a renewed Christian life. Thus the awakenings drew many Americans together into a network of believers that spanned the country. The awakenings also touched the lives of thousands of black slaves, who were rapidly embracing Christianity.

By the middle of the 18th century settlers in British America had a great deal in common. Most of them spoke the same language, sang the same songs, lived under the same law, and worshipped the same God. They were all shaped by the common struggle to clear the wilderness and to build a new life in a new land. From this shared experience was emerging a new people.

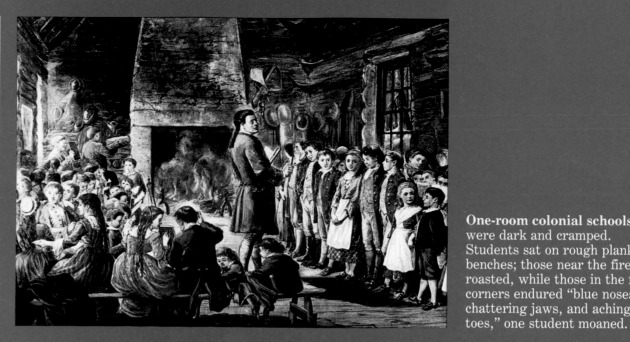

One-room colonial schools were dark and cramped. Students sat on rough plank benches; those near the fire roasted, while those in the far corners endured "blue noses, chattering jaws, and aching toes," one student moaned.

This "deadfall" rattrap (below) helped colonists fight furry pests, some of which came to America on European ships.

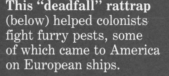

This cannon stove is named for its round shape. Cast-iron stoves, made popular by Germans, warmed better than fireplaces and used less wood.

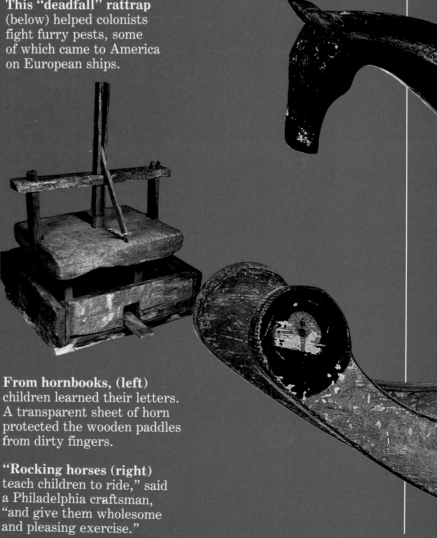

From hornbooks, (left) children learned their letters. A transparent sheet of horn protected the wooden paddles from dirty fingers.

"Rocking horses (right) teach children to ride," said a Philadelphia craftsman, "and give them wholesome and pleasing exercise."

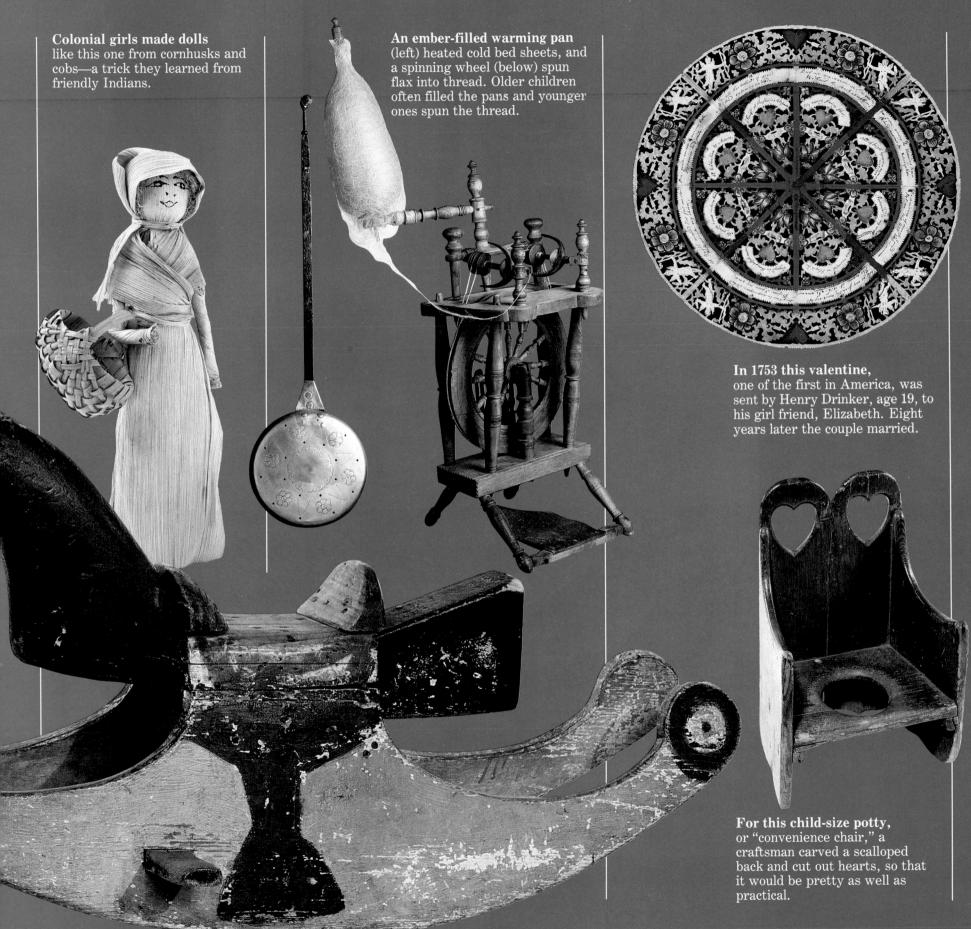

Colonial girls made dolls like this one from cornhusks and cobs—a trick they learned from friendly Indians.

An ember-filled warming pan (left) heated cold bed sheets, and a spinning wheel (below) spun flax into thread. Older children often filled the pans and younger ones spun the thread.

In 1753 this valentine, one of the first in America, was sent by Henry Drinker, age 19, to his girl friend, Elizabeth. Eight years later the couple married.

For this child-size potty, or "convenience chair," a craftsman carved a scalloped back and cut out hearts, so that it would be pretty as well as practical.

· FROM · Colonies TO States

The Road to Independence 1763-1783

erched on high cliffs, the fortress-city of Quebec guarded the main approach to Montreal and the great North American empire of the French. On September 13, 1759, just before dawn, British soldiers landed at the foot of the cliffs and wound their way up a steep path to the top. They found themselves outside the town walls on a plateau called the Plains of Abraham. Their leader, a pale, red-haired young general named James Wolfe, drew them up in battle formation. Quebec's defender, the Marquis de Montcalm, lined up his men outside the town gates and gave the order to advance. The British held their ground as the French approached and then released a burst of musket fire that sent the French fleeing. Near the town gates, the marquis was fatally shot. James Wolfe was also hit. As he lay dying, he learned he had won Quebec.

This clash on the Plains of Abraham was a decisive battle in the latest round of a struggle between Britain and France that had been going on for years. The prize was nothing less than North America itself. France finally admitted defeat. The Treaty of Paris, signed in 1763, forced the French king, Louis XV, to give up all the lands he claimed on the continent of North America.

The American colonists considered Wolfe a hero. They had taken part in all the wars against France and had often been victims of French attacks. They were afraid that as long as the French remained in America, the French might one day drive them right off the eastern shore into the Atlantic.

After the war the government in London took steps to tighten its grip on the empire it had won. In October 1763 King George III handed down a proclamation telling the colonists that they were not to cross the Appalachians to settle. The British wanted to make peace with the Indians on the new lands, so that they might take over the fur trade that the French had been forced to abandon.

King George then announced plans to keep an army of 10,000 men in the New World at all times for what he called "imperial defense." The events of the spring were on his mind: Pontiac, chief of the Ottawa Indians, had united a dozen tribes in revolt against British rule and had set the frontier ablaze with warfare from New York to Virginia.

When 10,000 men eat three meals a day, somebody has to pay the bill. King George now decided that the American colonists must do this. Were they not, after all, the ones who would get the most protection? In order to get the colonists to pay, the British Parliament passed the Stamp Act in 1765. The act placed a tax on newspapers, licenses, calendars, playing cards, and even dice. The money raised by the taxes would cover some of the army's bills.

How would this work? Suppose you are publishing a newspaper called the *Pennsylvania Journal*, which you sell for three pennies. Beginning November 1, 1765, you will have to buy a one-penny stamp from a royal agent for each copy of the *Journal*. People who buy the *Journal* will now have to pay an extra penny for it.

In passing the Stamp Act, the Parliament in London broke a rule that the colonists thought of as the very foundation of the British

Wounded by French muskets, British Gen. James Wolfe lies dying as his troops fight on for control of Quebec. This 1759 battle—the last major conflict of the Seven Years War in America—ended with the French soldiers' rapid retreat from heavy British fire. Americans, allied with the British, cheered the French defeat and honored Wolfe in song:
  "The drums did loudly beat,
    colors were flying,
  The purple gore did stream,
    and men lay dying,
  When shot off from his horse
    fell this brave hero,
  And we lament his loss in
    weeds of sorrow."

French Militiaman of the Seven Years War

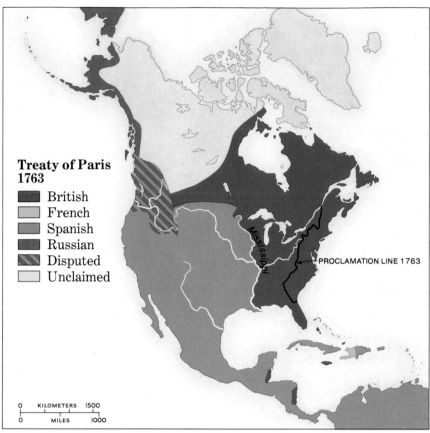

Treaty of Paris 1763

■ British
□ French
▨ Spanish
▨ Russian
▨ Disputed
□ Unclaimed

PROCLAMATION LINE 1763

Mississippi

KILOMETERS 1500
MILES 1000

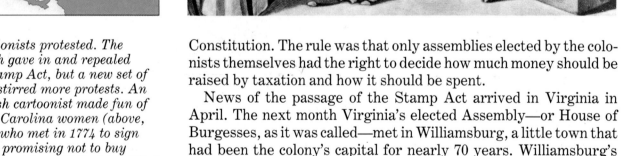

The Treaty of 1763 ended the Seven Years War and broke up France's North American empire. Britain won Canada and split the Louisiana Territory—which stretched from the Appalachians to the Rockies—with France's ally, Spain. Britain took Louisiana east of the Mississippi River; Spain gained the western land. American jubilation over Britain's victory quickly cooled when King George III handed down a proclamation forbidding settlement west of the Appalachian Mountains.

When the British required revenue stamps (right) for everyday items, such as newspapers and playing cards,

the colonists protested. The British gave in and repealed the Stamp Act, but a new set of taxes stirred more protests. An English cartoonist made fun of North Carolina women (above, right) who met in 1774 to sign a pact promising not to buy British goods until the king lifted unfair taxes.

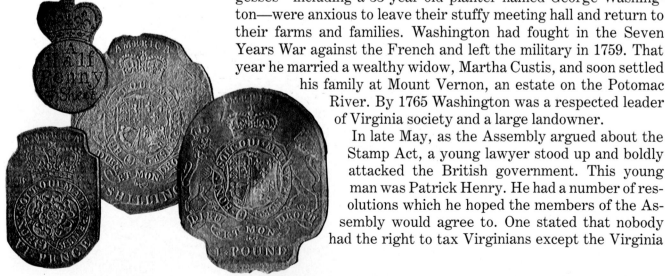

Constitution. The rule was that only assemblies elected by the colonists themselves had the right to decide how much money should be raised by taxation and how it should be spent.

News of the passage of the Stamp Act arrived in Virginia in April. The next month Virginia's elected Assembly—or House of Burgesses, as it was called—met in Williamsburg, a little town that had been the colony's capital for nearly 70 years. Williamsburg's 200 houses were clustered between the York and James Rivers in a land of broad plantations, stately mansions, and slave cabins.

The southern spring had come and almost gone. Most of the burgesses—including a 33-year-old planter named George Washington—were anxious to leave their stuffy meeting hall and return to their farms and families. Washington had fought in the Seven Years War against the French and left the military in 1759. That year he married a wealthy widow, Martha Custis, and soon settled his family at Mount Vernon, an estate on the Potomac River. By 1765 Washington was a respected leader of Virginia society and a large landowner.

In late May, as the Assembly argued about the Stamp Act, a young lawyer stood up and boldly attacked the British government. This young man was Patrick Henry. He had a number of resolutions which he hoped the members of the Assembly would agree to. One stated that nobody had the right to tax Virginians except the Virginia

Patrick Henry
1736-1799

N o one could say that young Patrick Henry was especially industrious or talented. What he liked to do was fish, fiddle, and roam the Virginia woods. The only thing unusual about him was his "sending" voice. When he "sent" his voice, he could be heard a half a mile away, which was handy for calling the dogs.

But what Patrick needed was to earn his living. He failed as a storekeeper and as a farmer but found his calling in the law. His first big case came along in 1763. Arguing against the king's right to tell Virginians how much to pay their preachers, Patrick suddenly got mad and began sending his voice over the courtroom. Up and down he sent it, and when he'd finished, the audience cheered. Patrick had become an orator, and, as it turned out, this was just what America needed.

Two years later as a member of Virginia's governing body, Patrick sent his voice out so boldly against the Stamp Tax that there was a cry of "Treason!" In 1775 he transfixed his audience by pretending to stab himself with a letter opener as he cried, "Give me liberty or give me death!" A man in the balcony was so excited he spit a wad of tobacco into the audience below.

When war broke out, "Liberty or Death" became the battle cry of the country. Patrick was elected governor of Virginia and reelected four times. And his voice never lost its magic. Indeed, people said it was an experience just to hear Patrick Henry announce the weather.

JEAN FRITZ

Patrick Henry speaking at a Virginia courthouse, 1763

Assembly itself. Henry bluntly told the burgesses that if the king were allowed to tax the colonists as he pleased, it would mean the end of the colonists' freedom. When Henry compared King George to earlier tyrants in history who had been overthrown for their crimes, some of his listeners cried "Treason."

As news of the debate spread through town, a law student, Thomas Jefferson, hurried to the House of Burgesses. Jefferson was 22 years old. The son of a tobacco grower, he had come to Williamsburg in 1760 to attend the College of William and Mary. In 1769 he would be chosen a member of that same Assembly where he now heard Patrick Henry speak.

When the debate was finished, the House of Burgesses passed Henry's resolutions, and they appeared in many newspapers. Soon the country was alive with protest against the Stamp Act. Committees that called themselves the Sons of Liberty organized demonstrations. Bonfires blazed. Straw figures symbolizing the king's taxmen hung in nooses from trees. The stamp sellers got a clear message: *resign your jobs or get out of town.* Early in 1766 the British government gave in and repealed the Stamp Act. The colonists celebrated the good news.

New Taxes Arouse the Colonists

The next year a new British finance minister, Charles Townshend, persuaded Parliament to pass new taxes—or, as he called them, "duties"—on a number of items that the colonists imported from England, like glass, tea, paper, and lead.

The Townshend Duties sparked the same kind of resistance that the Stamp Act had. This time Massachusetts led the fight from its capital, Boston, a prosperous seaport of 15,000 people.

The Sons of Liberty asked Bostonians to boycott British goods until the Townshend Duties were withdrawn. Women of all ages formed the Daughters of Liberty and joined the "Don't Buy British" movement. They took up spinning and weaving in order to clothe their families with American-made cloth.

Now the government in England decided there must be no more resistance; the colonists must be made to obey the law. In October 1768 a fleet of warships dropped anchor in Boston harbor, with cannons trained on the town. Soldiers landed with drums rolling and flags flying. Some pitched their tents on Boston Common.

The British troops remained in Boston for 18 months. The Bostonians resented their presence and grew more and more angry at reports of British bad manners, brutality, and drunken behavior. Soldiers and civilians traded jeers and sometimes blows.

On March 5, 1770, the tension in Boston boiled over: British soldiers opened fire on a threatening mob. Five Bostonians died. The incident—described by extremists as the Boston Massacre—fueled the colonists' anger against the British.

On the very day of the Boston shooting, Parliament, concerned about the boycotts, voted to withdraw the Townshend Duties,

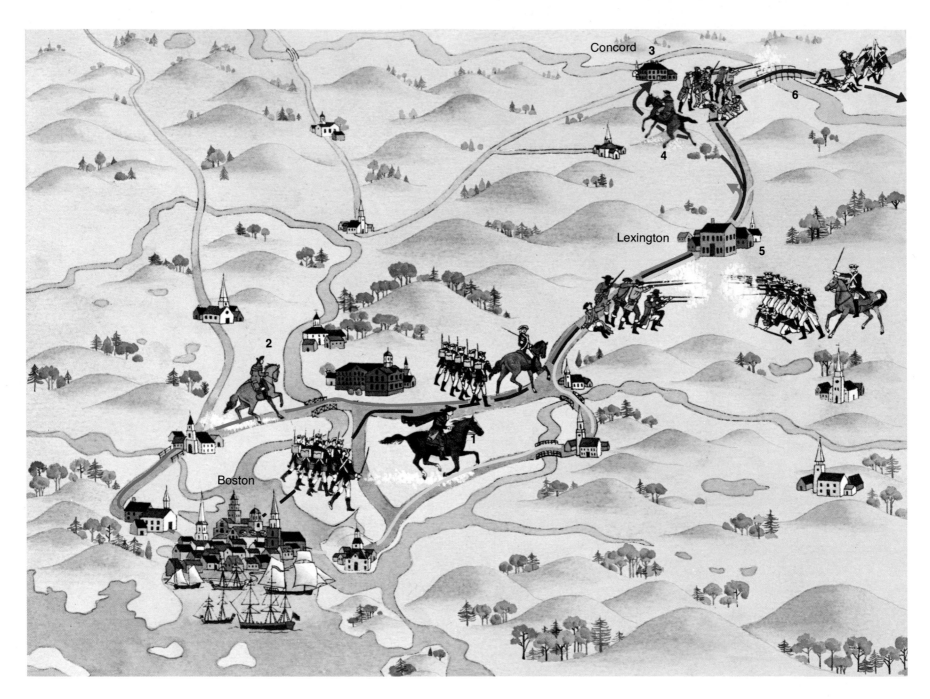

"The British Are Coming!"

- ➡ British Redcoats
- ➡ Paul Revere
- ➡ Will Dawes
- ➡ Dr. Samuel Prescott

Racing across the Massachusetts countryside, Paul Revere (1) and William Dawes (2) warn their countrymen that the redcoats are coming. A British force of about 700 men had hoped to surprise Concord (3) and seize colonial ammunition; but on the night of May 18, 1775, patriots caught wind of the plan and dispatched the two riders to alert the militia.

At Lexington Dr. Samuel Prescott (4), a patriot physician, joined Revere and Dawes. Near Concord a British patrol stopped them and took Revere prisoner. Dawes fled on foot; Prescott spurred his horse over a stone wall and galloped on to Concord to spread the news. By the time 180 of the redcoats reached Lexington (5), about 70 militiamen had lined up on the village green to meet them. Although badly outnumbered, patriot Capt. John Parker urged his men to stand firm. No one knows who fired the first shot, but when the volleys stopped, eight militiamen lay dead. The redcoats marched confidently on to Concord, where more than 300 of the militia awaited them. The British destroyed some ammunition and food supplies in town and then confronted angry militiamen at North Bridge (6). An exchange of fire killed three redcoats and two rebels. With more militiamen arriving, the British turned around and began their march back to Boston.

except for a tax on tea. Soon the British troops sailed away.

Most people rejoiced at this victory, but Sam Adams, who led the Boston resistance movement, looked ahead to fresh struggles. Adams had failed as a businessman, but he was a superb politician, organizer, and writer. In 1772, at age 50, he persuaded townspeople to set up a committee to "enter into correspondence" with other towns in Massachusetts to discuss common complaints. This Committee of Correspondence was actually a "shadow government" that could organize resistance to the British throughout Massachusetts whenever the time came. Soon the Boston committee was in touch with more than 80 other committees in Massachusetts alone. Other colonies set up similar networks.

In 1773 the British tried again to make Americans pay taxes. The scheme was to bring a huge amount of tea over from India and to sell it at a price so low, tax included, that the colonists would not be able to resist buying it. But they resisted. In New York, Philadelphia, and Boston, colonists stopped sailors from unloading the tea. When Thomas Hutchinson, the royal governor of Massachusetts, made clear his plans to unload it under the protection of troops, Bostonians took action. On December 16, 1773, colonists disguised as Indians boarded three tea ships in the harbor, seized 340 tea chests, and dumped them into the sea.

The British swiftly punished this act of defiance, known as the Boston Tea Party. In May 1774 they sailed back into Boston harbor and prepared to blockade the port, cutting off its trade. *Pay for the spoiled tea*, the king told the Bostonians, *or starve*.

The Continental Congress Assembles

On May 27 a group of Virginia lawmakers met. They called upon patriots in all the Colonies to elect delegates to a Continental Congress to decide what to do in this new crisis. In September, 56 men—mostly merchants, lawyers, and large landowners—assembled in Philadelphia. The Virginia delegation included George Washington and Patrick Henry. John Adams, an ambitious young lawyer and cousin of rebel leader Sam Adams, came from Boston.

As John Adams and the rest of the Massachusetts delegation rode by coach to Philadelphia, people waved and cheered them. "As we came into [New Haven]," Adams wrote in his diary, "all the bells in town were set to ringing, and the people, men, women, and children, were crowding at the doors and windows as if it was . . . a coronation." Hot, dusty, and tired, they arrived in Philadelphia on August 29 after nearly three weeks on the road.

Adams's wife, Abigail, waited at home with a heavy heart. America and Britain, clearly enough, were moving toward war. On her shoulders alone had fallen the burden of running the Adams farm and caring for their five children. "The great anxiety I feel for my country, for you, and for our family," she wrote her husband, "renders the day tedious and the night unpleasant. . . . Did ever any kingdom or state regain its liberty when once it was

Rebel sharpshooters crouched behind this wall and fired at redcoats retreating from Concord to Boston. Near this spot, "a great many lay dead and the road was bloody," a veteran recalled. The redcoat uniform in this modern photograph shows what obvious targets the British were. Of the rebels a British officer wrote: "I never believed . . . they would have attacked the King's troops, or have had the perseverance I found in them."

73

British naval guns belch smoke and deadly fire from Boston's Charles River as redcoats stream ashore to take a rebel stronghold at the Battle of Bunker Hill. By early afternoon on this sweltering day, June 17, 1775, more than two dozen barges had ferried troops across the water. At first the well-ordered redcoat columns "advanced with confidence," one officer recalled. The patriots, low on ammunition, waited with grim resolve from their position on Breed's Hill, just below Bunker Hill. "Don't fire until you see the whites of their eyes," a patriot officer was said to have instructed his men. The first colonial volley killed 96 redcoats and sent others scurrying down the hill. A second clash killed even more. On the third assault the British took the hill as the militiamen ran out of gunpowder and retreated. No day of fighting proved more costly to the British than the struggle on Breed's Hill. With more than a thousand redcoats killed or wounded, Gen. Henry Clinton called the battle "a dear bought victory. Another such would have ruined us."

Candles burn (left) in the Pennsylvania State House as they did on the evening of July 4, 1776, when the Continental Congress adopted the Declaration of Independence. In a painting from the period (above), delegates confer as Thomas Jefferson presents his draft of the declaration to John Hancock. The declaration severed political ties between Britain and America and provided an enduring statement of human rights: "We hold these truths to be self-evident, that all men are created equal, that they are endowed by their Creator with certain unalienable Rights, that among these are Life, Liberty and the pursuit of Happiness."

invaded, without bloodshed? I cannot think of it without horror."

When the Continental Congress met in early September, it decided to send a letter to the king, urging him to lift the Boston blockade. A short time later the delegates approved resolutions calling on the people of Massachusetts to arm themselves and urging all Colonies to stop trading with Britain.

Soon militiamen—the troops raised and paid for by the individual Colonies—were marching up and down on village greens, and towns were gathering supplies of ammunition. Americans prepared to fight a government which they no longer trusted, which they viewed increasingly as an enemy.

In Boston the commander in chief of the British forces, General Sir Thomas Gage, became concerned about reports of stockpiled munitions at Concord, about 20 miles to the west. On the night of April 18, 1775, Gage sent his troops to seize the supplies and arrest two rebel leaders, Sam Adams and John Hancock.

Thanks to early warnings from Paul Revere and William Dawes, the militia was waiting when the redcoats arrived. At Lexington, a town on the way to Concord, the redcoats faced 70 militiamen— eight of whom died in this first exchange of fire of the Revolutionary War. At Concord the redcoats destroyed a small store of supplies, met resistance at North Bridge, and at 3 p.m. began the long march back to Boston. Armed colonists hid behind stone walls and trees and picked off the redcoats as they passed, turning the march into a bloody retreat. Long after nightfall, Gage's troops

Continental Soldiers and their Gear

The Continental Army, George Washington lamented, had "very little discipline, order or government" at the beginning of the Revolutionary War. As the war progressed, his soldiers learned European military drill—and combined it with their own determination and frontier know-how to defeat the redcoats, one of the world's best-trained, best-equipped armies.

Equipment was scarce for both Continental soldiers and the state militia, and uniforms even scarcer. Soldiers wore whatever they could find—sometimes next to nothing. Many dressed like this rifleman—in a linen hunting shirt, moccasins, and leggings. These sturdy outfits, based on Indian garb, proved so practical that General Washington said he preferred them for the whole Army.

But the regulation uniforms, finally ordered in 1779, were wholly different. Soldiers, like this officer, received dark blue coats with different colored facings to designate different units. Even after the introduction of the uniform, supplies came slowly and whole regiments sometimes had to report "not fit for duty for want of clothing."

Cartridge (actual size)

Musket ball

Gunpowder

"Prime and Load!" It took 15 hectic seconds for a Revolutionary War soldier (below) to ready his musket for firing. After grabbing a ball and powder cartridge (left), the soldier bites it open (1) and pours a little gunpowder into his musket's priming pan (2). He pours the remaining powder down the barrel and drops the musket ball after it, along with the cartridge paper to hold the ball in place (3). With his ramrod the soldier pushes paper, ball, and powder snug against the barrel (4). At "Fire!" he pulls the trigger (5), which sends a flint scraping against metal to create a spark. The spark ignites the gunpowder in the pan. This in turn explodes the powder in the barrel and sends the musket ball hurtling toward its target.

Spiraling grooves cut along the inside of a rifle barrel (left) helped rifle balls reach their marks. When a rifle fired, the grooves put a spin on the ball, propelling it farther and more accurately than the musket ball could fly. The rifle (left, center) proved effective at such battles as Bemis Heights, Kings Mountain, and Cowpens, but it had serious drawbacks. Compared with the musket (far left), the rifle took a long time to load. By the time a soldier forced his rifle ball tightly down the barrel, the enemy could be on him with a bayonet. The rifle itself had no bayonet, a necessity for fighting at close range or in damp weather when wet flints and gunpowder made firearms useless. Because of these disadvantages, the musket remained the primary weapon of the Revolutionary War.

were still limping wearily back to town. A thousand campfires burning in the surrounding fields told the British that they themselves were now under siege.

When Congress met three weeks after Lexington and Concord, it decided to raise an army of 20,000 men. These men were called "Continental soldiers" because they promised to fight for a full year anywhere on the continent that the commander in chief might send them. Congress appointed George Washington commander in chief of all American military forces, both the Continental troops and the militia. General Washington hastened to join the Massachusetts militia that was besieging Boston. He made his headquarters in the village of Cambridge, at a college named in honor of John Harvard, a Puritan minister.

Abigail Adams's dismay, as she saw the country inch daily toward war, was shared throughout the Colonies. Most colonists hoped that reconciliation with Great Britain was still possible. The British, with a population of eight million, controlled the world's greatest empire and could put large armies in the field and keep them there. Britain boasted well-trained generals, factories to cast cannons, and a navy that commanded the seas.

The Americans, by contrast, were a poor and scattered people with no navy and no money to raise and supply a big army. They numbered at most 2,260,000 people, of whom 500,000 were black slaves who would not be permitted to fight. Thus many colonists thought reconciliation made much more sense than war.

" 'Tis Time To Part"

In January 1776, while the British were still bottled up in Boston, a pamphlet called *Common Sense* appeared. Its writer was Tom Paine, a poor English immigrant who had arrived in Philadelphia two years earlier. Paine boldly defended the idea of independence.

" 'Tis time to part," he told his readers. Americans must decide to be free and tell the world. If Congress proclaimed independence, he argued, Americans could send agents to Europe to win help for the American cause in men, money, ships, and guns. "The sun never shined on a cause of greater worth. 'Tis not the affair of a city, a county, a province, or a kingdom; but of a continent—of at least one-eighth part of the habitable globe." Paine's *Common Sense* was a sensation; tattered copies passed from hand to hand.

Soon the Continental Congress was caught up in the rush of enthusiasm to be rid of Great Britain. In June 1776 it set up a committee to prepare a Declaration of Independence. Thomas Jefferson, the committee's chairman, wrote the first draft, which the committee gave to Congress at the end of June. Congress adopted the declaration July 4.

In the declaration, Jefferson explained that Americans, like all people, had a right to "Life, Liberty and the pursuit of Happiness," but that the British government had failed to protect these rights. To prove this charge, he listed bad things the British had done, like

At ease in a British camp on Manhattan Island, one soldier sharpens his sword while others play checkers, swap tales, and visit the barber. The British soldier usually led a hard life. Food from home often came moldy and late. His uniform (below) looked attractive but was impractical. Brimless hats provided little protection, and the canvas and wool suits were hot and heavy. On one summer march near New York City, 63 redcoats collapsed from heatstroke and nine died.

Fire rages through New York City after the British seize control from fleeing American troops in September 1776. The British blamed rebel extremists; George Washington, too, thought "some good honest fellow" might be responsible. Redcoats chased Washington's army as far as Pennsylvania. "Our little handful is daily decreasing," the general wrote. In three months the British had captured more than 4,000 of his men.

From the saddle, General Washington directs his men across the Delaware River on a daring mission to capture Trenton, New Jersey. Contrary to this artist's view, dangerous ice-choked waters and blinding snow hindered the nighttime crossing. Desperate situations require "desperate remedies," Washington said, explaining his decision to launch the bold raid.

keeping an army in the Colonies and making the colonists pay for it. For these reasons, Jefferson told the world, the American Colonies had decided to become free and independent states, with full power to make war, "conclude Peace . . . and to do all other Acts and Things which Independent States may of right do."

Messengers soon rode out of Philadelphia with news of the declaration. People assembled on town commons and in public squares to hear the news. Those who supported independence, the patriots, cheered and set off fireworks. Soldiers marched and fired guns.

But not everyone greeted the Declaration of Independence with such enthusiasm. Many people still opposed independence and remained loyal to the crown. No one knows exactly how many of these "Loyalists," or "Tories," there were, but their numbers ran to many thousands. They lived in all classes of society, in the towns, in the countryside, on the frontier.

Even some slaves and indentured servants were Loyalists, especially after the governor of Virginia had promised them freedom if they joined the British forces. "I do . . . declare," Governor Dunmore had said in his emancipation proclamation of November 7, 1775, "all indentured servants, Negroes or others, [belonging to rebels] FREE, that are able and willing to bear arms, they joining His Majesty's Troops as soon as may be. . . ."

Loyalists made a valuable contribution to the British side as soldiers, sailors, writers, and spies. On many battlefields Americans confronted not only British soldiers but other Americans as well. This gave the struggle the character of a civil war.

A Plan to Divide the Colonies

At the same time Americans were declaring their independence, the British launched a campaign to end the rebellion. Their plan was first to take New York City, then occupy the Hudson Valley and the Lake Champlain waterway with ships and troops. Success in this operation would seal off the New England states from all the others. The crown could then move ahead at its own pace to reconquer New England and after that the rest of the country.

At first all went well for the British. Their troopships and men-o'-war streamed into New York harbor while Congress was debating whether to declare independence. "So vast a fleet," one observer wrote, "was never before seen together in the port of New York . . . the multitude of masts carries the appearance of a wood." The new British commander in chief, General Sir William Howe, landed his forces on Staten Island. On August 27 he struck, falling first on the American encampment at Brooklyn village, then upon Manhattan. Washington's men fled in panic northward to White Plains, westward across the Hudson, southward through New Jersey to the Delaware River. The British took hundreds of prisoners; many were teenage boys. Behind the British lines a young Connecticut officer named Nathan Hale was caught spying. The British hanged Hale on September 22. He was reported to have said from

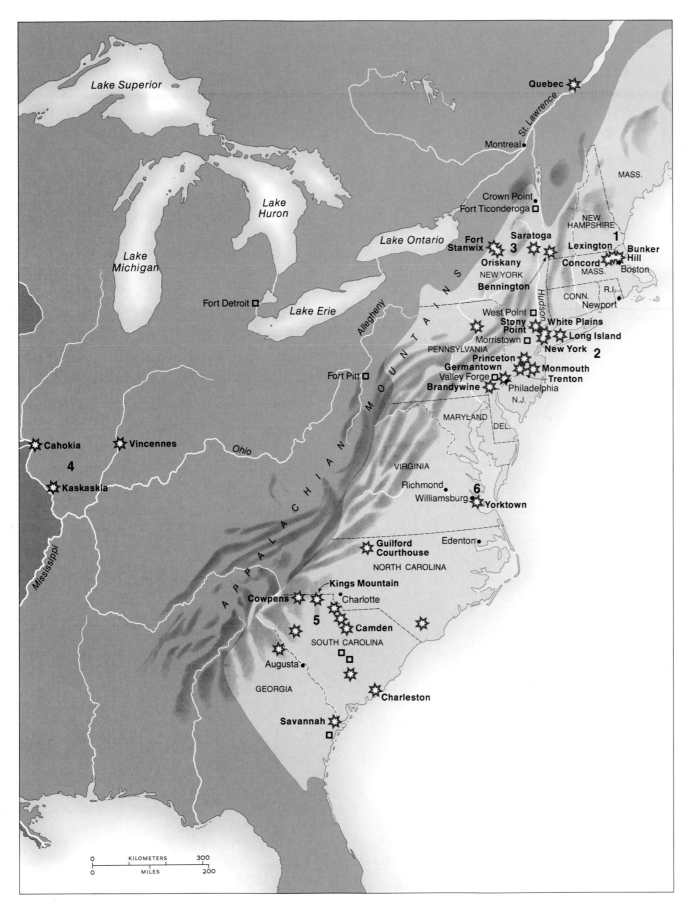

Battles of the Revolution

▨	British America
▢	The Thirteen Colonies
▩	Spanish Possessions
✷	Battles
▢	Forts

A barrage of gunfire at Lexington and Concord and a bloodbath near Bunker Hill (1) plunged the American Colonies into the war for independence in 1775. The following year British troops attacked on Long Island (2), then swept into New York City, forcing Washington to retreat to White Plains. From there the redcoats chased the rebels south. At Trenton and Princeton patriot troops scored victories before wintering at Morristown.

In July 1777 Fort Ticonderoga fell to the British. In September and early October, Americans lost costly battles at Brandywine and Germantown. But soon after, the tide of war shifted with a patriot victory at Saratoga (3).

Patriots suffered through winter at Valley Forge but in spring cheered the news that France would join their cause.

Meanwhile in the West (4), George Rogers Clark led the capture of British-held posts at Cahokia, Kaskaskia, and Vincennes. By mid-1779 his successes established American control from the Appalachians to the Mississippi.

In late 1778 the British moved south (5) where Loyalist support was strong. In December redcoats captured Savannah. Charleston and Camden fell in 1780. Patriots took revenge with victories at Kings Mountain and Cowpens, and inflicted heavy casualties at the battle of Guilford Courthouse.

With the Deep South in arms against him, Lord Cornwallis moved to Virginia. While he awaited reinforcements at Yorktown (6), the French and Americans closed in by land and sea and forced him to surrender on October 19, 1781.

Trenton: A Desperate Gamble

*"Der Feind!" The Enemy!
Warning shouts woke Hessian
soldiers sleeping off a Christmas
binge in Trenton, New Jersey, in
1776. But the warnings came too
late for these German troops
fighting for the British.*

*Half-frozen patriot troops had
crossed the ice-choked Delaware
and marched through sleet and
snow to launch a surprise attack.
General Washington ordered the
raid as a final act of desperation:
The enlistments of most of his
men were due to expire December
31. Only a victory would keep
them fighting—and keep the
patriot cause alive.*

*Outside Trenton, Washington
split his 2,400 men into two
groups. One followed the River
Road (1), the other moved along
the Pennington Road (2), and
both entered the town at the same
time. As most of the patriots
fanned out to encircle the 1,650
startled Hessians, others placed
cannons at the end of the main
streets (3) and opened fire.*

*The German commander, Col.
Johann Rall, ordered his men to
charge the patriot position at the
north of town. But as the blue-
uniformed Hessians advanced,
cannonballs tore into their
ranks. The Hessians regrouped,
advanced, but again found
patriot fire too heavy. As smoke
and confusion enveloped Trenton, Rall ordered a retreat to
the south—but patriot troops
blocked the bridge over
Assunpink Creek (4). Rall next
ordered his men to an orchard (5)
on the edge of town. Patriot fire
mortally wounded Rall before
he got there. As his men entered
the orchard, American units
closed in (6) to prevent escape.
Surrounded, the leaderless
Hessians surrendered.*

*The Americans had dealt
the British a severe blow:
About 100 Hessians killed or
wounded, more than 900 captured. Most important, the
victory rekindled patriot spirit.
As a British observer wrote,
"they are all liberty mad again."*

peake Bay and marched northward early in September to occupy Philadelphia. George Washington offered resistance and then fell back. In December 1777 Washington took his army into winter quarters at Valley Forge, about 20 miles from Philadelphia.

In the spring good news arrived from France. King Louis XVI, impressed with American fighting abilities in the 1777 campaigns, had signed an alliance with the United States. The two countries would fight together against their common enemy. At Valley Forge, men marched, cannons boomed, fifes squealed. The officers had a party with wine and cheese, and drank toasts: "To the King of France! To the American States!"

The British received the news with gloom. What had started as a mere colonial rebellion had suddenly exploded into a costly, bloody war that pitted the British empire not only against the American Colonies but against France, along with her ally, Spain. More than three years had passed since the first shots of the war rang out at Lexington. What did the British have to show for the money they had spent and the blood they had shed? Only Manhattan, Philadelphia, and a tiny island called Rhode Island in Narragansett Bay.

At the same time France announced support for the American cause, General Howe was relieved as commander of His Majesty's forces. General Sir Henry Clinton, a skinny, sour-faced, humorless man, replaced him. Clinton pulled his troops from Philadelphia to New York and devised a new plan. He would invade the South.

The War Moves South

In December 1779 Clinton started south with an armada of nearly 9,000 British, Hessian, and Loyalist soldiers. Five months later they took the key southern port of Charleston, South Carolina, and with it 5,500 patriot prisoners.

Clinton then sailed back to New York where he schemed to take over West Point, an American fort on the Hudson River. He left Lord Charles Cornwallis in the South to finish destroying patriot opposition. In August 1780 Cornwallis routed General Gates at Camden, South Carolina. Gates's defeat led Congress to remove him. The new commander of southern troops was Nathanael Greene, who had proved his fighting ability at Saratoga.

Cornwallis now planned to move his army through North Carolina in three columns. Maj. Patrick Ferguson commanded one of the columns made up of Loyalists who were hated by the patriots for their brutality and marauding ways. Camped on Kings Mountain, a rocky height near the North Carolina border, Ferguson wrote Cornwallis that he had "taken a post where I do not think I can be forced. . . ."

But the patriot militia stormed Kings Mountain and overran it. In a bloody fight that pitted Americans against Americans, the whole Loyalist force—all 1,100 men—was killed, wounded, or taken prisoner. James Collins, a sixteen-year-old fighting with the patriot militia, watched as "the wives and children of the poor Tories came in, in great numbers. Their husbands, fathers, and brothers

A Traitor to the Cause

Benedict Arnold as a colonel, 1776

Peggy Arnold as sketched by John André, 1778

George Washington called him "The bravest of the brave." He was an early hero of the Revolution. Yet Benedict Arnold died in disgrace, a traitor.

On the battlefield, Arnold led his men fearlessly. At Saratoga in 1777, the temperamental general defied orders to remain in the rear and furiously charged British lines. Swinging his sword and shouting encouragement, Arnold heroically directed American forces toward victory until a bullet shattered his leg.

Off the field, Arnold feuded with fellow officers and quarreled with Congress over his promotion and expenses. Twice Arnold threatened to quit the Army, but both times George Washington convinced him to stay.

When the Americans regained control of Philadelphia in 1778, Washington made Arnold its military commander. There Arnold met and married Peggy Shippen, daughter of a well-known family that was loyal to the British.

The newlyweds lived lavishly, spending more than they could afford. In 1779 a court-martial tried Arnold for using his post to enrich himself. Although cleared of most charges, Arnold fumed. Had he not risked his life in battle? He deserved a raise and a promotion, not a court-martial!

With thoughts of revenge and making money, Arnold sent a message to John André, a British major who'd kept company with Peggy during the British occupation of Philadelphia.

Three patriots capture John André.

The hanging of John André, Tappan, New York, 1780

Arnold told him he was ready to help defeat the American cause.

In August 1780 Arnold persuaded Washington to name him commandant of West Point, a strategic fort overlooking the Hudson River. Seven weeks later the new commandant met secretly with André on the riverbank. After much haggling the two agreed: Arnold would turn over the plans of West Point for 10,000 pounds sterling. André set off for British lines, but 15 miles from safety, three American scouts stopped and searched him and found the plans in his socks.

When Arnold learned of André's capture, he excused himself from a meeting with Washington's aides and raced on horseback to the Hudson. He jumped into his barge and was rowed 18 miles to the safety of the *Vulture*, a British warship.

The Americans hanged André as a spy. Arnold was never caught. He joined the British and fought against his countrymen. After the war, Arnold and his family moved to England. But he never got the honor or wealth he expected and died at age 60, a lonely and bitter man.

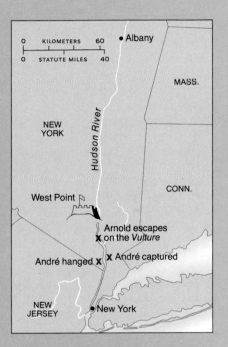

West Point: Guardian of the Hudson

An American fort called West Point controlled the strategic Hudson River Valley—and with it the fortunes of a new nation. Had the British succeeded in capturing it, warships like the Vulture would have plied the river's course, helping split the Colonies in half. Fate foiled Benedict Arnold's treacherous plan—and kept the fort George Washington called "the key to America" in patriot hands.

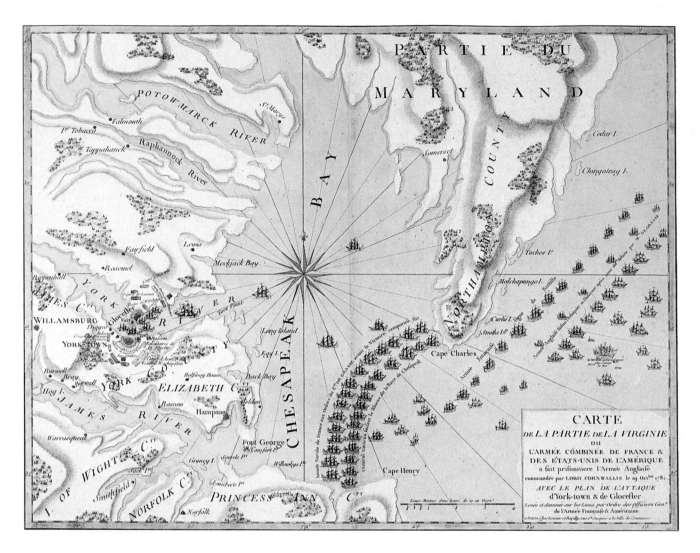

lay dead in heaps, while others lay wounded or dying. . . ."

Three months later, in a South Carolina cow pasture called Cowpens, Greene's troops drew the British into a carefully laid trap and after an hour's bloody combat again inflicted heavy losses. To avenge this disaster, Cornwallis stripped his troops of excess baggage and took off after Greene and his men. For weeks Greene eluded Cornwallis. Finally on March 15, 1781, the American commander confronted the outnumbered British at the town of Guilford Courthouse in North Carolina and killed or wounded a quarter of Cornwallis's men. Discouraged with the progress of the southern campaign, Cornwallis decided to head north to Virginia. After a long march he settled down in Yorktown at the tip of the York River peninsula on Chesapeake Bay. Here Cornwallis felt safe because supplies and reinforcements could be brought by sea.

Actually, Cornwallis was far from safe. When General Washington learned that Cornwallis had settled in Yorktown, he moved his troops there as rapidly and secretly as possible. With him was a large French force. As the armies marched south, a French fleet of 24 men-o'-war under Admiral de Grasse was racing from the West Indies. It arrived off Chesapeake Bay in early September and

A French battle plan (above) illustrates the siege of Yorktown and the naval blockade that defeated the British in 1781. France's Admiral de Grasse arrived in time to block a British fleet that was coming to rescue Lord Cornwallis from French and American land forces. On September 5, 1781, de Grasse's fleet moved out of Chesapeake Bay to face attacking British ships. The two-and-a-half-hour battle (right) left four British ships badly damaged. Realizing the French blockade could not be broken, the British fleet sailed back to New York leaving Cornwallis's army with no choice but surrender.

In endless white columns, marching French soldiers join American forces as they besiege the British base at Yorktown in October 1781. While allied officers confer, men at the right race from the path of a British cannonball. Puffs of smoke rise from the American and French cannons that pound the British position in the center. During the 20-day siege, 16,000 French and American soldiers steadily closed in on the 8,000-man British force. After sustaining hundreds of injuries and severe damage to their artillery, the redcoats surrendered on October 19.

The Treaty of Paris in 1783 formally ended the Revolutionary War and recognized the United States as an independent country. Britain granted the new nation all its land from the Atlantic Ocean to the Mississippi River and from Canada to Florida.

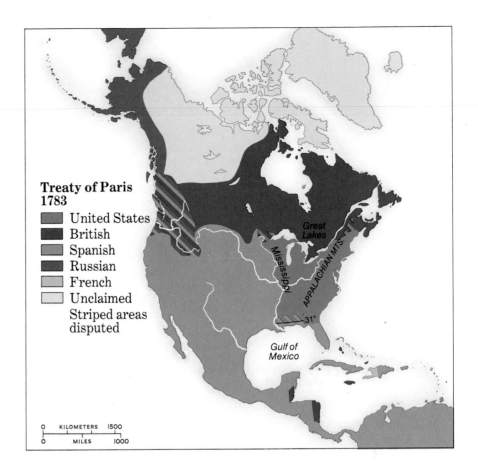

Treaty of Paris 1783

- United States
- British
- Spanish
- Russian
- French
- Unclaimed
- Striped areas disputed

quickly beat off a British fleet that had come to help Cornwallis. On September 28, a scorching hot day, 16,000 French and American troops laid siege to Yorktown by land.

Three weeks later Cornwallis's sick, demoralized 8,000-man force gave up their battered base. As Washington watched from horseback, the weary and defeated redcoats walked out between lines of American and French soldiers. They marched, an American Army doctor recalled, "in a slow and solemn step, with shouldered arms, colors cased and drums beating a British march."

The defeat at Yorktown was a colossal disaster for the British; it meant the end of the war.

John Adams, Benjamin Franklin, and John Jay skillfully negotiated the Treaty of Paris, which was signed in 1783. The British recognized the United States as an independent country and surrendered all the land between the Appalachians and the Mississippi River, which they themselves had won from France in 1763.

Americans won a great deal from the Revolutionary War—independence, a vast amount of land, the right to trade with whom they pleased, the right to run their own affairs without British interference. But the ideals of freedom and equality set forth in the Declaration of Independence remained only partly fulfilled. Millions of black people continued to be slaves, and millions of women took second place to men. As for the Indians living in North America in 1783, many of them continued to struggle for their own independence in the years that followed.

A quilt takes shape with help from many hands. Colonial era quilting bees combined sewing and sociability—and made a necessary task enjoyable.

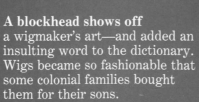

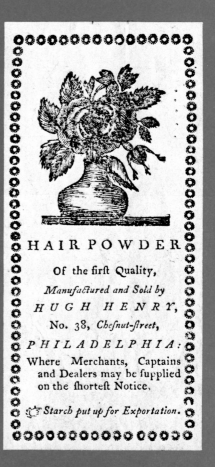

A homemade wooden doll entertained a young girl in the 18th century. Resourceful colonists made dolls from apples, corncobs, and scrap materials.

A blockhead shows off a wigmaker's art—and added an insulting word to the dictionary. Wigs became so fashionable that some colonial families bought them for their sons.

"Hair Powder of the First Quality" kept a wig's color. Even men who didn't wear wigs used the powder to make their own hair look wig-like.

Colonial bills appeared in the Revolutionary War but quickly lost their value. Foreign coins were considered more secure.

"Sucking bottles for children," advertised in 1764, were made of pewter, a metal alloy used in colonial times to make everything from cups and plates to ice cream molds.

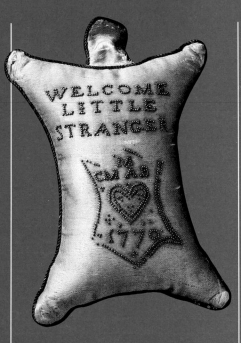

"Little Strangers"—newborns— were often welcomed into colonial homes with satin pincushions. Hung on the front door, the cushions announced a birth to friends and neighbors.

Two little colonial boys solemnly pose like adults for a portrait. The boy on the left, about six years old, has reached an important milestone: His skirts have been exchanged for trousers. Children of this era were expected to act grown-up; their clothes were not usually meant for play.

Badge of Military Merit, designed by George Washington, honored soldiers of extraordinary courage in the Revolutionary War. The award is known today as the Purple Heart.

THE EARLY REPUBLIC

Launching the Nation 1783-1815

In 1783 the Revolutionary War was over. Roads teemed with ragged, penniless soldiers heading home. George Washington, writing that year, described them as people who had "shed their blood or lost their limbs in the service of their country, without a shelter, without a friend, and without the means of obtaining any of the necessaries or comforts of life, compelled to beg their daily bread from door to door."

Congress had not paid many of the soldiers their wages because the government had no money. In 1777 Congress adopted the Articles of Confederation, a plan for solving the problems that faced the new federal government. This document containing 13 separate articles, or items, became the first Constitution of the United States. One article gave Congress the power to ask the states for contributions to pay the wages of the soldiers and other government expenses. This sounded fine, but because Congress had no power to demand the contributions, many states failed to make them. There was little Congress could do about it.

In May 1787, four years after the end of the war, 55 men arrived in Philadelphia for a meeting. Some came on horseback, some by coach, and others by ship. Selected by the different states as delegates, they came to discuss how the Articles of Confederation might be changed to make the federal government work better. The men who came to this meeting, called the Constitutional Convention, were some of the most talented leaders in the country. Alexander Hamilton, a lawyer, came from New York. Hamilton had been caught up in the Revolution by his late teens. A fellow officer remembered him as "a mere boy, of small, slender and delicate frame, with his cocked hat pulled down over his eyes, [marching] beside a cannon, patting it every now and then as if it were a favorite . . . plaything." In 1776 Hamilton had commanded a New York artillery company and had won Washington's admiration for coolness under fire and skill in handling both men and guns.

Benjamin Franklin, 81 years old and a resident of Philadelphia, served as a Pennsylvania delegate. Franklin had earned his reputation before the Revolution by representing Pennsylvania and other Colonies in London and serving the Continental Congress as its commissioner to France. There he helped negotiate the 1778 French-American alliance that brought about Britain's defeat at Yorktown. Another Pennsylvania delegate was James Wilson, a skillful debater.

George Washington came to Philadelphia to represent Virginia. He brought with him a fellow planter, James Madison, the only delegate to keep a careful record of the discussions that summer of 1787. A third Virginia delegate, Edmund Jennings Randolph, had been an aide to George Washington in the Revolutionary War and, later, the governor of Virginia.

Other influential Southerners at the Philadelphia meeting were Pierce Butler and Charles C. Pinckney, both of South Carolina. Butler had been a

A pillar of strength, George Washington stands on a platform and speaks to delegates at the Constitutional Convention in Philadelphia in 1787. Through the hot summer, 55 men from all over the new land wrangled over the kind of government their nation should have. "I almost despair," wrote Washington as the bickering raged. But on September 17, one by one, the delegates drew a quill pen from an inkstand—perhaps the same silver one (left) that now stands in Independence Hall—and signed the United States of America into life.

"The decorations of the ships, the roar of cannon, and the loud acclamations of the people" impressed George Washington as he was rowed up New York's East River (left) to take office as first President of the United States in 1789. Huge crowds greeted their hero all along his route from Mount Vernon—his estate in Virginia—to New York, then the nation's capital. Choirs sang, children tossed flowers, even some porpoises frolicked around the ornate barge. "Well," said one newspaper, "he deserves it all."

"Come along Bobby," sneers the devil in a 1790 cartoon (right). Behind him an obedient Robert Morris, one of the signers of the Declaration of Independence, carries New York's Federal Hall off to Philadelphia. Congress held its first meetings in that hall. But then the lawmakers decided to build a new capital at what is now Washington, D.C., and to meet in Philadelphia until it was ready. Senator Morris's foes—including this artist—cried foul; they said Morris engineered the move to increase the value of land he owned in Philadelphia.

British officer who came to the Colonies before the Revolution, married an heiress, and settled down to grow cotton and rice. Pinckney had been captured by the British during the Revolution and later exchanged for British officers captured by General Washington's troops.

The convention delegates assembled in the Pennsylvania State House (later called Independence Hall). They elected George Washington to preside. All agreed that "nothing spoken in this House be printed or otherwise published . . . without leave." Guards stood at the doors, and the street was covered with gravel to muffle the noise of carriages.

Week after week the delegates debated in the awful summer heat. By early September they had produced a new Constitution for the United States. Like the other delegates, Pierce Butler was worn out by the long summer's effort. But, as he wrote to a friend, if the new Constitution became the law of the land, he would feel rewarded "for my share of the trouble, and a summer's confinement which injured my health much."

The new Constitution, in its first Article, said that Congress "shall have the power to lay and collect taxes." These nine words spelled out the essence of the change which the Philadelphia delegates were proposing. For the first time the federal government would be granted a power which the American people had denied the British government itself. The power to tax citizens is crucial to government. With this power the federal government could raise the money to supply an army, build a navy, hire public servants, and set up courts and jails to make sure its laws were obeyed.

Perhaps the most difficult problem for the delegates was deciding what the makeup of a permanent Congress should be. After much debate they divided Congress into two lawmaking groups. The first, the House of Representatives, would be elected by popular vote. Each state would be given a number of representatives in

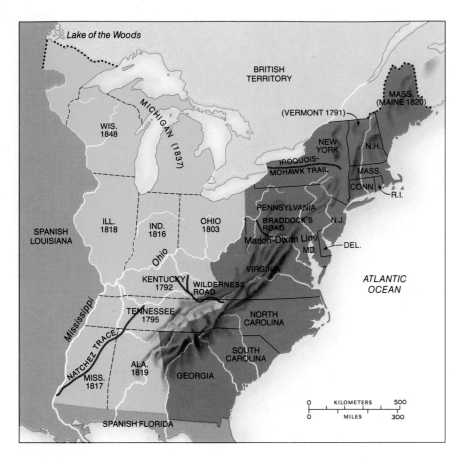

The Old Northwest and The Old Southwest 1791

- Old Southwest—slavery permitted
- Old Northwest—slavery banned
- Original 13 colonies
- Roads and trails
- .... Indefinite international boundary

The United States of America at its beginning stretched down the Atlantic coast and spilled over the Appalachian Mountains as far as the Mississippi River, where Spanish claims began. By 1791 Congress had carved from these western lands two huge tracts later known as the Old Northwest and Old Southwest.

Rough trails grew into busy roads as trading swelled and settlers headed for the new lands. In the Northwest Ordinance of 1787, Congress had provided for governors and judges and had set the pattern for the creation of new states. When the population of an area reached 5,000 free male adults, they could elect a legislature and pass laws. When it grew to 60,000, they could apply for statehood.

Slavery had been a sore point since colonial times. To ease the problem, Congress allowed slavery in the Old Southwest and banned it in the Old Northwest. A line drawn in the 1760s to settle a land dispute became the border between slave states and free states—the Mason-Dixon Line.

proportion to its population. States with more people would have more representatives and, therefore, more votes.

The delegates had a hard time working out the details of this plan. Were representatives to be allotted to a state in proportion to its *total* population or in proportion to its total *nonslave* population? If representatives were allotted in proportion to total population, then states like Virginia or South Carolina, with many slaves, would have more votes. Obviously the slaves themselves would not be allowed to vote or have any say in choosing representatives. In the end the delegates included three-fifths of the slaves in figuring both a state's representatives and the taxation it must pay. This agreement came to be known as the "three-fifths compromise."

The delegates also set up a second lawmaking group in Congress called the Senate. Each state, whether large or small, could elect two senators. The purpose of the Senate, said Edmund Randolph, "is to control the democratic branch" of Congress. "If it be not a firm body, the other branch being more numerous . . . will overwhelm it." No proposal could become law until it had been passed by both the House of Representatives and the Senate.

The new Constitution gave Congress the power to raise and maintain an army and a navy, to deal with Indian affairs, to operate a mail service, and to control trading activities between states as well as with foreign countries. One important clause also gave Congress the right "to provide for calling forth the militia to execute the laws of the Union, suppress insurrections and repel invasions." If there were an uprising or slave revolt in a state, the federal government could bring in militiamen to put it down.

Under the Constitution, Congress would make the laws. A President, chosen by special electors and holding office for four years, would see that they were carried out. He would also be Commander in Chief of the armed forces and would make treaties with the Indians and with foreign countries. He would appoint judges, ambassadors, and a Cabinet—a group of people who would advise him and head the departments of government.

The Struggle to Ratify

Article Seven declared that the new Constitution would become the law of the land if and when the people in nine of the thirteen states ratified, or approved, it. From December 1787 until June 1788 special meetings also called constitutional conventions were held in all states to discuss the proposed Constitution. Those who favored it were called Federalists, and those who opposed it were called Antifederalists.

During these months three leading Federalists, Alexander Hamilton, James Madison, and John Jay, wrote a series of essays known as the Federalist Papers. Here they presented all their arguments for ratifying the Constitution. Without a strong government, they asked, how would it be possible to stop the states from fighting over land, trade, and control of key ports? How would it be possible to build an effective national defense against foreign enemies?

At that time few Americans wanted a strong national government. The memory of British rule was recent and painful. Such a government could tax its citizens without their permission and send troops against them. Had Americans fought the Revolution only to replace one strong government with another?

Until now the Constitution was mostly a list of "do's." The Antifederalists proposed adding a list of "don'ts." The government, said the Antifederalists, cannot punish people who speak or write against it. It cannot stop them from meeting in halls or on the streets merely because it doesn't like what they have to say. It cannot tell people what to think or stop them from worshiping God in any way they please. It cannot declare people guilty of crimes and send them to jail without first giving them a fair trial.

The Federalists saw the sense of the Antifederalist position. They agreed to add their list of "don'ts," or a bill of rights, to the Constitution once it was ratified. With this promise 11 states had voted to ratify by the summer of 1788, and so the Constitution was declared ratified. Soon after Congress added to it a list of ten additions, or amendments—the Bill of Rights.

A collector of taxes collects a coat of tar and feathers instead (above) from Pennsylvania hill folk enraged by a tax on home-brewed whiskey. The cartoon at left shows another of the hated tax men. He has confiscated two kegs of whiskey "to make the farmers pay for drinking their own grog." Tempers finally exploded in the brief Whiskey Rebellion of 1794. Federal troops quickly snuffed out this first challenge to the government's power to tax.

John & Abigail Adams
The Presidential Years
1797-1801

Abigail Adams hotly denied any suggestion that woman was secondary to man. "If man is Lord," she said, "woman is *Lordess*." Certainly Abigail and John had a partnership in their marriage and shared a passion for politics. When away from Abigail, John moaned, "I want my talkative wife."

But when it came to John's running for President, they had mixed feelings. John couldn't bear the thought of being rejected. Outspoken Abigail hated the prospect of being "fastened up hand and foot and tongue to be shot at." And once John was in office, Abigail found the criticism hard to take. When John was called "old, querulous, bald, blind, crippled, toothless Adams," it was almost too much.

Yet in spite of a Presidency filled with international crises, frictions within his party, and slander, Abigail and John wanted a second term. They waited for the results of the voting in the new white President's house to which they had recently moved. But when John's defeat was announced, the Adamses were weighed down with grief. They had just learned their son Charles had died.

Heartsick, they returned to the farm in Massachusetts where they had always found peace. Soon John was writing that he had "exchanged honor and virtue for manure" and Abigail that she could be seen "skimming" milk "at five o'clock in the morning."

JEAN FRITZ

104

In the spring of 1789 the United States held its first elections under the new Constitution. George Washington was chosen President, and a Federalist majority was elected to Congress. At noon on April 30, 1789, the new President arrived at Federal Hall in New York City, the nation's first capital. Washington took an oath to defend the Constitution. A huge crowd cried, "Long live George Washington, President of the United States!"

In the early 1790s the Federalist Party was at the height of its popularity. With men like George Washington, John Adams, and Alexander Hamilton at its head, it organized the first government to wield power under the Constitution. Secretary of the Treasury Hamilton's far-reaching financial program included the first Na-

On Jenkins Hill in the new city of Washington, a young nation built a Capitol to house its Congress and Supreme Court. Elegant carriages gather while workmen labor on the lawn in this painting of 1800 (below). Today the hill is called Capitol Hill, and there this old building still stands. It is now part of the North Wing (see sketch below) of a Capitol Building about six times as long.

tional Bank, a tax on imports, and a plan to repay the country's debts. But in spite of all their achievements, the Federalists soon lost much public support because they started to pass unpopular laws. For example, one of Hamilton's schemes was to pay the federal war debt by putting a tax on whiskey. This tax fell hardest on the backwoods people of Pennsylvania, Virginia, and North Carolina. Whiskey was their main cash "crop," which they sold to buy things they could not make—like guns, bullets, axes, and cooking pots.

When Congress passed Hamilton's tax, frontier farmers were furious. What was this but the Stamp Act all over again? The farmers organized into groups of "Whiskey Boys" who seized the collectors, tarred and feathered them, and drove them out of town.

In 1794 Washington, at Hamilton's urging, decided that it was time to stop this "insurrection" against the federal government. He pointed to the Constitution, which gave Congress power to call up the militia. In August 1794 the government gathered 15,000 militiamen in Philadelphia, the country's new capital. President Washington and Secretary Hamilton led them out of town.

The troops marched to the frontier town of Pittsburgh and back again in two months. They arrested scores of people and brought back 22 prisoners to Philadelphia for trial. The Whiskey Rebellion cost the taxpayers thousands of dollars. It cost the Federalists, too, because it earned them the hatred of many people.

In 1796 George Washington's second term as President came to an end. After a farewell address in which he urged his country to steer clear of entangling alliances with foreign governments, Washington waited in Philadelphia to see John Adams take the oath of office as President. In March 1797 he climbed into his coach and headed back to Mount Vernon, his Virginia home. The father of his country died there on December 14, 1799.

Thomas Jefferson, Adams's Vice President, was the leader of the group that opposed Hamilton's economic policies. Farmers, craftsmen, shopkeepers, and frontier people loved Jefferson because they thought he stood for the rights of common people rather than a strong central government. In the 1800 presidential election this group—who called themselves Republicans—supported Jefferson against Adams, again the Federalist candidate, and Jefferson became President. Thus the nation's first political parties rose out of disagreements over Hamilton's policies.

All of Louisiana?

When Jefferson took office in 1801, he faced a crisis in the West. Napoleon Bonaparte, a French general who would soon make himself Emperor of France, had forced Spain to give back the western part of the Louisiana Territory, which France had lost in 1763. It included all the land from the Mississippi River to the Rocky Mountains and the port of New Orleans. Westerners could no longer float their produce down the Mississippi to New Orleans in order to ship it to the eastern states and to Europe. *Do something!* they urged Jefferson.

Jefferson at once sent a special agent, James Monroe, to Paris. He told Monroe and the American Ambassador to France, Robert Livingston, to try to buy New Orleans from Napoleon. In April 1803 the two men were struck dumb with surprise when Napoleon offered to sell them not only New Orleans but *all* of the western Louisiana Territory as well for $15 million.

Napoleon had good reasons for this decision. He needed money for a new war with France's old-time enemy, England. He hoped that selling Louisiana to the Americans would be like throwing a bone between two dogs: Britain and the United States would fight over it. Who knows, he thought, the Americans might even enter the war against England on his side.

President Thomas Jefferson (below) had an idea: Why not buy New Orleans from the French? The nation needed to control this gateway to the Mississippi Valley. Napoleon had a better idea: Why not sell him the whole Louisiana Territory? Thus Jefferson sealed his nation's greatest bargain—and doubled its size. In this 1803 painting New Orleans basks beneath an eagle, symbol of the nation that just bought it for 4 cents an acre.

New Orleans in 1803

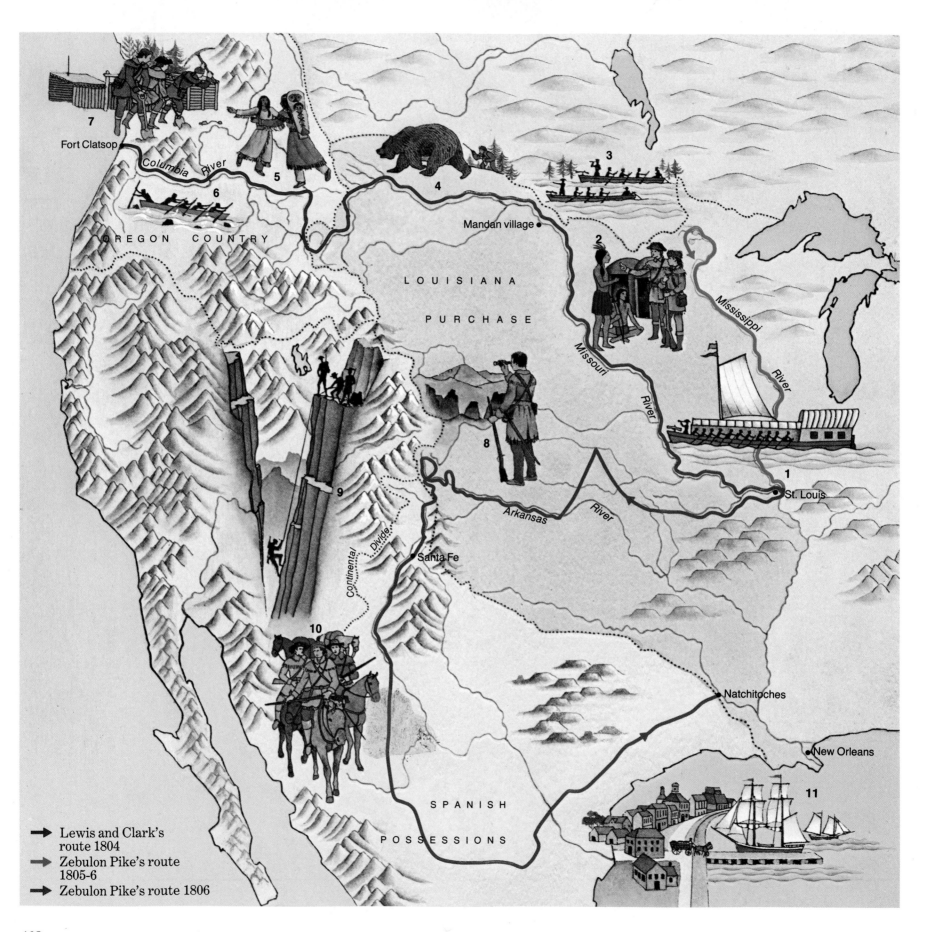

Fort Clatsop

7

Columbia River

5

6

OREGON COUNTRY

4

Mandan village

3

2

LOUISIANA

PURCHASE

Missouri River

Mississippi River

8

9

St. Louis

1

Arkansas River

Continental Divide

Santa Fe

10

Natchitoches

New Orleans

SPANISH

POSSESSIONS

11

→ Lewis and Clark's route 1804

→ Zebulon Pike's route 1805-6

→ Zebulon Pike's route 1806

Adventuring in an Unknown Land

What lay out there in the vast Louisiana Territory? Strange beasts? Unfriendly tribes? Cliffs and rapids? Westward went the explorers—Lewis and Clark in 1804, Zebulon Pike in 1805 and 1806—to find all this and more.

Meriwether Lewis, William Clark, and about 40 companions left St. Louis in a 55-foot keelboat (1) and two smaller craft. On the Missouri River they spent the winter among friendly Mandan and Arikara Indians (2). In spring they pressed on in small boats (3) to the foothills of the Rockies, where they met grizzly bears (4) and other unfamiliar wildlife. With them went only one woman, a Shoshone Indian guide named Sacajawea. She found her people (5)—a tribe she hadn't seen since she was captured as a child—and persuaded them to supply horses. The travelers soon left the Louisiana Territory, battling fierce rapids (6) as they struggled to the Pacific. There they built Fort Clatsop (7), a log shelter where they spent a rough winter before returning to St. Louis in 1806.

The U. S. Army also began to explore. Lt. Zebulon Pike probed the upper Mississippi in 1805, then headed west from St. Louis with 21 men in 1806. That November he saw a great peak ahead (8) and decided he could reach it in a day. Three days later, shivering in deep snow, he gave up. Pike never climbed Pikes Peak. But he did explore dark, deep Royal Gorge (9) on the Arkansas River. Lost, hungry, and cold, he strayed into Spanish territory (10). The Spaniards found him near Santa Fe and let him go home after questioning.

Journals of explorers told the nation much about the new land stretching from New Orleans (11) almost to Canada.

Smoke billows from a recreated Mandan Indian village (below) in North Dakota. Such sights greeted Lewis and Clark as they explored the Louisiana Territory. Told by President Jefferson to record what they saw "with great pains and accuracy," they crammed journals with notes and drawings. "This is a faint likeness of the Cock of the Plains," Clark wrote around a sketch of a sage grouse (lower) on this journal entry from 1806.

Fort Abraham Lincoln State Park, N.D.

Page from William Clark's journal

One day while soaking in the bathtub, Napoleon mentioned his decision to his brothers Lucien and Joseph. They were upset. Joseph said that he would defy Napoleon by speaking against the sale in public. Napoleon, angry, rose suddenly from the tub. "It is my idea," he yelled, "and I shall go through with it." His fury spent, Napoleon fell back into the bathwater. A wave of warm, soapy water hit Joseph and drenched him from head to toe. When Jefferson heard of the agreement in June 1803, he could not believe his ears. He was going to sign a treaty that would double the size of the United States.

Exactly how big was Louisiana? Nobody knew for sure. Thomas Jefferson ordered an Army expedition, headed by a young Virginia officer, Meriwether Lewis, and Lewis's friend, William Clark. Jefferson asked them to explore the territory and, if possible, to find a water route across the Rockies to the Pacific Ocean.

Lewis and Clark started west in the spring of 1804. From St. Louis their expedition traveled up the Missouri River to its source in Montana. They crossed the Rocky Mountains on Indian horses in bitter cold, built canoes, and followed the Columbia River as it descended toward the Pacific. In September 1806, two years and four months later, they made their way back to St. Louis.

Lewis and Clark brought back word about the Indians they had met and about the wildlife that flourished in the great West. In his journal of the trip, Clark wrote that the Nez Perce of the Pacific Northwest were "Stout likely men, handsome women, and very dressy in their way." The men wore "white buffalo robe or elk skin dressed with beads," and "the women dress in a shirt of ibex or goat . . . skins which reach quite down to their ankles."

Lewis and Clark also saw a grizzly bear. "It was a male not fully grown . . . at 300 pounds. . . . it is a . . . furious and formidable animal, and will frequently pursue the hunter when wounded."

Close behind Lewis and Clark came American traders with blankets, guns, tools—goods aplenty to swap for the Indians' furs. Close behind the traders came government crews to build fortified trading posts. From a high bluff—made even higher by an artist's imagination—Fort Osage (opposite) looked down on traders' barges, Indian lodges, and the muddy Missouri River. Nearby a settlement grew—the Kansas City we know today.

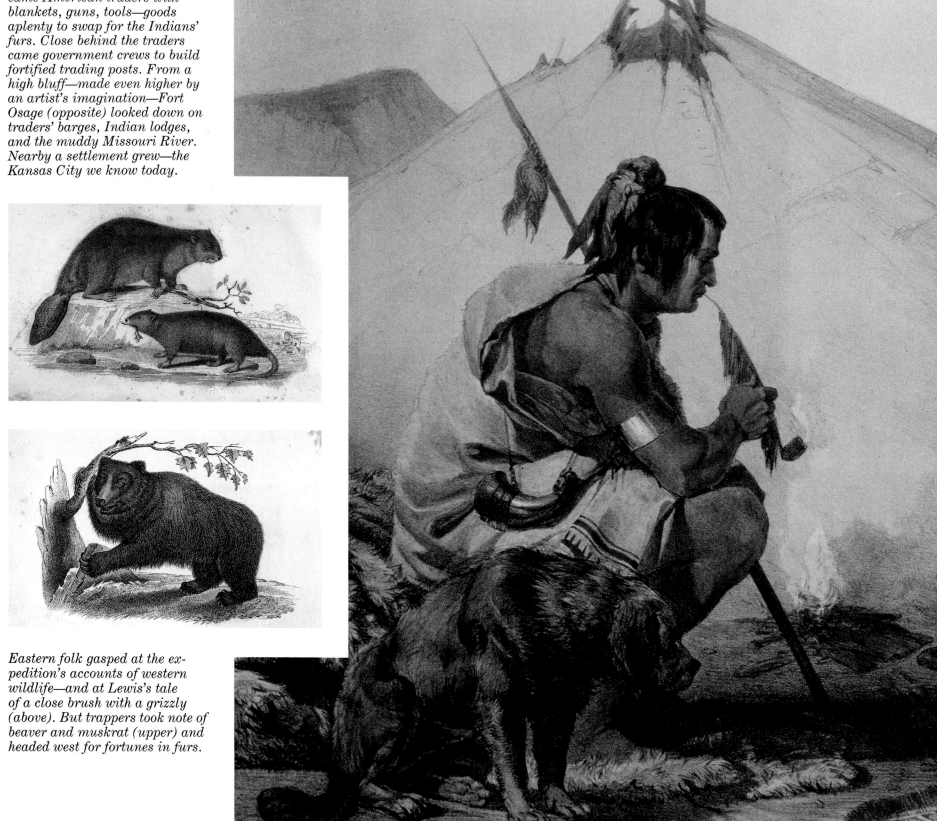

Eastern folk gasped at the expedition's accounts of western wildlife—and at Lewis's tale of a close brush with a grizzly (above). But trappers took note of beaver and muskrat (upper) and headed west for fortunes in furs.

Fort Osage about as it looked in the 1820s

When Lewis and Clark returned to St. Louis, France and England were still at war. At first the United States took no side in the struggle. Its merchant ships sailed with cargoes both to English and French ports. But soon the British and French Navies began seizing hundreds of American vessels. The British wanted to cut off supplies from France, and the French wanted to stop supplies from reaching England. Americans were particularly angry at the British because the British seized not only ships and cargoes but also American sailors and forced them into its service.

In 1806 the American Navy was still very small. It was inadequate to protect merchant ships at sea from British search and seizure, so Jefferson forbade U. S. ships to sail into foreign ports. By 1808 American ports were crammed with idle ships and idle men. The country's foreign trade had almost stopped.

That same year Jefferson's second term as President ended, and James Madison succeeded him. Madison shared Jefferson's wish to stay out of a war with England. But soon a group of congressmen, known as the War Hawks, began to call for war. Their leaders were Henry Clay of Kentucky and John C. Calhoun of South Carolina. In 1810 Clay and Calhoun began to demand that the government declare war against England. Their speeches were received with enthusiasm throughout the West and the South.

Why were the War Hawks so keen on war? The seizure of American sailors was not the only issue. The Indians had also become a serious problem to settlers moving west. By 1800 Tecumseh, a Shawnee Indian from the Ohio Territory, had gained a reputation among frontier tribes as a brave warrior. He had led his people against the whites who tried to take their lands and urged other tribes to unite and resist the white men also. "Where today," he asked his listeners, "are the Pequot? Where the Narragansett, the Mohican? . . . They have vanished before the avarice and oppression of the white man as snow before a summer sun."

Anxious to keep the Indians as friends in case of war, the British in Canada encouraged them to resist the advancing settlers. The mere thought of an Indian-British alliance made the War Hawks furious. They hoped that war would drive the British from the New World and break the back of Indian resistance.

In the spring of 1812 James Madison gave in to the pressure. He and many of his Republican followers felt that all other ways of solving the problem with England had failed and that war was now necessary to preserve their party. He sent the British his final word: *Stop the search and seizure or face war*. The British did not want to go to war with the United States. They were already caught up in a life-and-death struggle with France in Europe. But they agreed too late to Madison's demand. Congress declared war against Great Britain on June 18.

A Needless War

The war lasted for two and a half years in a series of battles that gave no final victory to either side. British and American men-o'-war exchanged cannonballs on the Atlantic Ocean, Lake Champlain, and Lake Erie. Soldiers fought along the northern frontier from Lake Champlain to Lake Michigan. The war even reached Washington, D. C., the nation's capital since 1800. In August 1814 the British Navy sailed into Chesapeake Bay, landed troops on the banks of the Patuxent River, and briefly occupied the new city. Many buildings were damaged by fire, including the President's house, later called the White House.

In the struggle, some Indian tribes took the British side, some the American. Tecumseh and many of his warriors fought alongside British troops. At the Battle of the Thames, north of Lake Erie, on October 5, 1813, hundreds of Indian braves died, including Tecumseh. Indian opposition to the advance of white settlers in the Northwest was over.

In the part of the South known as the Mississippi Territory, a group of Upper Creek Indians had listened to Tecumseh's appeal for warfare against the whites. On their way home from Florida, where they had gone to get ammunition from the Spaniards, a party of Creeks was attacked by white militiamen. Hundreds of white men, women, and children, fearing retaliation, fled to stockades which had been built for protection against Indian attack. At Fort Mims, a stockade on the Alabama River, Maj. Daniel Beasley, who was in charge, scoffed at the settlers' fears. But at noon on August 30, 1813, as drums beat for the midday meal, the Creek warriors attacked. The settlers fought with desperate courage, but almost all 500 of them were killed.

The Fort Mims massacre triggered an all-out war against the Creeks. A Tennessee militiaman, Gen. Andrew Jackson, was given command. He was 47 years old and a veteran of the Revolutionary War. A New Orleans native who saw him in 1814 wrote, "A small leather cap protected his head, and a short blue Spanish cloak his body. His high boots . . . were long innocent of any polish.

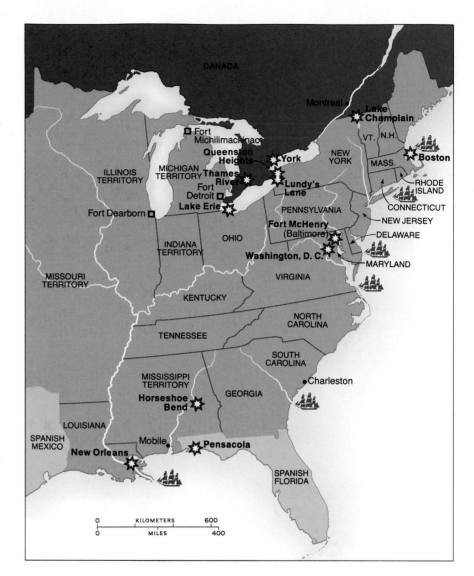

The War of 1812

🚢 Blockade
▫ Fort
✶ Battle site

Combat raged over land and sea (above) as the United States and Britain clashed in the War of 1812. The U. S. Army struck feebly into Canada, at Queenston Heights and Lundy's Lane, but won the Battle of the Thames in October 1813. Within a year the British seized and set fire to Washington, D. C. From there they sailed north to Baltimore, only to retreat before heavy artillery at Fort McHenry. The tiny U. S. Navy grappled triumphantly on Lakes Erie and Champlain with the powerful

British fleet—but Britain ruled the seas. War's end came with a peace treaty in late 1814 that pronounced a virtual draw. But news of the treaty arrived late. The last major battle—a stunning American victory at New Orleans—took place two weeks after the signing.

Lurching backward, the warrior-statesman Tecumseh falls at the Battle of the Thames in Ontario. With him fell the dream of an Indian nation united against the intruding Americans. Pictures like this showed various versions of the Shawnee chieftain's death in this battle, but no one knows how he really was killed.

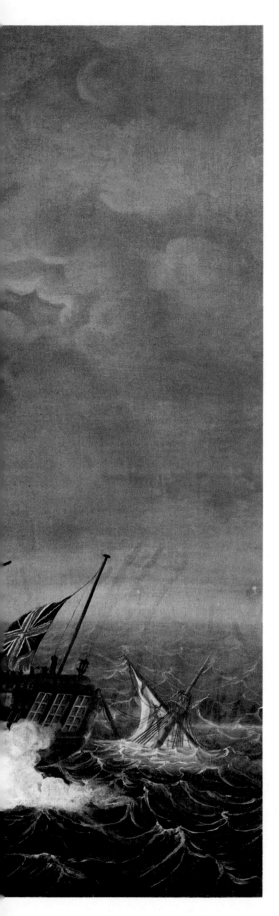

British sailors in the War of 1812 cheer from their boats (above) as their comrades burn Washington, D. C., on an August evening in 1814. One congressman mourned to see "The Capitol wrapped in its winding sheet of fire."

American sailors also tasted triumph. Cannons booming, Stars and Stripes rippling, their 44-gun frigate Constitution *batters the British frigate* Guerrière *(left) off the Maine coast. "Huzza," one of the American sailors was said to have shouted of his ship, "her sides are made of iron." Now restored, Old Ironsides keeps an honored place as the oldest ship in the U. S. Navy.*

His complexion was sallow, and unhealthy, his hair iron gray, and his body thin and emaciated. . . . But a fierce glare shone in his bright and hawk-like eyes."

From November 1813 until March 1814, Andrew Jackson and his Tennessee militia battled the Creeks. At Horseshoe Bend on March 27, 1814, nearly a thousand Creek men, women, and children lost their lives. Their power to hold up the white settlers' advance into the Mississippi Valley was broken.

In the spring of 1814 the long struggle of Britain and its European allies against Napoleon ended with the collapse of France. Britain could now turn its full attention to unfinished business in the New World and challenge the American claim to Louisiana.

In December 1814 the British Navy landed an army 15 miles east of New Orleans. It was a formidable striking force of 10,000 men, strengthened by veterans of the Napoleonic wars. President Madison had placed Andrew Jackson, fresh from his victories over the Creeks, in charge of the city's defense.

The Americans were mostly Kentucky and Tennessee militiamen. They threw up mud walls six miles below New Orleans in a narrow strip of land between the Mississippi River and a wilderness of cypress swamps. Here on January 8, 1815, American gunners and riflemen waited as the scarlet-clad British marched to the

Ships battering Fort McHenry, Baltimore harbor

attack, half-hidden in the morning mist. American fire cut them down like grass under a scythe. The British lost over 2,000 men in a half hour. The American casualties were only 70. "The field," a Kentucky soldier wrote, "looked at first glance like a sea of blood." Ten days later the British withdrew to their ships.

Thus ended one of the most decisive battles ever fought in North America. It was finally clear that the United States, not Britain, would control the port of New Orleans, the commerce of the West, and the land from the Mississippi to the Rockies.

The following month, February 1815, a peace treaty arrived in Washington, D. C. British and American representatives, meeting in the Belgian town of Ghent, had already signed it on Christmas Eve. The Treaty of Ghent called for a halt to the fighting. Neither western lands nor boundary lines, nor search and seizure of American ships and sailors were mentioned. But both sides learned something from the long and unnecessary struggle. The British discovered they could no longer hope to win back what they had lost in the Revolution. The Americans found they would have to learn to live next door to the British in Canada.

New York City held a big celebration when news of the treaty arrived. Thousands of people came out to the streets with candles and torches in their hands, cheering and weeping. Bells pealed and cannons boomed. American ships could sail the seas and trade with the whole world again. The way was open to the West—a new era was about to begin.

British generals reel in defeat as American generals press on to victory in this fanciful lithograph of the Battle of New Orleans. Americans hailed the battle's hero, Gen. Andrew Jackson, and later elected him their seventh President. Here he rides his rearing horse and directs his troops as they fire over a wall of cotton bales. Neither side knew that a treaty to end the War of 1812 had been signed in Belgium two weeks earlier.

Out of the War of 1812 came an anthem to stir a nation's heart. From a ship in Baltimore harbor (opposite) an American lawyer named Francis Scott Key watched a British fleet pound Fort McHenry in 1814. "By the dawn's early light" he saw the fort's flag still "so gallantly streaming." On the back of an envelope he scrawled the words now sung as our national anthem. "The rockets' red glare, the bombs bursting in air" seem oddly underplayed in this artist's serene view of war's violence.

117

Pieces of Our Past
1783-1815

The Samels family smiles across the years from a portrait painted in 1788. Freed from British rule, Americans often continued their English life-style, including—as in this painting—a taste for tea.

Unicorns and mounted swordsmen strut on this hand-painted chest from eastern Pennsylvania. Called a dower chest, it may once have held linens, clothes, and other treasures a young woman took with her when she married.

A leather fire bucket (below) identifies both its owner and its date. Volunteer firefighters sometimes lined up in bucket brigades, passing such buckets hand-to-hand to put out a blaze.

A wooden whirligig pokes fun at a schoolmaster. The hornbooks he holds are actually paddles that make his arms twirl in the wind.

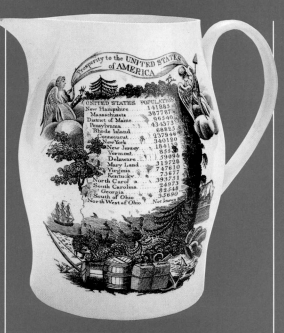

Into this tin bank clanked some of America's earliest coins. Perhaps the bank held big copper pennies like the ones below. They show Liberty's head on one side. On the other, a chain of 15 links stands for the 15 states in 1793, when such cents first were made.

A pitcher made in England held America's population on its side. Nearly four million people were counted in the first census in 1790. "North West of Ohio," says the pitcher, "Not known."

Samplers like this one showed off a girl's skill with a needle. In days when clothing was often homemade, girls learned sewing at an early age. Stitched in fine detail, this sampler is signed only "AF 1804."

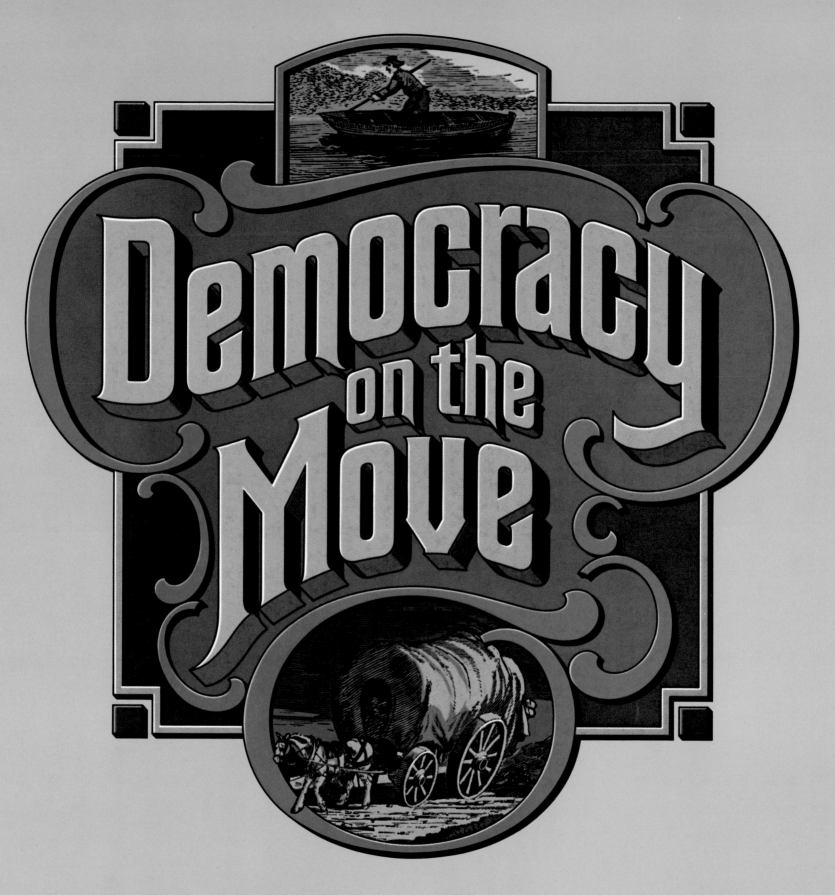

Democracy on the Move

America Looks West 1815-1848

After the War of 1812 American settlers turned toward the West. The vast and fertile lands beyond the Appalachian Mountains attracted tens of thousands of pioneers eager to sink their roots—and plows—into fresh, dark soil. Here the pure waters of lakes and streams swarmed with fish, and the forests teemed with game. Over the next 30 years the population of these new lands rose from less than a million people to more than five and a half million.

Settlements grew quickly in the lands along the Mississippi and Ohio Rivers. To bustling towns, such as Cincinnati, farmers brought food and other products for shipment to eastern or southern markets. They returned home with axes, plows, guns, cloth, and other goods manufactured in the East. This growing western business in turn gave a boost to factory production in New England and the central Atlantic states of New York, New Jersey, and Pennsylvania. More and more machines were built and housed in large sheds that eventually became factories and mills. First waterpower, and later steam power, made the machines run.

Francis Cabot Lowell, a Boston merchant, helped pioneer America's textile industry after returning from a visit to cloth-making mills in England. He and other wealthy Bostonians set up a factory at Waltham, Massachusetts, in 1813. Here, for the first time, the entire cloth-making process—spinning thread, weaving and dyeing fabric—took place under a single roof. In 1822, after Lowell's death, his partners began an even more ambitious project. They built an entire town in Massachusetts, named it Lowell, and brought in young women from the country to run the machines. Eventually children also worked in the mills. In less than 15 years the workers of Lowell were turning out 750,000 yards of cloth a week—almost enough to reach from Lowell to Washington, D. C.

Early mill towns were not the shabby, dingy industrial cities they later became. One worker, an 11-year-old girl named Lucy Larcom, later recalled that nature "came very close to the mill gates . . . violets and wild geraniums grew by the canals; long stretches of open land between the corporation buildings and the street made the town seem country-like."

Even so, Lucy, who had been forced to go to work to help support her brothers and sisters and widowed mother, grew to hate factory work. Life amid the "buzzing and hissing and whizzing of pulleys and rollers and spindles" seemed dull and tiring to a child who would have been happier playing in the fields or studying in school. But, as she later wrote, "alas, I could not go. The little money I would earn—one dollar a week . . . was needed in the family."

Getting goods from factory to consumer was an enormous problem in a day when roads were little more than rutted trails in dry weather and impassable quagmires when it rained. But improvements came steadily in the years following the War of 1812. One of the biggest was the steamboat, a craft perfected by Robert Fulton of Pennsylvania. After experimenting in Paris, Fulton returned to the United States and built the 150-foot-long *Clermont*. On September 10, 1807, a crowd watched the *Clermont* leave its wharf in

Rivers served as highways for Americans on the move in the early 1800s. Boxy flatboats (upper) carried entire families and their belongings to new homes beyond the Appalachians. Such boats drifted with the current, steered to shore and into faster currents with oarlike "sweeps." Flatboats had another use: When a family reached their destination, they broke up the boat and used its lumber to build a house.

Road travel often turned to nightmare, as in this drawing (lower) by a visiting Russian diplomat. It took the coach, called a "diligence," a full day to travel the 30 miles from Trenton to Philadelphia, a journey that left the traveler thoroughly "crushed, shaken, thrown about . . . and bumped."

Iron mills and foundries (below) turned out a growing flood of metal and machines in the 1830s —the muscle to power America's industrial revolution. Pennsylvania's rich deposits of coal and ore helped make it a leading manufacturer of iron rails, tools, and machines.

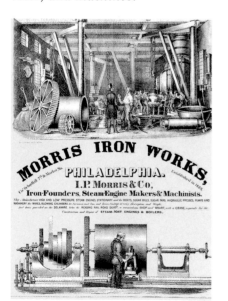

lower Manhattan and move into the Hudson River for a trial run of 150 miles to Albany. As smoke and sparks belched from the funnel, huge paddle wheels on each side of the boat began to turn, scattering spray behind them. The onlookers gaped at the strange sight. But, noted one member of the crowd, as the *Clermont* picked up speed, "this feeling gave way to undisguised delight, and cheer after cheer went up from the vast throng."

After its trial run the *Clermont* went into service as a passenger boat, and within 20 years hundreds of other steamboats were churning up and down the nation's waterways.

At about this time railroad builders were working to put steam engines on wheels, laying iron rails, and establishing railroad lines to haul passengers and freight.

A network of canals also began to grow. These man-made ditches, linked with rivers and filled with water, carried bulky cargo, such as wheat and coal, on barges hauled by teams of horses or mules. The greatest project of its kind during these years was the Erie Canal, a mammoth construction job that employed thousands of immigrant Irish laborers and cost more than seven million dollars to complete. When opened in 1825, the 360-mile-long canal linked the town of Buffalo, on Lake Erie, with the Hudson River at Albany. Thus it helped open up vast new areas of the Midwest to settlement and provided cheap, easy, and safe transportation between the East Coast and the Great Lakes region. Westward-bound settlers could travel by barge from Albany to Buffalo for

At the dawn of modern transportation, horsepower gives way to steam power on the Providence, Rhode Island, waterfront (above).

The DeWitt Clinton (below), one of America's earliest steam locomotives, chugged 16 miles between Albany and Schenectady, New York, in 1831. The nation's first passenger-hauling locomotive, the Tom Thumb, *went into service a year earlier.*

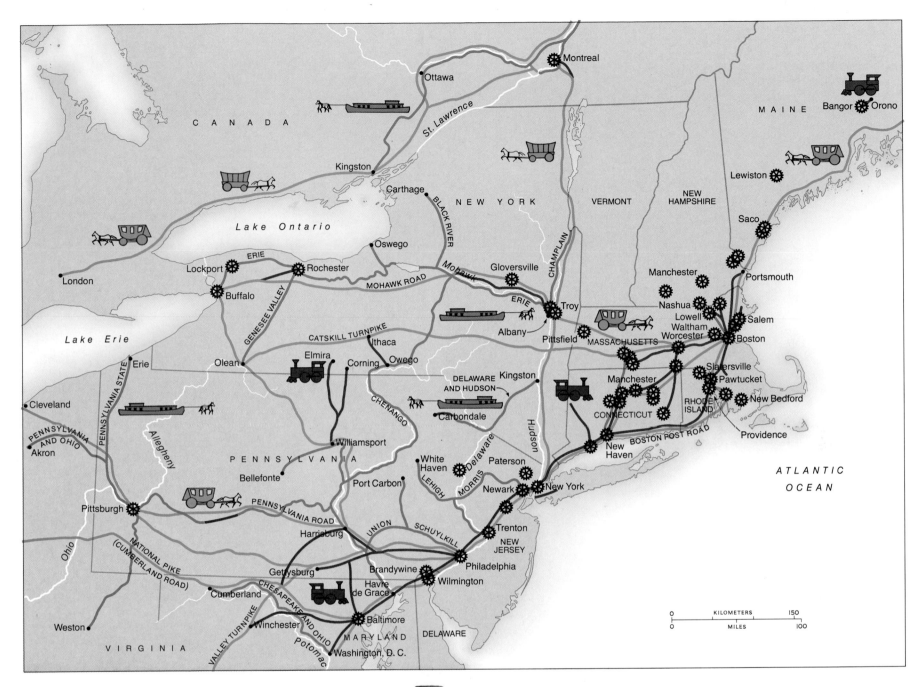

CANADA

Ottawa

Montreal

St. Lawrence

MAINE

Bangor • Orono

Kingston

Carthage

Lewiston

NEW YORK

VERMONT

NEW HAMPSHIRE

Saco

Lake Ontario

Oswego

BLACK RIVER

CHAMPLAIN

Portsmouth

London

Lockport

ERIE

Rochester

Manchester

Nashua

Buffalo

MOHAWK ROAD

Mohawk

Gloversville

Lowell

Salem

ERIE

Troy

Waltham

Lake Erie

GENESEE VALLEY

CATSKILL TURNPIKE

Ithaca

Albany

Pittsfield

Worcester

Boston

Erie

Olean

Elmira

Corning

Owego

MASSACHUSETTS

Cleveland

PENNSYLVANIA STATE

Allegheny

CHENANGO

Kingston

DELAWARE AND HUDSON

Manchester

Slatersville

Pawtucket

PENNSYLVANIA AND OHIO

Akron

Carbondale

Hudson

CONNECTICUT

RHODE ISLAND

New Bedford

PENNSYLVANIA

Williamsport

Delaware

LEHIGH

White Haven

Paterson

New Haven

BOSTON POST ROAD

Providence

Bellefonte

Port Carbon

MORRIS

Newark

New York

ATLANTIC OCEAN

Pittsburgh

PENNSYLVANIA ROAD

UNION

SCHUYLKILL

Trenton

NATIONAL PIKE (CUMBERLAND ROAD)

Harrisburg

NEW JERSEY

Ohio

Gettysburg

Brandywine

Philadelphia

Weston

Cumberland

CHESAPEAKE AND OHIO

Havre de Grace

Wilmington

VALLEY TURNPIKE

Winchester

Potomac

Baltimore

DELAWARE

VIRGINIA

Washington, D.C.

MARYLAND

KILOMETERS   0 — 150

MILES   0 — 100

Industry and Transportation, 1840

⚙ Industrial center
— Road
— Canal
— Railroad

An expanding network of roads, canals, and railroad lines by the mid-1800s linked the major industrial and commercial centers of the United States.

Women and children worked up to 70 hours a week at low-paying jobs in New England textile mills like the one in Lowell, Massachusetts (below). Such work, wrote one mill hand, "was not, and could not be, the right sort of a life for a child."

The workers at right operate carding machines that comb fibers into loose coils that will later be spun into yarn or thread. Here a young girl helps pack the coils into cannisters.

eight dollars—and tens of thousands of them did. In the first year of operation alone, more than 40,000 passengers traveled west on 13,000 boats, barges, and rafts of all kinds.

Most of the nation's roads were little more than backwoods trails in 1814. They also began to receive attention. Private companies improved many of the roads and then hung long poles called turnpikes across them. After a traveler paid a toll for the right to use the road, the gateman swung the turnpike to let him through. One of the greatest new highways was the Cumberland Road, built by the federal government. The Cumberland, or National Road, as it was also known, started at the town of Cumberland in western Maryland and by 1840 reached 600 miles to Vandalia in central Illinois. Over it traveled countless wagons and carriages as well as horses, mules, cattle, hogs, and sheep bound for eastern markets.

The Rise of Cotton

The new canals and roads could not have been built without the efforts of the immigrants who flocked to America's shores. In the 33 years from 1815 to 1848, some three million people fled from the poverty and hunger that gripped much of Europe to start new lives in the United States. By far the largest number of immigrants—six of every ten—came from Ireland.

Centuries earlier, the English had invaded Ireland, seized its green and rolling acres and turned its people into landless peasants. Early in the 19th century, the hopes of many poor Irish people turned to the United States. During the 1820s some 50,000 Irish crossed the Atlantic; in the 1830s more than three times that number came. Over the next decade the flood turned into a tidal wave, for in 1845 famine hit Ireland, caused by a blight that rotted the potatoes so many of the Irish depended on for food. During the famine years perhaps a million Irish people died, and one and a half million more left their homeland for America.

Many of the immigrants found jobs in mills that made thread and cloth. Such mills used up enormous quantities of raw cotton, which by 1850 became firmly established as America's most valuable crop. Most of the cotton was grown on plantations, cultivated and picked by slaves brought from Africa. How this happened is one of the most important and tragic chapters in American history.

In 1792 a young graduate of Yale College named Eli Whitney, while visiting a plantation in Georgia, met some planters who talked about a farming problem. Their coastal plantations grew a type of long-fibered cotton that could be easily separated from the seed. Because this long-fibered cotton could be grown only in a small coastal area of the South, the planters could not produce enough to meet demand. So they wanted to try another variety of cotton—a hardy, short-fibered kind that would grow over a wider area. But the short-fibered cotton clung so tightly to the seed that separating the fluff from the seed was difficult.

Whitney pondered the problem, then set to work on a solution in the spring of 1793. "All agreed," he wrote to his father, "that if a

The Erie Canal: Triumph of a Wilderness Waterway

"Little short of madness," declared Thomas Jefferson when told of a plan to build a 360-mile-long canal that would link Lake Erie with the Hudson River—and the Atlantic Ocean. The proposed canal would cut across the wilds of northern New York State between Albany and Buffalo. A series of locks would raise and lower boats and barges over hilly stretches in between—the most ambitious project of its kind the world had yet seen.

Critics scoffed, but one man did not. He was DeWitt Clinton, a former mayor of New York and an avid supporter of the canal project. He saw the Erie Canal as an ideal way to move people and goods cheaply between the Atlantic coast and the Midwest. In 1817, the year work began on the canal, he predicted, "The day will come in less than ten years when we will see Erie water flowing into the Hudson."

Thousands of workmen, including 3,000 newly arrived Irish immigrants, flocked to the project, drawn by the prospect of generous pay—80 cents a day, a ration of whiskey, and all the pork, venison, squirrel, and corn bread they could eat.

Work crews cleared trees, dug a 40-foot-wide trench, and diverted streams to supply the canal with water. At Lockport (opposite, lower) they dug and blasted stair-stepping locks over a rocky ledge. They also built 10-foot-wide towpaths (opposite, upper) for the horses and mules that would haul boats

A horse-drawn canal boat

Clearing the towpath

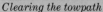

A bow lamp

and barges along the canal.

Hundreds of men died on the job—many of them killed in accidents while blasting through rock or dying from malaria and other fevers caught while working in mosquito-filled swamps and wetlands.

In spite of such problems the canal was opened in 1825. DeWitt Clinton—now governor of New York State—inaugurated the waterway with a nine-day barge ride from Buffalo to New York City.

Cannons boomed along the way, flags flew, feasts and speeches were given. And in New York harbor, amid great fanfare, Governor Clinton dumped a keg of Lake Erie water into the broad Atlantic Ocean.

Soon boats and barges of all descriptions—including the passenger craft at left—were plying the new waterway. At night, lanterns (upper right) swayed from the bows of canal boats, reminding onlookers of fireflies. No one joked about the "Big Ditch" anymore. Now they called it the "Grand Canal" and lined up in droves to buy tickets on westbound boats. Towns along the canal prospered from the traffic. One proud citizen summed up the project with these words: "They have built the longest canal, in the least time, with the least experience, for the least money, and to the greatest public benefit."

The locks at Lockport, New York

Irish immigrants, driven from their homeland by famine and poverty, arrive at New York in 1847. Risking their lives on a voyage of six weeks or more, two million Irish crossed the Atlantic before the Civil War, attracted to America by the promise of jobs and plentiful food. "Every day is like a Christmas Day for meat," exulted one immigrant.

Posters (below) advertised fares as low as $12.50.

machine could be invented which would clean the cotton [fast], it would be a great thing both to the country and to the inventor." By summer of the same year, he put together a device that could comb the fiber from the short-fibered cotton—a cotton engine, or "gin."

Driven by a horse, a water wheel, or a steam engine, Whitney's machine cleaned 50 times more short-fibered cotton an hour than could be separated by hand. The gin made Whitney famous but not rich. Planters simply built their own gins without telling Whitney or paying him the inventors' fee he was entitled to.

The Spread of Slavery

Cotton "ginning" soon became widespread, but even so the cotton itself still had to be planted, tended, and harvested by hand. Because cotton plantations now began to spread rapidly across the South, more slaves than ever were required to work in the fields. The task of cultivating the crop was, at best, tedious and backbreaking. As Solomon Northup, a free black man who had been a slave for 12 years, wrote near the end of his life, "the overseer or driver follows the slaves on horseback with a whip. . . . If one falls behind, or is a moment idle, he is whipped. In fact the lash is flying from morning until night, the whole day long."

At harvesttime in late summer, the slaves went into the fields with large sacks hung around their necks. From first light until dark, they dragged the sacks up and down the rows of plants, filling them with fuzzy cotton bolls.

Not all slaves worked at hard farm labor under brutal masters. Some worked as house servants and were relatively well fed and clothed. Others worked in towns as craftsmen and clerks. But whatever the job and however kindly treated, every slave suffered the agony of knowing that he or she was a prisoner for life—subject at all times to a white person's whim and command.

Most slaves could own nothing, not even the clothes they wore. Slave families could be, and often were, broken apart—sold on the auction block to the highest bidder or deeded in wills, like furniture and livestock. A slave who defied a white person risked severe punishment—a flogging, or even death.

Slaveholders tried to justify their position with arguments that black people were subhuman—uncivilized and inferior beings who did not share the white man's urge to be free. To support the myth, slave states passed laws designed to keep slaves subservient and ignorant. Teaching a slave to read and write became a crime. Underlying many of these laws, of course, was the fear that rights and privileges granted to slaves would lead to rebellion and insurrection—and the destruction of the plantation system which, by 1850, included nearly three million slaves. Thus the United States became one of history's notable slave empires.

While slavery grew, white American men enjoyed more and more democracy. In the early 1800s most states had laws limiting the vote to white males who owned property and paid taxes. By the 1850s most states had removed the property requirements. Voting by paper ballot replaced voice voting. Most states allowed voters to elect the men who would choose the next President, instead of having state legislatures pick the presidential electors.

Removing the Southeastern Tribes

As settlers moved southward toward Florida and westward into the fertile Mississippi Valley, they encountered Indians who had lived in the region for centuries—including the Choctaws, Chickasaws, Creeks, Cherokees, and Seminoles. Most of these people farmed, herded, and hunted. Three of the tribes, Choctaws, Chickasaws, Creeks, lived in what are now Mississippi and Alabama. The Cherokees inhabited the southern Appalachian Mountain area, mostly in Georgia. The Seminoles, a mixed racial group that included Creek Indians and escaped black slaves, lived in the forests and swamps of Spanish Florida.

After 1815 southern planters, land agents, and politicians, led by military hero Andrew Jackson, plotted to uproot the Indians from their lands so that the region could be opened to cotton plantations. In return the Indians were promised land on the prairies west of the Mississippi, a special "Indian Territory." The federal government also promised them seeds and tools. Those who didn't want to farm would be free to hunt buffalo.

But the Indians resisted the idea of giving up their southeastern homelands. They had a strong attachment to the land they lived on and considered it their rightful home. So over the next 20 years, the government took land from the Indians bit by bit. State and government agents asked the Indians to give up one piece of land, then another, and another. Often tricked and bribed, the Indians sold or gave away parcels of land, hoping to be left in peace on the land they still held. But the Indians hoped in vain. The more land they gave up, the more the government demanded from them. The Creeks, for example, by 1832 had lost about 25 million acres—an area almost the size of present-day Mississippi.

When Andrew Jackson became President of the United States in 1829, he drew up and sent to Congress the Indian Removal Act that authorized the President to remove the southeastern tribes from their lands in exchange for territory west of the Mississippi River. The act also provided funds—and troops—to move the 50,000 to 60,000 Indians involved. Many congressmen felt that it was cruel and unjust to uproot the Indians. They charged the government with planning to carry out its program at gunpoint. The bill passed in both Houses—but barely.

Jackson then drew up a new treaty for each tribe, while the southern states passed laws to seize the remaining Indian lands. Jackson and Martin Van Buren, who succeeded him in the White House in 1837, carried out the removal plan with almost total success. But one group of Seminoles resisted in a series of battles and skirmishes that went on for six years. The Seminoles eventually lost most of their Florida land, but at a high cost to the government—1,500 troopers' lives and 20 million dollars.

Slaves in Sunday finery visit the "Big House" to exchange pleasantries with the master and mistress (left). Rituals such as this often included games, races, wrestling bouts, and swapping small gifts—eggs, a new cap or pair of gloves, a jug of molasses, a plug of tobacco. But such pleasant scenes masked a far darker reality: the everyday hardships and brutality that most slaves were forced to endure.

Cotton became "King Cotton"— the chief crop of the South—by 1820 after a young tutor on a Georgia plantation invented a machine to quickly separate the fluff from the seed. The inventor, Eli Whitney, put together his cotton (en)gin(e) in 1793. Rollers with wire bristles enabled a field hand (above) to process 50 times more cotton than he could when plucking seeds by hand. From 3,000 bales sold in 1790, cotton production soared to more than two million bales a year by 1850.

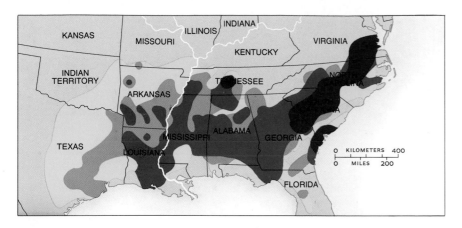

"Removal" poorly describes what actually happened to the Choctaws, Chickasaws, Creeks, Cherokees, and Seminoles. When the Army told the Indians they must go, many left home quietly, bidding tearful farewells to the familiar trees and streams and hills of their ancestral lands. But some stayed in their cabins, and others went into hiding in the forests. James Mooney, a historian of the Indian people, recorded what happened next: "Squads of troops," he wrote of one incident, "were sent to search out with rifle and bayonet every small cabin hidden away in the coves or by the sides of mountain streams. . . . Families at dinner were startled by the sudden gleam of bayonets in the doorway and rose to be driven with blows and oaths along the weary miles of trail. . . . Men were seized in their fields, or going along the road, women were taken from their spinning wheels and children from their play."

The Indians were forced to travel from 500 to 1,000 miles to get to the new Indian Territory, now the state of Oklahoma. Many of them had to walk all the way, a journey of up to six months known as the "Trail of Tears." Because the government failed to supply the Indians with enough food, blankets, clothing, and medicine, thousands of them died along the way. As one witness described the scene along the trail: "Some carry a downcast, dejected look bordering upon the appearance of despair; others a wild, frantic appearance as if about to burst the chains of nature and pounce like a tiger upon their enemies."

The old and the young suffered most. Old people died in each other's arms as they huddled for warmth in the carts that carried them. Many children walked the frozen trail in bare feet and died of cold and exhaustion.

When the Indians were driven across the Mississippi, the territory of the Louisiana Purchase was still just what it had been for hundreds of years—an expanse of waving grassland, the home of the buffalo that grazed there in uncounted millions and of the Plains Indians who hunted them. West of the 100th meridian—which runs down the center of present-day North and South Dakota—the land was an almost treeless plain with only a few inches of rainfall a year. The summers were a torment of heat, tornadoes, and drought; the winters brought numbing cold and blizzards. Mapmakers of the day labeled it the "Great American Desert."

A whole new way of life dawned for southern planters when the cotton gin was introduced. Before then, long-fibered "lowland" cotton could be grown only in a few hot and humid coastal areas. With the problem of seed removal conquered by Eli Whitney's invention, vast new lands could be planted profitably with hardier, short-fibered "upland" cotton. The map shows how far— and how fast—southern growers "cottoned" to their new crop. Cotton's rapid spread also triggered an explosion of slavery: from less than 700,000 slaves in 1790 to more than two million slaves 40 years later.

A Mississippi riverboat, paddle wheels churning to keep it nosed ashore, takes on bales of cotton from a nearby plantation—and firewood to fuel its boilers. The arrival of steamboats on the Mississippi River in 1811 revolutionized trade and communications over an area almost as big as Europe. Freight and passengers now could be carried upriver almost as easily as down—and at far less cost than by road. River ports became boomtowns. By 1851 the St. Louis waterfront was described as a "forest of smoke stacks" and America's western lakes and rivers carried more freight than Britain's entire merchant fleet.

Removal of Indian Tribes from the Southeast 1830-1840

Lands and Routes of Removal

- Cherokee
- Creek
- Chickasaw
- Seminole
- Choctaw

Forced at bayonet point from their homes in the East, members of the Cherokee tribe (left) undertake a midwinter trek to new homes in a harsh and unfamiliar land called "Indian Territory" (later Oklahoma). Disease and lack of adequate food and clothing took a toll of more than 4,000 Cherokee Indians alone along a line of march that became known as the "Trail of Tears." Lamented a Creek woman: "I have no more land, I am driven away from home . . . Let us all go, let us all die together."

The map traces the routes of the five southeastern tribes exiled from their homelands between 1830 and 1840—part of the government's program to rid the East of Indians.

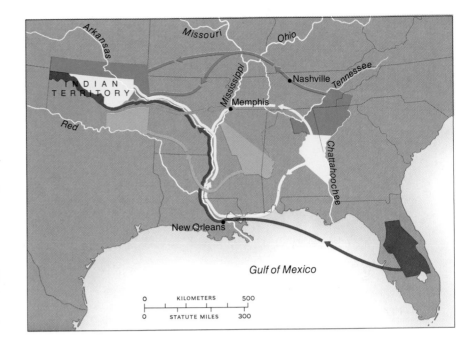

Beginning in the 1820s, pioneering families set out to cross that harsh land, lured by what lay beyond. To the west and the southwest spread the vast provinces of New Mexico and California. These lands had belonged to Spain since the 16th century, but few Spaniards had seen fit to settle there. To the northwest lay the Oregon country, stretching from the Rocky Mountains west to the Pacific Ocean and from Spanish California north to the Russian colony of Alaska. Britain and the United States claimed ownership of parts of Oregon but were content for the time being to enjoy what they called "joint occupancy."

The Santa Fe Trail became the first of the great new routes across the plains. From near Independence, Missouri, it led some 900 miles to Santa Fe, now the capital of New Mexico. Traders traveled the trail, carrying cotton goods from the United States to exchange for Mexican silver, furs, and mules. Pioneers, too, used the trail, seeking new lands to settle in California.

The Oregon Trail, blazed in 1832 by Nathaniel Wyeth and a crew of New Englanders equipped with amphibious, wheeled canoes, also started near Independence. It followed the Platte River westward across what is now Nebraska and Wyoming. In Wyoming the trail forked. Settlers bound for Oregon continued northwestward along the Snake River into present-day Idaho and beyond. Those going to California headed southwest along the California Trail through what is now Nevada.

Travelers setting out either for Oregon or Santa Fe assembled at Independence or a nearby town to gather supplies and form their wagon trains. They chose leaders and guides to check the route, pick river crossings, scout for campsites, set up camps, and organize guard duty.

Most treks began in the spring, when fresh grass grew abundantly along the trail, providing food for the oxen and cattle, horses and mules. Once started, the wagon trains crawled along, covering 15

Wayne City landing on the Missouri River, 1840s

Wagon with a full load

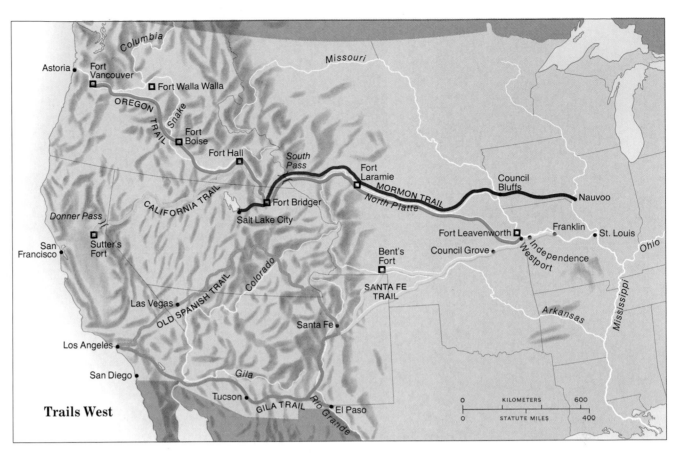

Trails West

Many trails led west (map), but none were easy, and all brought grief and hardship to hundreds of pioneering families at the height of the westward migration during the 1840s and 1850s. The Oregon Trail alone claimed some 34,000

lives—most from accidents or cholera. About one grave was dug for every 100 yards. Many families also faced disaster in Indian raids or when their oxen gave out (below, left).

Steamboats such as the ones landing near Independence, Missouri (above, left), brought many settlers west to begin the last long leg of their overland trek. At such jumping-off places travelers formed wagon trains, bought supplies, and loaded wagons with family belongings (opposite, lower).

or 20 miles a day. There was also plenty of work to do. Wagons crossing a creek often sank to their floorboards in mud. Men, mules, and oxen had to haul them free. Crossing a swampy stretch required building a road of saplings and brush, so the wagons wouldn't sink in. The pace of the slowest wagon became the pace of the entire expedition. A single accident, such as the breaking of a wheel or axle, could mean long delays for repairs.

Most wagon-train leaders tried to reach a campsite by mid- or late afternoon. Arriving at a likely place, the wagons were drawn into a circular formation to provide a corral for the larger animals and to serve as a defensive ring in case of Indian attack. Campfires were lit and the evening meal prepared. In fair weather the pioneers spread rugs or buffalo skins and slept in the open under the stars. Travelers often found the prairies touched with a life and beauty of their own. Grassy expanses, green and gold, stirred in the wind like ocean waves beneath an immense bowl of blue sky. In the early summer wild flowers bloomed, mingling so thickly with the grass that children might imagine themselves walking on a carpet in paradise.

Life existed in a thousand forms on the plains. Francis Parkman, a young Harvard graduate traveling the Oregon Trail in 1846, described a country "dotted far and wide with countless hundreds of buffalo." In another place, he wrote, "gaudy butterflies fluttered about my horse's head; strangely formed beetles . . . were crawling upon plants that I had never seen before; multitudes of lizards, too,

An ox lies down to die.

Chimney Rock on the Oregon Trail, visible up to 30 miles away, served as a beacon to westward-bound wagon trains, such as this one fording the Platte River in Nebraska. Earlier arrivals on the far side already have drawn their wagons into camping formation.

So many of these wagons rolled along the Oregon Trail that in Wyoming their wheels left deep ruts in the sandstone that still remain (below).

Sam Houston
1793-1863

As a boy on a Tennessee farm, Sam Houston filled his head so full of hero stories, he couldn't be bothered to do chores and didn't like being bossed by his four older brothers. So at 16 he ran away and joined the Cherokees. The chief, Oolooteka, adopted Sam and renamed him "The Raven."

But when the War of 1812 came along, Sam left the Indians to become a soldier. After that he decided it was time to get ahead in the world. So he became a lawyer, a successful one. Elected twice to represent Tennessee in Congress, in 1827 he put on a black satin suit and a red sash, ran for governor, and won.

Sam expected to be happy, especially after he married young Eliza Allen. Instead after three months Eliza packed up and went home. Why? Neither Sam nor Eliza would tell, but people blamed Sam and turned against him. So Sam gave up his governor's office, put on his Indian blanket, and went back to the Cherokees.

Sam grew restless again. Texas, still under Mexican rule, looked as though it might need a hero soon, so off Sam went. And when the Texans wrote their declaration of independence, Sam was first to sign it. When Texas defeated Mexico at the Battle of San Jacinto, Sam was in command. The battle lasted 20 minutes, and though Sam fought with his right leg shattered and a boot full of blood, the battle was the turning point of his life.

Sam later became president of the Republic, and when Texas won statehood, he served as a senator and finally governor. But to Texans Sam Houston remained "the hero of San Jacinto," and that suited him fine.

JEAN FRITZ

A wounded Sam Houston accepts Santa Anna's surrender, April 23, 1836.

were darting like lightning over the sand." At an Indian encampment on the Platte River, Parkman described a scene in which "warriors, women, and children swarmed like bees; hundreds of dogs, of all sizes and colors, ran restlessly about; and, close at hand, the wide shallow stream was alive with boys, girls, and young squaws, splashing, screaming, and laughing in the water."

There was also a dark side to crossing the prairies and plains. Pioneer travelers lived in fear that the Indians might plunder their supplies and steal their horses and cattle. They dreaded the ordeals brought by heat and drought and summer storms that could shred a canvas wagon cover and pelt the train with hailstones as big as hens' eggs. Lightning killed many travelers. So did disease, snakes, turbulent rivers, and kicking horses. Trailside graves—some just mounds, others marked with simple headboards—told of heartbreak and tragedy: "John Hoover. Died June 18, 1849, Aged twelve years. Rest in peace, sweet boy, for thy travels are over." And on a nameless grave, "The remains of a dead man dug up by wolves, and reburied."

Settlement of the far West reached new heights during the 1840s and 1850s. In one year alone, 1845, more than 2,500 pioneers traveled the Oregon Trail. The following year more than 5,000 members of the Mormon Church, fleeing persecution in the East, trekked on foot to the Great Salt Lake area of what is now Utah. Here, under the guidance of their leader, Brigham Young, they set up self-contained communities where they could worship free from outside interference.

The War Against Mexico

Mexico had gained its independence from Spain in 1821. At first the new nation eagerly sought to attract settlers to its great, empty borderland province of Texas and welcomed immigrants from the United States. So many came to eastern Texas, attracted by the mild winters and fertile valleys, that in a few years the Mexican government became alarmed and tried to stop further immigration. Some of these new citizens were defying Mexican law by bringing slaves with them. They also demanded self-government and refused to become Catholic like other Mexicans. By the early 1830s the Americans in Texas had gone so far as to set up their own rules. It was too much for Mexico's President, Gen. Antonio Lopez de Santa Anna. In 1836 he marched north to place Texas under military rule. The Texans reacted by declaring their independence at the village of Washington-on-Brazos in March 1836. They wrote their own constitution, which, among other things, declared slavery lawful. In April they defeated Santa Anna's army at the Battle of San Jacinto. With their own general, Sam Houston, as president, the Texans set up an independent republic and applied for admission to the United States.

Neither President Jackson nor his successor, Martin Van Buren, was eager to accept Texas into the Union. Texas had huge, empty western lands that might one day be made into slave states. Surely

Under the eye of her Mexican captors, Susanna Dickinson and her baby depart the Alamo, a church mission where 188 Texans —including her husband— died in a 13-day battle against 4,000 Mexican troops. Susanna was sent out to discourage other Texans from rebelling against Mexican rule.

With freedom won in 1836, Texas soon adopted its famous Lone Star flag (above).

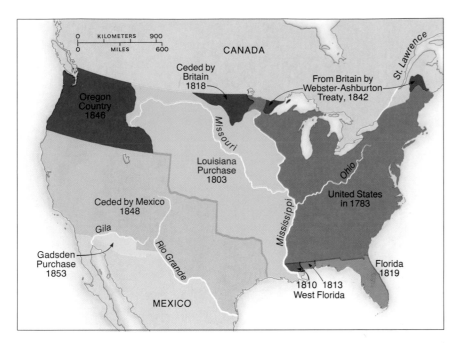

Territorial Gains 1783-1853

Growing by leaps and bounds, the United States expanded from the Mississippi River to the Pacific coast in 45 years. From France came the Louisiana Purchase (green). Spain was persuaded to give up its claims to Florida and the northeastern Gulf coast (orange). Mexico ceded much of the Southwest after the Mexican-American War (gold and yellow), and from Britain came half the Oregon Territory and other areas along the boundary with Canada (red).

Gunsmoke wreathes the heights of Chapultepec during the last major battle of the 1847 war with Mexico. The building, then used as the governor's palace and training school for young cadets, occupied a site where once had stood the famed "Halls of Montezuma," a palace built by the Aztecs. Now it guarded the western approaches to Mexico City. On September 13, after furious assaults by U. S. troops under Gen. Winfield Scott, Chapultepec fell. Among the heroes of this engagement were teenaged Mexican cadets—Los Niños, the Boys—who died defending their position, and a young American lieutenant, Thomas Jonathan Jackson, who later would gain fame as "Stonewall" Jackson.

this would stir up trouble among Northerners, who were becoming more and more angry about the westward expansion of slavery. Also Mexico did not recognize Texas's independence. Admitting Texas into the United States could easily lead to war with Mexico.

In 1844 the Democrats chose as their presidential candidate James K. Polk of Tennessee. He ran for office on a platform that promised "all of Texas, and all of Oregon." The Democrats hoped to win northern approval for new slave territories in the South by promising an equal amount of free territory to the North. Polk won the election then moved to put his program into effect, even though such action would trigger a war with Mexico. Victory over Mexico would also enable the United States to seize California, a rich territory with valuable ports. As newspaperman John O'Sullivan wrote and many people believed, it was the nation's "manifest destiny to overspread the continent allotted by Providence."

Preparing for war, President Polk first came to terms with England about Oregon. The two countries agreed to split Oregon Territory along the 49th parallel, the present boundary with Canada. The northern part went to Great Britain, the southern part to the United States. Then in the spring of 1846 Mexican and U. S. Cavalry patrols clashed on the northern bank of the Rio Grande River. This gave Polk the excuse for war he wanted.

In 1846 and 1847 the United States invaded Mexico. The result was the total defeat of Mexican forces. In February 1848 the United States imposed a treaty of peace on Mexico at the town of Guadalupe Hidalgo. Mexico surrendered Texas, New Mexico, and California—an empire of land reaching from the Gulf of Mexico to the Pacific Ocean.

Some people in the United States warned that slaveholders would take their slaves into the lands won in the war. Victory, they claimed, would spark a quarrel between slaveholders and the opponents of slavery that could endanger the Union itself.

A Yankee peddler, nattily dressed and traveling the primitive roads of the nation in a horse-drawn wagon, provided rural families with everything from candles to calicoes.

Sturdy, decorated sled called the "General Taylor," after the hero of the Mexican War, brought thrills and spills to youngsters of the 1840s.

The "reed bonnet," proper attire for any young lady of the mid-1800s, had a reed or wire frame that helped to shape the gathered fabric.

A scrimshaw doll, carved from a whale's tooth by a Nantucket sailor, had movable arms and legs—and sported fancy, high-laced boots.

A "bandbox,"—this one showing a scene of the Erie Canal—made a handy place to store frilly hats and dresses.

Fancy bellows made of wood, leather, and metal around 1820, saved a lot of huffing and puffing when starting a fire in the hearth.

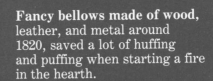

"McGuffey's Eclectic Reader" was used to teach millions of school children throughout the United States how to read after it came out in 1836.

The sturdy mug made a suitable "reward for diligence" for young scholars who might otherwise be inclined to shirk their lessons.

THE WAR FOR THE UNION 1848-1865

It was January 24, 1848. A carpenter named James Marshall and his crew were building a water-powered sawmill for trader John Sutter along a river in California. Something yellow glittered at the bottom of the waterway that Marshall's men had been digging. Marshall scooped up the glittering object and looked at it carefully. "It made my heart thump," he later recalled. "I was certain it was gold."

Marshall's discovery triggered a rush of gold seekers to California. During 1849, the first year of the Gold Rush, more than 80,000 people swarmed into the territory. The enthusiastic new Californians drew up a constitution and asked Congress to admit them to the Union as a state—a "free" state where slavery would not be permitted.

California's petition for statehood led to new debate in Congress over an old issue: the spread of slavery in the United States. The issue had first arisen in 1819, after Missouri asked for admission to the Union as a slave state. This set off a bitter dispute that ended in 1820 when Congress enacted the Missouri Compromise. This law permitted slavery in some parts of the West and banned it in other parts.

Working out an agreement between North and South had been difficult in 1820; in 1850 it would prove to be even harder. Most white Americans, in both North and South, believed that slaves had no claims to citizenship. They felt that black Africans were uncivilized and could never fit into white American society. But Northerners and Southerners came to different conclusions about this belief. Northerners wanted to prevent the spread of slavery in America by forbidding it in new states. Southerners opposed any law that might weaken the institution of slavery; they wanted a new slave state for every new free state admitted to the Union.

Although they argued fiercely about the spread of slavery, neither Northerners nor Southerners worried much about whether slavery was fair to the slaves themselves. But after the Missouri Compromise of 1820, a movement arose that gradually changed the way many Americans thought about slavery. It was called the "abolitionist" movement because its goal was to abolish all slavery.

One of the movement's first great leaders was William Lloyd Garrison, a young New England newspaper editor. Garrison felt that slavery was cruel, brutal, and contrary to democracy and that it should be abolished everywhere. On July 4, 1829, the 24-year-old Garrison gave an Independence Day speech in Boston. It was his own personal declaration of war against slavery. "The slaves," he said, "are entitled to the prayers, and sympathies, and charities of the American people." Garrison was pleading for what was then an unpopular vision—an America in which white people would accept black people as equals.

A small group of New Englanders listened to Garrison's ideas, shared his concerns, and banded together to help him. In 1831 Garrison and his friends began publishing a newspaper called the *Liberator*. And in 1833 the American Anti-slavery Society was organized in Philadelphia. Soon abolitionist groups were springing

A cartoon (upper) pokes fun at would-be gold miners rushing to California in 1849, but the journey facing the "forty-niners" was grim. Some of them spent eight months on ships sailing west around the tip of South America. Many died on overland wagon-train routes.

Prospectors (lower) swirled pans of silt or shoveled dirt into strainers to sift out the gold. "I tell you this mining among the mountains is a dog's life," one forty-niner wrote home. Some miners struck it rich, but the time quickly passed when "fortunes could be obtained for picking them up."

An auctioneer calls for bids on a mother and child at a slave sale in Missouri (below). Before the auction the slave trader exhibited his "merchandise," giving buyers a chance to examine the people being sold just as if they were horses or cattle. Slaves had to let prospective buyers stick fingers in their mouths to inspect their teeth, poke and pinch them all over, and make them bend, twist, and walk around to show that they were able-bodied.

Parents and children, husbands and wives say good-bye forever to each other (right) as a slave family is torn apart by the sale of some of its members. A former slave named Josiah Henson recalled the terrible day when his family was sold at auction: "My brothers and sisters were bid off first, and one by one, while my mother, paralyzed with grief, held me by the hand."

148

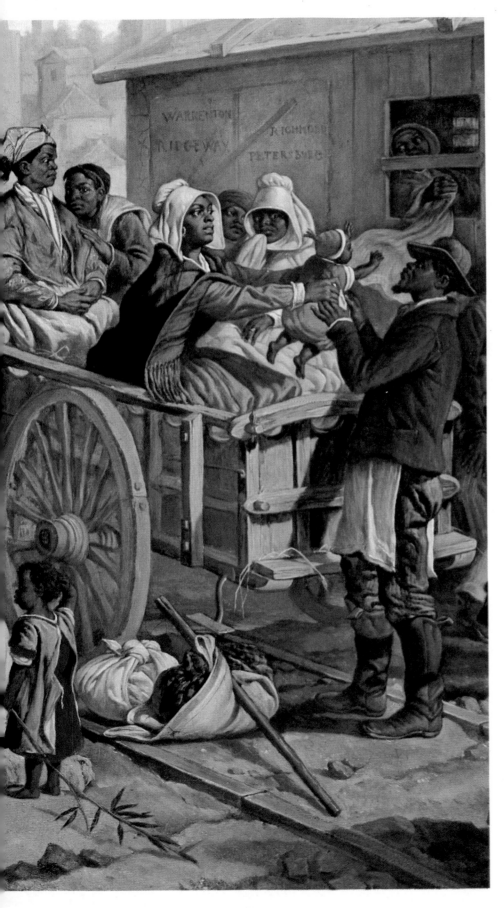

The Missouri Compromise of 1820 was designed to settle the long, bitter dispute over the spread of slavery into the western territories. The Compromise divided the lands of the Louisiana Purchase into two parts. Slavery would be permitted in the area south of the latitude of 36° 30' but forbidden in lands north of that line—except for the new State of Missouri. Since Maine would enter the Union as a free state, the admission of Missouri, a slave state, would maintain the balance of power in the U. S. Senate between slave states and free states.

The Compromise of 1850 was pieced together by a Congress anxious to save the Union. It banned the slave trade—but not slavery itself—in Washington, D. C., and admitted California as a free state, but postponed the question of whether slavery would be banned in the Utah and New Mexico Territories. It made the federal government responsible for catching and returning runaway slaves and required citizens, if asked, to help the federal officers.

Territorial Compromises

- Slave states and territories
- Free states and territories
- Decision left to the territory

Missouri Compromise 1820

Compromise of 1850

up all over the North. At first the abolitionists met a storm of opposition. Mobs jeered their speeches, threw rocks and rotten eggs at them, and smashed their printing presses. Garrison himself barely escaped an angry Boston mob in 1835.

In 1841 a young escaped slave from Maryland stood up at a meeting in Nantucket, Massachusetts. His name was Frederick Douglass. He was not yet a polished speaker, but his stories of the suffering he had endured held his audience spellbound. This was the start of Douglass's career as a speaker for the abolitionist movement. Some people found his stories hard to believe, but there was no arguing with the scars on his back.

Year by year, Douglass and his fellow abolitionists persuaded a growing number of Northerners that slavery was evil and that its further spread into the western lands had to be stopped.

In 1850, after months of angry debate over California's statehood, Congress passed a set of laws that tried to satisfy both North and South. These laws are known as the Compromise of 1850. One of the laws, passed to please the South, was the Fugitive Slave Act. It made the federal government responsible for hunting down

"So you're the little woman who wrote the book that made this great war," President Lincoln is reported to have said when he was introduced to Harriet Beecher Stowe. Her book, Uncle Tom's Cabin, *was a heartrending story of the cruelty of slavery. First published during 1851-52 as a serial in an abolitionist newspaper, then in 1852 as a book,* Uncle Tom's Cabin *strengthened and spread anti-slavery sentiment among* *Northerners, already angered by the Fugitive Slave Act of 1850. More than 300,000 copies of the book were sold within a year. Southerners claimed that the book was not true to life. They called Mrs. Stowe a "vile wretch in petticoats."*

runaway slaves and returning them to their owners. This law also required citizens to help the federal officers if asked, and it imposed a severe penalty for helping a runaway.

Long before the abolitionist movement began, slaves in America had frequently taken matters into their own hands and run away from their masters to seek freedom. Sympathetic people, both black and white, helped these fugitive slaves travel along secret escape routes to the North and into Canada. The people who gave help to the runaways were called "agents," their homes were "stations," escorts were "conductors," and the routes the fugitives took were the "Underground Railroad." Now, under the new law, people risked being sent to prison and heavily fined for every runaway they helped.

The Fugitive Slave Act pleased the slave owners of the South, but Northerners were shocked by its harshness. Many people simply ignored the law and went on helping runaways. Four years later, another new law brought more dismay to the North. Stephen A. Douglas, a powerful Democratic senator from Illinois, pushed a bill through Congress that would allow settlers in Kansas and Nebraska to decide for themselves whether to permit slavery.

Anger at the passage of Douglas's bill—known as the Kansas-Nebraska Act—swept the North. Town by town, state by state, people met, set up committees, and created a new political organization—the Republican Party. Its major goal was to stop the spread of slavery in the West.

Soon after Douglas's bill became law, elections for a territorial legislature in Kansas were announced. Pro-slavery forces streamed into Kansas from Missouri to influence the elections. These men were heavily armed and beat up or chased away many Kansans who were against slavery. Thus, in March 1855 a pro-slavery legislature was elected. But anti-slavery forces in Kansas drafted their own constitution banning slavery. By 1856 Kansas had two governments and its own civil war, which gave the territory the nickname "Bleeding Kansas."

A Piece of Property

In 1857 the Supreme Court dealt the anti-slavery cause a setback when it ruled in the *Dred Scott* case. Dred Scott was a slave whose master had taken him from the slave state of Missouri to the northern part of the Louisiana Purchase. Back in Missouri, Scott's master died, and Scott sued his master's heirs for his freedom. He had been taken to an area where Congress had banned slavery, Scott said, and this made him a free man. Not so, said the Court. A slave is only a piece of property, and under the Constitution the Congress could not take people's property away from them. Therefore, Congress had no power to forbid slaveholders from taking slaves into American territories.

In 1858 Illinois Republicans chose a 49-year-old lawyer named Abraham Lincoln to run against Douglas for the U. S. Senate. Lincoln's mother and father were farmers from Kentucky who had crossed the Ohio River and settled in Illinois. Lincoln had educated

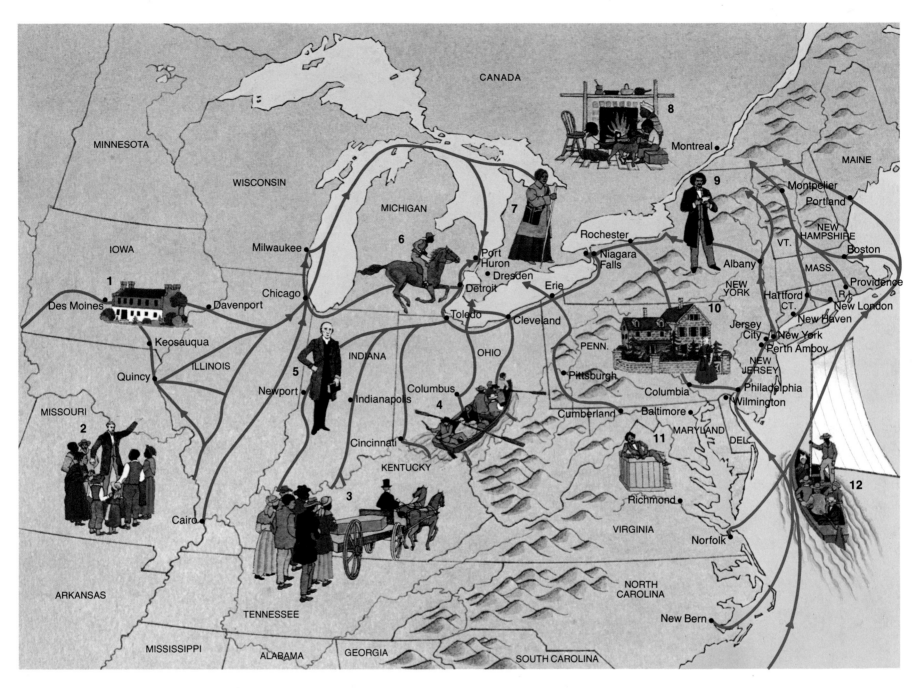

Escape to Freedom

The secret routes and daring operators of the Underground Railroad helped thousands of fugitive slaves find freedom in the North and Canada. Some of the Railroad's people, places, and events have become legendary. Benjamin Pearson built his house in Iowa (1) with a trapdoor and a secret basement where he hid runaway slaves. Bold John Brown (2) liberated slaves in Missouri and led them across ice and snow to Canada. Master of disguise, John Fairfield posed 28 slaves as a funeral procession and marched them to freedom (3). Jane Lewis, a black woman, regularly rowed fugitives across the Ohio River (4). Nicknamed "President of the Underground Railroad," Levi Coffin (5) assisted more than 3,000 runaway slaves. Escaping on a stolen horse, Henry Bibb (6) coolly passed as a free man all the way from Indian Territory to Canada. Called Moses by her people, Harriet Tubman (7) escaped to the North and then made many perilous trips back to the South to escort other slaves to freedom. Fugitives set up colonies in Canada (8), but after the Civil War more than half returned. Fiery orator Frederick Douglass (9), born a slave, devoted his life to the fight for black rights. Pennsylvania abolitionist Lucretia Mott (10) helped black Union Army veterans buy land for a community they named La Mott in her honor. Slave Henry "Box" Brown (11) had himself shipped from Richmond to Philadelphia in a wooden crate. Many slaves stowed away on ships (12) or paid profiteering boatmen high fees to take them north.

151

Frozen and fearful, a runaway slave family huddles in a snow fort built by Quaker children. Slave catchers on horseback search in vain while the children pretend to play. A true story, this act of courage occurred in the mid-nineteenth century at Plymouth Meeting, Pennsylvania, a well-known stop on the Underground Railroad. Thousands of slaves braved such dangers and hardships for a chance at freedom. Former slave Henry Bibb wrote that he journeyed "nearly forty-eight hours without food or rest . . . through cold and fear . . . pelted by the snow storms through the dark hours of the night, and not a house in which I could enter to shelter me from the storm." Many white people helped the fugitives, but for the most part it was the daring and ingenuity of blacks themselves that won them their freedom.

himself, become a lawyer, and settled in Springfield, the state capital. One observer recalled that "his clothes hung awkwardly upon his giant frame; his face was of a dark pallor without the slightest tinge of color; his deepset eyes looked sad and anxious."

In a series of campaign debates, usually held before large, noisy crowds, Lincoln and Douglas argued about slavery. Both men agreed that blacks were not equal to whites. But Douglas was not bothered by slavery, while Lincoln insisted that it was immoral and that its growth had to be stopped.

Douglas won the election, but the debates made Lincoln famous throughout the land. Republicans began to think of him as a possible candidate for the 1860 presidential election.

In October 1859 an abolitionist named John Brown and 18 of his followers seized the U. S. Armory at Harpers Ferry, Virginia (now West Virginia). Brown planned to establish a stronghold of freed slaves who would use force to liberate their brothers and sisters in the South. But he was soon captured, convicted of murder, conspiracy, and treason, and then hanged. Lincoln denounced Brown and insisted that the Republicans had no plans to organize revolts or liberate slaves. But Southern slaveholders were not convinced. They warned that if the Republicans won the 1860 elections, the South would leave—secede from—the Union.

There were four major candidates in the election. The North voted strongly for Lincoln, and he won. True to their threat, the southern states began to secede. South Carolina went first, followed by Mississippi, Florida, Alabama, Georgia, Louisiana, and Texas. Delegates from these states met at Montgomery, Alabama, in February 1861—a month before Lincoln was inaugurated—and established the Confederate States of America, with former U. S. Senator Jefferson Davis as president. These Confederate States quickly began to take control of the U. S. government lands, buildings, and military posts within their borders.

Fiery John Brown exhorts the nation to rise up against slavery in this painting, done 82 years after his death. In October of 1859 Brown and 18 other men captured the U. S. Armory at Harpers Ferry (below), trying to start a slave revolt. The exploit was doomed from the start and Brown was hanged, but his memory and example lived on in legend and song. Children today still sing about "John Brown's Body."

The Union and The Confederacy

- Union states
- Slaveholding Union states
- South Carolina: seceded first, Dec. 1860
- Deep South: seceded Jan.-Feb. 1861
- Upper South: seceded April-May 1861
- Separated from Virginia 1861, admitted to Union 1863
— Boundary of the Confederacy

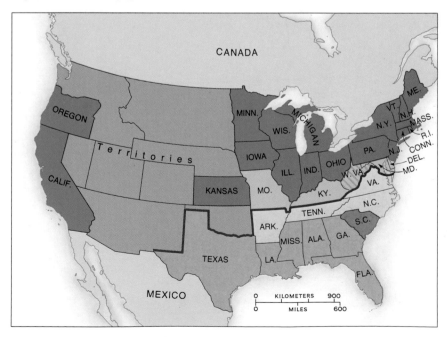

By mid-1861, 11 states had joined the Confederacy. Lincoln kept the border states (light blue) from seceding by refusing to free the slaves. "We would like to have God on our side," he said, "but we must have Kentucky."

Battles of the Civil War

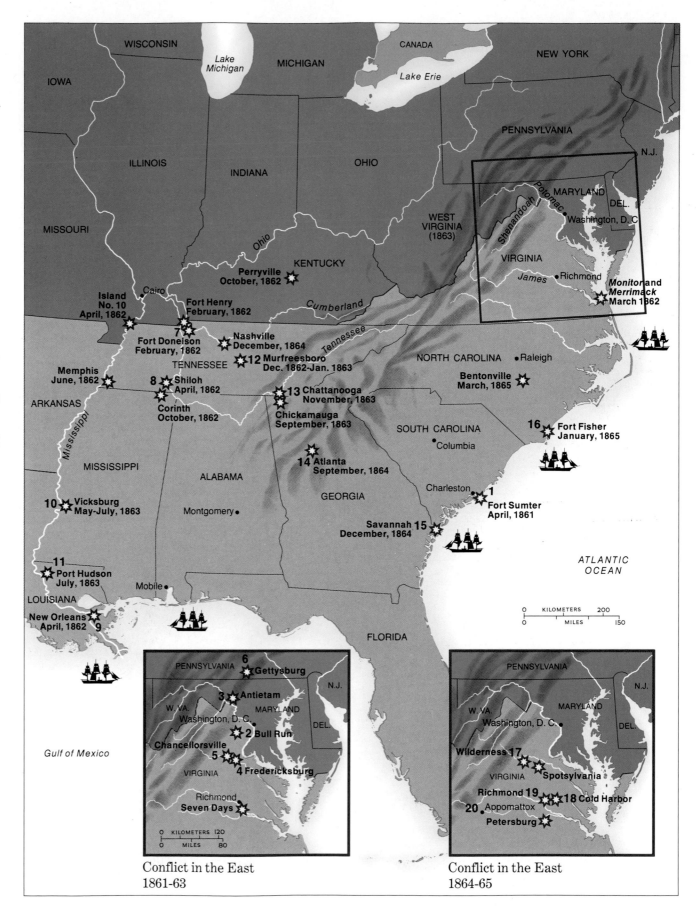

Legend:
- ■ The Union
- ■ The Confederacy
- ✪ Battle Sites
- ⚓ Union Blockade

Fort Sumter (1) felt the first fury of the Civil War in 1861. Appomattox (20) saw the war's end in 1865.

The South lacked industries, but from its plantations poured bales of cotton to trade for European supplies and weapons. The North shut off such trade with a slowly tightening blockade of Southern ports.

On land, battles raged across the South, especially in Virginia. There (left inset), Confederates stunned the Union Army at Bull Run (2) in 1861. But when the Rebels lunged northward in 1862, Union forces stopped them at Antietam (3). Confederate Gen. Robert E. Lee won fresh victories at Fredericksburg (4) and Chancellorsville (5) in 1862 and 1863. Again his army drove northward until they were stopped at Gettysburg (6).

The capture of Forts Henry and Donelson (7) in 1862 won fame for Union Gen. Ulysses S. Grant. Weeks later at Shiloh (8) he barely staved off a bloody attack. But Union ships took New Orleans (9). Vicksburg (10) and Port Hudson (11) surrendered in 1863. Now the Union controlled the entire Mississippi, slamming shut the South's door to vital supplies from the West.

A string of battles from Murfreesboro (12) and Chattanooga (13) to Atlanta (14) and Savannah (15) in 1863 and 1864 tore the South apart. The surrender of Fort Fisher (16) in January 1865 completed the Union blockade of the Atlantic. In Virginia (right inset) Grant battered the outnumbered Lee southward. From the Wilderness battle (17) through the bloodbath at Cold Harbor (18), Grant pounded on until Richmond (19) was his. Cornered at Appomattox (20) in April 1865, Lee surrendered.

Conflict in the East
1861–63

Conflict in the East
1864–65

Lincoln did not want to use force against the southern states, but there were two points on which he would not give ground: Slavery could not expand into new territory, and no state had the right to leave the Union.

On April 12, 1861, the Confederates—also called Rebels or Rebs, because they were in rebellion against the U. S. government— opened fire on Fort Sumter, a U. S. Army battery in the harbor of Charleston, South Carolina. Three days later, Lincoln called out 75,000 volunteers to put down the rebellion. On hearing that news, the legislatures of Virginia, Arkansas, Tennessee, and North Carolina voted to join the Confederacy. The Confederate capital was moved from Montgomery to the Virginia state capital, Richmond. The Civil War—or the War Between the States, as it was called in the South—was under way.

The Northern, or Union, side seemed to have all the advantages for fighting a major war. It had 23 states with a population of about 21 million. The 11 Confederate States had just 9 million people— and about one third of them were slaves. The North had many more

The first shots of the Civil War blaze from the cannons of Charleston, South Carolina, in this engraving by Currier & Ives. On a shoal in the harbor sits Fort Sumter, manned by about 75 U. S. troops. On April 12, 1861, a Confederate mortar shell exploded over the fort in the darkness before dawn. All day and into the next afternoon the guns roared. More than 3,000 shells flew before the fort surrendered. Not a man was lost on either side—but more than half a million would die in the war that followed.

Billy Yank and Johnny Reb

"I'm a raw recruit with a brand-new suit" went a Civil War soldiers' song. The Union infantryman's blue wool uniform (right) was tough and practical, but rarely fit well; one soldier described it as "a wilderness of overcoat and breeches." Each soldier carried his own weapons and equipment. He soon discarded all but the bare essentials. These included his wool blanket and waterproof rubber blanket, which he rolled together over his shoulder. A canteen carried his precious water supply. All other personal odds and ends he tossed into his haversack, a shoulder bag made of painted cloth. Many Union infantrymen carried a rifle-musket. This rugged weapon was accurate to a range of about 500 yards. The bayonet hanging at the soldier's waist was intended to be fixed to the end of the rifle, but he used it more often as a roasting stick or a can opener than as a weapon.

The haversack (below) was a Union or Confederate foot soldier's traveling household. It bulged with eating utensils and his rations of coffee and sugar, hardtack and salt pork, and vegetables and fruit foraged on the march. The soldier's personal effects might include his soap and razor, a flask, a sewing kit called a "housewife," a deck of cards, a book, stationery, and pictures of his loved ones.

The Confederate Cavalry left the Union in its dust during the first two years of the Civil War. Many Southern horsemen—expert riders from childhood—brought their own horses to battle. Traditionally, a cavalryman charged his foe on horseback, with saber drawn, but such a dramatic fighting style was useless against foot soldiers with rifles. The Confederate cavalryman (above) abandoned the saber for a revolver and a firearm. He was as likely to fight on foot as on horseback. Eyes of the army, the cavalrymen kept track of the enemy's maneuvers and were often the first troops at the scene of battle. In a typical action (above), cavalrymen dismounted, leaving their horses in the rear, and advanced with rifles in a skirmish line ahead of the main body of soldiers.

159

Union sailors pose on board the Monitor.

factories and more than twice as many miles of railroad track. Neither side put much importance on the North's greater riches—for neither side expected that it would have to fight a long war.

When the war started, soldiers and civilians on both sides were full of high spirits and sure that they would whip the other side in a few weeks of easy fighting. War songs reflected this lighthearted mood. A popular Southern one went like this:

> *Soldier boy, O soldier boy, a soldier boy for me,*
> *If ever I get married, a soldier's wife I'll be.*

In July 1861 Union troops under Gen. Irvin McDowell made their first attack. They marched from Washington into Virginia with the

Confederate torpedo

Merrimack *(left) battles the* Monitor *(right).*

aim of capturing an important railroad center at Manassas Junction. Civilians with picnic baskets tagged along to watch. But the war suddenly became horrifyingly real. Twenty-five miles southwest of Washington, Confederate troops under Generals Pierre Beauregard and Joseph E. Johnston stopped the Yankees at the village of Manassas, near a little stream called Bull Run. Many soldiers on both sides died in the hard-fought battle. The Union men streamed back to Washington, hanging their heads in shame, while the Rebs rejoiced, singing:

> *Yankee Doodle wheeled about,*
> *And scampered off at full run,*
> *And such a race was never seen*
> *As that he ran at Bull Run.*

Yankee and Rebel soldiers alike had now learned that the war would not be a Sunday picnic. Over the next few years, they often would be forced to live off the land, scavenging for food. They frequently had to march hundreds of miles between battles. In the

Union "powder monkey"

Smoke billows as the ironclad Merrimack *(Confederate) and* Monitor *(Union) fight to a draw at Hampton Roads, Virginia, on March 9, 1862. Unlike wooden ships, ironclads could withstand cannonballs. But no ship was safe from the floating mines called torpedoes.*

The navies of both sides played a vital role in the Civil War. Crews often included young boys—powder monkeys—who fetched gunpowder for cannons.

161

The Battle of Antietam

"Try to imagine us laying there the balls going whiz, whiz, whiz . . . over our heads. . . ." Union soldier Joseph Pettiner had good reason to fear as he sprawled in a field near Sharpsburg, Maryland. For this day—September 17, 1862—was the bloodiest of the war. Private Pettiner survived unhurt, but more than 23,000 other men did not.

The Confederates had crossed the Potomac River into Maryland. Union troops caught up with them near Antietam Creek. The battle raged over several miles of farmland, but some of the worst fighting erupted here along the Hagerstown Pike (1). The early morning battle near the Miller farmhouse (2) has littered the cornfield (3) with bodies—some in Union blue, some in Rebel gray. Flames are devouring the Mumma family's farmhouse (4), burned by Confederates so that Union snipers cannot hide there. Part of the Rebel force has withdrawn to the West Woods (5) behind the tiny Dunker Church (6); other units have rushed to reinforce them. And there at mid-morning the Confederate soldiers wait for the attack they know is coming.

And here it comes. Out of the East Woods (7) march line after line of Union soldiers, like blue waves rolling toward the enemy. But the Rebels are ready—many more of them than the Union generals suspect. They jump out from behind trees and rocks (8). They pour out of the woods at either side. From fields to the rear they thunder on foot and horseback, nearly encircling the astonished Union soldiers in a deadly embrace of musket fire and cannon shot. In less than 30 minutes, more than 2,000 Union men will be gunned down.

Thousands more on both sides will fall as the battle rages. The day will end in a standoff that stops the Confederates' northward march.

Photograph taken after the battle at Antietam

winter, rain turned roads into rivers of mud, bogging down whole armies. In summer, soldiers churned up huge clouds of dust as they marched. "The faces become grimed out of all human semblance," recalled one Union soldier. "The eyelashes are loaded, the hair discolored, and the uniform turns to the color of the earth."

The Battle of Bull Run (now called First Bull Run because another big battle took place there a year later) set a pattern that would be repeated during the first year of the war in the East. Poorly led Northern armies were outmaneuvered—or at least stopped—by smaller, faster-moving Confederate forces under such great generals as Robert E. Lee and Thomas "Stonewall" Jackson.

Dismayed by the defeat at Bull Run, Lincoln replaced McDowell with red-haired Gen. George McClellan, who spent the rest of 1861 strengthening the Army of the Potomac, the main Union force in the East. Under McClellan's direction, the Army of the Potomac swelled in numbers and spent its time drilling and marching and learning camp routine—but not fighting.

From Shiloh Church to Antietam Creek

In February 1862 the fighting resumed. Union Gen. Ulysses S. Grant moved south through Kentucky and captured Fort Henry and Fort Donelson in northern Tennessee. Continuing southward, Grant's men were camped at Shiloh Church near the Tennessee River when, on April 6, the Confederates attacked. The Union was victorious, but at the end of two days of fighting, more than 23,000 Americans had been killed or wounded in the Battle of Shiloh.

Three weeks later, other Union forces seized the port of New Orleans, gateway to the Mississippi River.

Meanwhile, in the East, McClellan had finally sailed his army down the Virginia coast, landed it on the peninsula between the York and James Rivers, and cautiously began to move northwest toward Richmond. But in a campaign that became known as the Seven Days Battle, the Confederate forces commanded by Lee intercepted the far larger Union Army and forced it to retreat. Lee then moved northward. In late August he defeated another large Union force at the Second Battle of Bull Run. A few days later, Lee crossed the Potomac River into Maryland.

Lee's bold strike into the North was important for more than just military reasons. If he could give the Northerners a stinging setback in their own territory, they might lose their will to keep on fighting. Such a victory might also lead European countries to recognize the Confederacy as an independent nation. This would make it difficult for the Union to maintain its naval blockade of the South. If the blockade were lifted, Southern cotton could again supply British textile mills, and British guns, ships, other manufactured goods, and money would aid the South.

But it was not to be. McClellan rallied his forces and raced to meet Lee 55 miles northwest of Washington, near Antietam Creek, Maryland. A savage struggle took place there on September 17,

A grim President Lincoln meets with Gen. George McClellan soon after the Antietam battle (above). McClellan's men had outnumbered Lee's by almost two to one, but McClellan's slow and cautious use of his troops prevented a total victory over the Rebels. A month after this meeting, Lincoln replaced McClellan with another general.

In a grisly photograph taken two days after the Antietam battle, the twisted bodies of Confederate soldiers lie in a sunken road called Bloody Lane (opposite). Photographs showing the ugly realities of war were a shock to civilians, accustomed to the gentler images portrayed by painters (left).

"The Wounded Drummer Boy"
by Eastman Johnson

Battlefield Medicine

Union field hospital at Gettysburg

More than 600,000 men died in the Civil War, chiefly of disease and battle wounds. Many more were wounded and managed to survive.

While soldiers did their best to blow each other apart, doctors and nurses worked ceaselessly to mend broken bodies. Wounded men walked or were carried to a field hospital. Sometimes a horse-drawn ambulance wagon was available to transport them.

The field hospital might be a converted cow barn, mill or farmhouse, or just a group of tents beyond artillery range.

Once he reached the hospital, the soldier's ordeal had just begun. Battlefield medicine in the 1860s was sometimes closer to butchery than science. Most of the operations performed during the Civil War were amputations. Surgeons had no idea that germs caused infection or that cleanliness could save lives.

A door laid across two barrels often served as an operating table. Tubs caught gushing blood. Pails of dirty water and sea sponges were used over and over to clean wounds and hands. Scalpels and other instruments were merely wiped off. Luckily for the patient, chloroform and ether were usually available as anesthetics. Doctors also prescribed opium, morphine, marijuana, and whiskey. But for many men, the grisly surroundings were as frightening as the prospect of pain. A wounded colonel wrote his wife, "I could not help comparing the

Surgeon amputates a soldier's leg.

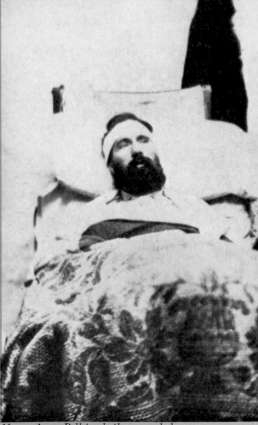

Nurse Anne Bell tends the wounded.

166

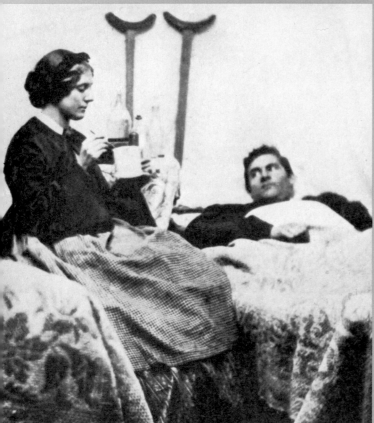

surgeons to fiends. It was dark & the building lighted partially with candles . . . near & around the tables stood the surgeons with blood all over them & by the side of the tables was a heap of feet, legs & arms."

Northern and Southern women did not sit idly at home during the war while the men suffered. Led by such activists as Dorothea Dix, thousands of Northern and Southern women broke tradition by working as nurses in general hospitals. At first, surgeons resisted sharing the all-male world of medicine with women, but nurses were sorely needed. The Confederate States passed a law in 1862 that gave "preference to females" as military nurses, matrons, and aides.

A few brave women served as nurses at the front lines of battle. Clara Barton, who later founded the American Red Cross, acted as a one-woman rescue squad, delivering bandages, splints, drugs, food, and candles to Union field hospitals by mule-drawn wagon. Once there, she helped to bandage wounds, extract bullets, and feed the patients. An admiring surgeon wrote of her, "if heaven ever sent out a holy angel, she must be one."

Above: Clara Barton. Below: surgeon's tool kit

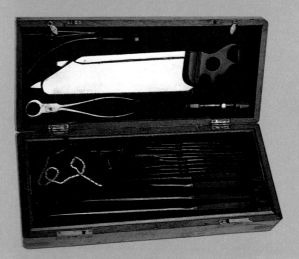

167

Union artillerymen practice loading cannons (above) before the battle at Chancellorsville in May 1863. But they practiced in vain. Union Maj. Gen. "Fighting Joe" Hooker, who boasted that he led "the finest army on the planet," lost this battle against a Rebel force that was half the size of the Union Army. General Lee's daring divide-and-conquer tactics confused Hooker and earned the Confederacy a stunning victory.

"Tenting Tonight" (above) was a popular Civil War song for soldiers on both sides. To pass the long hours between battles, Yankees and Rebels sang about the war and played banjos and harmonicas. Opposing armies sometimes serenaded each other across battle lines.

1862, that resulted in more than 23,000 casualties. Neither side was victorious, but Lee's northward invasion was halted; he withdrew his army across the Potomac.

Five days after Lee was stopped at Antietam, Lincoln gave the Confederacy an ultimatum. End your rebellion by January 1, he said, or I will emancipate—free—your slaves.

True to his word, on January 1, 1863, Lincoln proclaimed all slaves in Rebel areas to be "thenceforward, and forever free." The Emancipation Proclamation was a masterful political move. No European country would now be likely to help the South, since such help would support slavery.

The Proclamation brought new hope to the abolitionists. It also invited black people to join the Union forces. Frederick Douglass, by now a famous black leader, urged his people to rally to the Union cause. "The iron gate of our prison," he told them, "stands half open." The blacks responded; eventually, some 200,000 joined the Union forces, serving as soldiers, sailors, laborers, officers, and spies.

The Confederates, meanwhile, had dealt a serious setback to the Army of the Potomac. In mid-December Gen. Ambrose Burnside, who was McClellan's successor, crossed the Rappahannock River at Fredericksburg, Virginia, to battle Lee's army. The action was a disaster, resulting in 12,700 Union casualties in one day of fighting. Soon afterward, Lincoln accepted Burnside's resignation from command.

Stonewall Jackson wounded at Chancellorsville, May 2, 1863

Thomas "Stonewall" Jackson 1824-1863

Tom Jackson came from a proud western Virginia family and grew up to become a general in the Confederate Army. When Tom was two, his father died, leaving behind nothing but debts.

Tom was determined that *he* was not going to fail in life. But how could he be sure? He'd make rules, he decided, and follow them—no matter what. He'd tell the truth. He'd keep promises. He'd finish whatever he started. Once he fell into a creek on the way to church, but did that stop him? No, he went right on and sat through the service in his dripping clothes. If people laughed, he didn't care.

Whatever he wanted to do, he *could* do. He believed this and proved it again and again. At West Point he was such a slow learner that some doubted he'd get through, but he did, often staying up far into the night to memorize his lessons.

It was in battle, however, that Tom was at his best. He earned his nickname, Stonewall, at First Bull Run when his brigade stood firm in the midst of a retreat. As the Civil War went on, he made such a record for himself that Southerners loved to talk about him. *Remember the time he marched his men 400 miles in 40 days through the Shenandoah Valley, fought five battles, and defeated three generals?* An unlikely hero, Stonewall Jackson rode an undersized horse, wore a crumpled hat, and sucked lemons during battle. But he was a winner. Someone to brag about and laugh about at the same time.

In the end Stonewall was accidentally shot by his own soldiers at the Battle of Chancellorsville and tragically died a few days later.

JEAN FRITZ

In the spring the Army of the Potomac, now led by Gen. Joseph Hooker, renewed its Virginia campaign. Once more Lee soundly defeated the Union forces, this time at Chancellorsville. General Lee now moved his army quickly up the Shenandoah Valley to Pennsylvania and a second invasion of the North. As the Confederate Army marched forward, the Union rallied its forces behind still another new commander, Gen. George Meade.

On July 1 the two armies collided at a little Pennsylvania town called Gettysburg and fought for three days. It was a desperate battle. When it ended, more than 6,000 soldiers were dead; another 40,000 were missing or wounded. One observer wrote that "blood stood in puddles in some places on the rocks."

At Gettysburg, as in other battles, Americans killed Americans. Worse still, brothers sometimes killed brothers. One family of three brothers came from Philadelphia; two of them moved to New Orleans before the war began and then enlisted in the Confederate Army. The youngest brother, who had stayed in Philadelphia, joined the Union Army. After a battle, one of the brothers from New Orleans turned over the body of his dead enemy and, to his horror, saw that it was his youngest brother.

Lee's army limped back south, having lost more than a third of its men. Meade, his own army battered and battle-weary, did not have the strength to pursue.

On July 4, even before Lee began his retreat, news came that Grant had taken the fortress town of Vicksburg on the Mississippi River after a 47-day siege. With the surrender of Port Hudson five days later, the Union cut off Texas and Louisiana from the rest of the Confederacy and now controlled the entire river.

But a few months later, a large Confederate force led by Generals Braxton Bragg and James Longstreet defeated the Union troops in another bloody battle, this one near Chickamauga Creek in northern Georgia. Here the Rebels chased the Yankees all the way to Chattanooga, Tennessee. The Rebel victory, one of the few in the west, did not last long. General Grant took command of the demoralized Union forces and eventually drove the Rebels back into Georgia, after defeating them at Lookout Mountain and Missionary Ridge in Tennessee. The fighting came to a halt in December as both armies withdrew for the winter.

Grant Takes Command

Grant's victories earned him Lincoln's esteem—and a promotion. In March 1864, Lincoln gave Grant command of all Union forces. Here at last, Lincoln felt, he had a general who would fight to the bitter end, who would not make excuses or throw away opportunities by being too cautious.

Grant took command with a carefully planned strategy: He would use the Army of the Potomac to hammer away at Lee in Virginia—regardless of Union losses—until the South was defeated. Meanwhile, Grant's old western army, now under Gen. William T. Sherman, would attack the Confederacy from the west.

Describing the infamous Confederate prison camp at Andersonville, Georgia, a former inmate wrote, "Stronghearted, brave men who had almost gleefully faced the cannon's mouth . . . here sank almost in helpless despair." Built to hold 10,000, the stockade was packed with 33,000 wretched men. Shelterless, they devised crude tents from old blankets. A sewage-laden creek served as their water supply. Death

claimed 13,000 men, chiefly from disease, starvation, and exposure. In the painting at left, a guard shoots a prisoner who dared to cross the "dead line," a pine-board barrier around the perimeter of the camp. After the war, the prison commander, Henry Wirz, was convicted of war crimes and hanged. But conditions at other prisons, both Northern and Southern, were not much better. Southern captives suffered terribly from the cold, and food was meager. In the small sketch above, drawn by a Rebel prisoner at Point Lookout, Maryland, inmates skin and cook rats to stretch their rations.

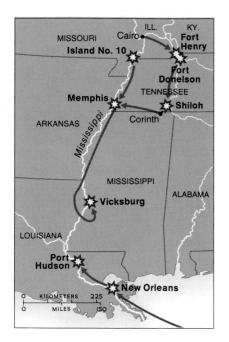

**The Civil War in The West
1862-63**

→ Union advance
✦ Battle site

*Yankee ironclads light the night
as they shell Island No. 10, a
Rebel battery on the Mississippi
River (right). Confederate river
fortresses toppled under the
North's combined land and naval
attacks in 1862 and 1863 (map,
above). Ironclads helped General
Grant's troops capture Forts
Henry and Donelson in February. On April 7 the Rebels were
defeated at Shiloh. The next
day Island No. 10 was captured.
Meanwhile, Union Admiral
Farragut's wooden fleet had taken
New Orleans on April 25 and
headed northward. Memphis
surrendered to Union ironclads
on June 6, opening the river as
far as Vicksburg. But it was not
until July 1863 that the last Rebel
fortresses, Vicksburg and Port
Hudson, surrendered, giving
control of the entire Mississippi
to the Union.*

Bold and decisive Union Gen. Ulysses S. Grant (below) gained national fame in the western river war, winning a string of battles while generals in the East bungled. Grant's demand for "an unconditional and immediate surrender" from the commander of Fort Donelson delighted Northerners, who began to call him "Unconditional Surrender" Grant.

Black Union volunteers (left) attack a Rebel stronghold at Charleston, South Carolina, in the summer of 1863, helping to launch a 22-month siege of the city. Almost half the men were killed or wounded in this attack; the dead included their leader, Col. Robert Shaw (with saber). In 1865, Charleston surrendered to another black regiment; proud soldiers took possession of the city where some had once been slaves.

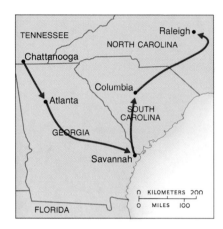

Sherman's Advance, 1863-65
General Sherman's troops rip up railroad tracks and burn buildings (above, right) in a rampage that destroyed the heart of the Confederacy. "We are not only fighting hostile armies, but a hostile people," Sherman claimed. In the final winter of the war, he led 62,000 men on a plundering march from Atlanta to the sea (map, above), capturing Savannah as a Christmas gift for President Lincoln. Sherman's troops then pressed northward through South Carolina and left Columbia, its capital, in ashes. In March 1865 a Rebel force of about 20,000 attacked the Union troops near Raleigh, North Carolina, but soon retreated. Three weeks later, General Lee surrendered.

Beginning on May 7, Sherman moved his army of 100,000 men along the railroad line from Chattanooga, Tennessee, toward Atlanta, Georgia. Opposing him were about half as many Southern troops under General Johnston. Each time Sherman tried to outmaneuver the Rebel force he was turned back or blocked by Johnston's brilliant tactics.

But the Yankees were too powerful to be stopped for long. They finally took Atlanta on September 2 and eventually burned much of the city to the ground—a blazing preview of what lay in store for the South. After resting and resupplying his men, Sherman started on a slashing march through the heart of Georgia to the seacoast city of Savannah. Seeking to wipe out the South's ability to continue supporting the war, Sherman ordered his troops to destroy everything of military value they came across: farms, factories, railroads, bridges, and public buildings. Sherman's men plundered everything in a 60-mile-wide path. They virtually destroyed the economy of Georgia, leaving its people to survive on the thinnest of rations. One 17-year-old girl later wrote, "Like statues mother and I stood looking on, and saw them take all the provisions we had, then kill the milk cows and other stock . . . and knew that now our last hope for food was gone."

After Sherman captured Savannah on December 21, he turned northward, fighting his way through the Carolinas against scattered Rebel forces. Grant, meanwhile, had begun his Virginia campaign, marching in pursuit of Lee. Somehow, General Lee

On April 9, 1865, in the parlor of Wilmer McLean's home at Appomattox Courthouse, Virginia (right), Ulysses S. Grant accepted Robert E. Lee's surrender. "Whatever his feelings," wrote Grant, "they were entirely concealed . . . but my own feelings . . . were sad and depressed. I felt like anything rather than rejoicing at the downfall of a foe who had fought so long and valiantly."

General Lee rode out among his men that afternoon to break the sad news of surrender. "The troops crowded around him, . . . anxious to touch his person or even his horse," one officer recalled. Lee, his voice shaking with emotion, said, "Men, we have fought through the war together. I have done my best for you. My heart is too full to say more." The next day, the defeated general rode home to Richmond.

managed to keep his tired, tattered army one step ahead of the Yankees. In battle after battle—the Wilderness, Spotsylvania Court House, Cold Harbor—Grant's forces suffered heavy losses—60,000 men in the first month. Finally, on June 15, Grant caught up with Lee at Petersburg, Virginia, just south of the Confederate capital. After failing several times to break through the Rebels' defensive lines, the Yankees settled down for a siege that lasted through the bitter winter of 1864-65.

In April of 1865, the Confederate forces at both Petersburg and Richmond slipped away and headed west. The Yankees followed in hot pursuit. Finally, after a chase lasting a week and covering 90 miles, Grant's forces surrounded Lee near the village of Appomattox Courthouse, Virginia. The Southerners had nowhere left to go.

Unwilling to see more men die in a lost cause, Lee surrendered to Grant on April 9. There was scattered fighting afterwards, but the war was over. In four years, the nation—North and South—had suffered more than a million casualties, including 360,000 Union dead and 260,000 Confederate dead. Ahead lay the task of making a bitterly divided country whole once again.

Croquet (left), a genteel sport imported from England, entertained war-weary Americans in the North and South. Women as well as men played this popular game.

A prancing pony (right) adorns a hand-cranked sewing machine in a design submitted to the U. S. Patent Office in 1858.

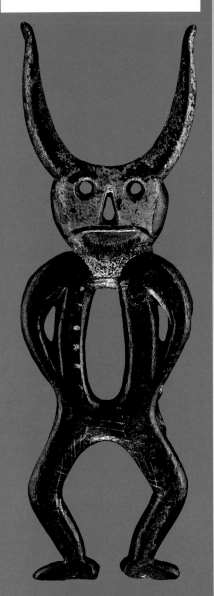

Comical cast-iron bootjack stands ready to help tug heavy boots off weary feet. The wearer steps on the demon's body, sticks a boot heel between the horns, and pulls.

Military toys were popular during the Civil War. Children who played the game "Running the Blockade" (above) had to evade a maze of enemy ships and other hazards to reach harbor safely. The platoon of wooden soldiers (right) marched when a child pulled its levers.

Confederate money, adorned with Stonewall Jackson's portrait, became worthless at war's end. The U. S. issued its first paper dollar, called a greenback, on August 1, 1862.

Tintypes—photographs printed on thin metal—comforted soldiers at war and their families at home. Above, a boy poses proudly beside his father. At top, a daughter's picture and one of her curls are tucked into a locket.

179

Rebuilding the SOUTH

The Struggle for Democracy 1865-1914

Abraham Lincoln had led the United States through the bloodiest war it had ever fought. But he had only five days to enjoy the peace that descended over the land. On the evening of April 14, 1865, he and his wife, Mary, went to see a play at Ford's Theatre in Washington, D. C. In the middle of the performance an unemployed actor and Southern sympathizer named John Wilkes Booth sneaked into the box where the couple sat. Bitter at the defeat of the South, Booth was out for revenge against the "tyrant" who had made it happen. He fired a shot at Lincoln's head. The unconscious President was carried to a house across the street and stretched out on a bed. As the news spread through the streets, a weeping crowd of people gathered outside. The Speaker of the House of Representatives and members of the Cabinet waited indoors. From time to time Mary Todd Lincoln approached her husband's bedside, and the sound of her sobbing filled the house. In the early dawn of April 15 Abraham Lincoln died.

Lincoln's death came at a time when the problems of winning the war were giving way to the even harder problems of managing the peace. The old pattern of society in the South—rich planters, small farmers, city people, and slaves—was shattered, and no one knew what would or should replace it. Throughout the country people disagreed strongly about the future of the freed black slaves. Northerners also disagreed with each other about how to treat the defeated Southerners. Were they traitors to be punished or brave fighters to be welcomed back into the American family of citizens? These matters urgently needed settling, because millions of homeless Southerners—black and white—did not know how to reconstruct their lives in the confusion of the war's end.

Union armies had destroyed huge areas of the South. Traveling through the region in 1865, a northern writer named John Trowbridge described what he saw. Everywhere plantations lay idle and in ruins. Whole sections of cities like Richmond and Atlanta were made up of "beds of cinders, cellars half filled with bricks and rubbish, broken and blackened walls, impassable streets. . . ." Small towns and villages too were crumbled and crushed.

Planters suffered much from the war. Some died, others lost sons, or faced ruin with the destruction of their lands. These were the big slaveholders whose fathers or grandfathers had settled in the fertile and well-watered river valleys. Their corn, sugar, cattle, horses, mules had been carried off, consumed, or destroyed. Plantation houses had been blasted and burned in the fighting or vandalized; weeds choked the fields.

Millions of other Southerners also suffered, especially in Virginia, South Carolina, and Georgia, states that had felt the full force of war. At the beginning of the war there were about five and a half million whites living in the Confederacy. Some of them owned farms, where they grew tobacco or cotton with the help of a few slaves and lived a good life. Millions more owned no slaves. Many owned only sandy, swampy, or worn-out land that nobody else wanted. They lived in tiny cabins, grew a few scanty crops, shot

Ford's Theatre becomes a stage for a mad actor's role in history as John Wilkes Booth shoots Abraham Lincoln (upper). That day the President had urged his Cabinet to treat the beaten South kindly. "With malice toward none," he had once said. His body went home to Illinois, pausing in cities along the way. A photographer caught mourners thronging the streets of Philadelphia as Lincoln's casket passes by (lower).

wildfowl, pastured half-wild hogs and cattle in the woods, and caught fish. These were the pinelanders of Georgia and the woodsmen who lived amid the hills and valleys of the Carolinas, Tennessee, and Alabama. Many of these men had fought valiantly for slavery and for their beloved leader, Gen. Robert E. Lee. Some 260,000 died; many others returned crippled or broken.

The collapse of the Confederacy brought freedom to the South's slaves, but it also brought suffering. As Union forces had fought their way through the South during the war, thousands of blacks followed them, leaving slavery behind. At the end of the war they were still following the troops, camping in makeshift shacks, often sick and starving. Other ex-slaves took to the roads in search of husbands, wives, and children torn from them by slave sales and by the confusion and bad luck of war. For some this search would continue for years. "I have a mother somewhere in the world," wrote the Reverend E. W. Johnson in an appeal for help to a newspaper. "I know not where. She used to belong to Philip Mathias in Elbert county, Georgia, and she left four of her children there about twenty-three years ago. . . . Her name was Martha and I heard that she was carried off to Mississippi by speculators."

The Freedmen's Bureau Helps Out

Just before Lincoln's death Congress created a special government agency called the Freedmen's Bureau to give emergency help to starving Southerners. Most of the people it helped were black. The Freedmen's Bureau found them jobs, provided food, and set up courts to settle legal disputes. The Bureau also supported schools for the ex-slaves. Men and women, old and young, flocked to these schools, which were set up in any place that could be found—in barns and sheds, in churches, even in the fields.

Both teachers and students ran risks. Some Confederate veterans turned on the black people. They blamed the blacks for their sufferings and felt outraged at the sight of them behaving as free men and women. Most white Southerners were unwilling or unable to accept black people as equals instead of humble, obedient servants. Some whites used violence to force the blacks back into their former lowly state. They burned schools and beat teachers and students. "There has been much opposition to the School," wrote Edmonia Highgate, who was teaching in 1866 in Lafayette Parish, Louisiana. "Twice I have been shot at in my room. My night school scholars have been shot but none killed."

In the spring of 1865 the Union government held the whole South in its hands. What would its future be? What would be the future of hundreds of thousands of black families thrown suddenly upon the world without land and without rights? The answers to such questions rested with the country's leaders in Washington, D. C.

At this moment Vice President Andrew Johnson succeeded the slain Lincoln as President. Born in Raleigh, North Carolina, of very poor parents, Johnson had moved to eastern Tennessee to earn his living as a tailor. When he was nineteen, his wife, Eliza,

182

Like ghosts of the fallen South, stunned citizens wander amid the rubble of Richmond in this photograph taken in April 1865. To keep Union troops from using the proud capital, Confederate soldiers set much of their city aflame before trudging away in defeat. Many went home—as did the soldier and his family in the painting below—to find only ruins there too. Peace was as hard as war for families who had to fight hunger and despair.

NORTH.
We don't want **THAT KIND OF IVORY**! We didn't raffle for that Elephant! We wont take him! We must drive him back where he belongs. There's no room for such a big black beast here.

SOUTH.
Big Black Sambo has broken from his keepers, and we can't chain him any more. But if we can't use him, we'll abuse him, and make him glad to come back to his hog and hominy.

taught him how to read and write. He soon entered politics and began to rise in the world. When the Civil War broke out, he was a senator from Tennessee, battling with the people who wanted to take the state out of the Union. He lost this struggle, but when Union troops occupied the state in 1862, Andrew Johnson returned as military governor. In this position he organized a new, loyal government for Tennessee. Republicans in Congress were pleased with the stern attitude he took toward plantation owners.

In 1864 Johnson was elected Vice President on Lincoln's ticket, and he became President the next year. John Trowbridge, who visited the White House in August 1865, described Johnson as having "strong features, dark, iron-gray hair . . . deep-sunk eyes, with a peculiarly wrinkled, care-worn look about them. . . ."

Once in the White House, Johnson's attitude toward the South began to soften. Between May and December 1865, when Congress was not in session, he went ahead by himself to "reconstruct" the South—that is, to set conditions the defeated states would have to accept in order to come back into the Union. His terms were generous. The southern states, he said, must accept the abolition of slavery, and they must withdraw the proclamations of 1860-61 that said they had left the Union. Southerners could be pardoned for rebellion if they took a new oath of loyalty to the United States. Even the Confederacy's top leaders would be forgiven for their treason if they appealed to the White House. Soon such petitions were pouring into Johnson's office; all summer long he signed them.

Blacks who once felt the bite of the lash now suffered the sting of cruel cartoons like this one of the 1870s. It mocks the ex-slaves who sought better homes in the North and West after the Reconstruction governments crumbled. The South offered blacks hard treatment and low pay—and the North, weary by then of war and wrangling, no longer really cared about their plight.

A photograph taken in Virginia about 1897 shows that a generation of freedom had brought little change in housing for southern blacks. Many lived in the same cabins they knew as slaves—"old and bare," wrote one historian, "built of rough boards," with "a fireplace . . . unsteady with age. . . . smelling of eating and sleeping, poorly ventilated, and anything but homes."

"My Lord, ma'am, what a great thing learning is!" Thus one former slave spoke for all as they now turned to another urgent need: education. In schoolhouses like this one (right)—and sometimes in tents and barns—teachers took up the task. In the 1866 photograph below, two children listen to lessons from a South Carolina schoolmarm. At first most teachers came from the North, sent down by church groups or the government's Freedmen's Bureau. Soon blacks could teach other blacks; by 1870 they filled half the South's teaching jobs.

Johnson showed little concern for the fate of the black people. He did not ask for promises that they would be fairly treated. And he put a stop to the Army's practice of dividing up captured plantations and giving the land to the freed slaves. In Georgia and South Carolina huge tracts of offshore and coastal lands had passed into the hands of freed blacks after Gen. William Sherman issued his Special Field Order Number 15 in January 1865. The area was under military rule, and Sherman saw the redistribution of the enemy's land as a way to take care of the many hungry and homeless ex-slaves who had attached themselves to his army. In other places, too, black people were farming lands from which planters had fled. Andrew Johnson issued orders that all plantation lands were to be given back to their former owners.

This decision was bad news for the blacks and was opposed by some of the Army officers who had helped carry out Sherman's policy. It was, however, welcome news to the white planters. At the moment of defeat panic had gripped them; now they began to breathe more easily. Nobody was going to be tried for treason, and nobody was going to lose his land. Planters began to look seriously

for workers to raise their crops. Soon many blacks found themselves back on the plantations as field hands.

During slavery days small groups of militiamen had patrolled the roads in the plantation districts. Their job was to watch for slaves trying to escape. Now, even though the war was lost and slavery outlawed, these patrols once more appeared in the South, which meant the return of a rule of terror. "Organized patrols . . . keep guard," wrote a Freedmen's Bureau official in September. "The unfortunate who attempts to escape, or he who returns for his wife or child, is waylaid or pursued with hounds, and shot or hung." By the end of 1865 there was little the Army could do to prevent such violence. Most of the Federal troops had returned North.

One by one the restored southern state governments now began to pass laws designed to force the blacks to go on living and working on the plantations. The blacks would not be allowed to vote, to move from place to place, to get better jobs, to mix with white people—to be treated in any way as full American citizens. These laws became known as the Black Codes; the first of these codes was passed by the state of Mississippi in November 1865.

"The Misses Cooke" teach their students in this engraving from 1866. Their simple schoolroom in Virginia recalls another in North Carolina, described in a letter from one of its teachers. "We are yet without curtains or shades. We borrowed chairs . . . and were obliged to provide other necessaries at our own expense. . . . We have now one hundred and seventy scholars and constantly increasing. We are surely 'Marching On.'" Not all the South marched with him. By 1870 only about one black child in ten went to school.

When the 39th Congress assembled in Washington in December, a large number of former Confederate politicians and officers were waiting to take seats. The Republican majority refused to seat them. Most Republicans didn't want to interfere with the rights of the states, nor did they wish to quarrel with Andrew Johnson. But, they argued, he had surely gone too far. A Reconstruction program that denied black people the right to vote and returned them to the mercy of their former masters made a mockery of the ideals for which the North had fought.

So Congress worked out its own Reconstruction plan. It approved the 14th Amendment to the Constitution, which the southern states were told they would have to ratify as a condition of reunion. The 14th Amendment gave citizenship to black Americans born in the United States and reduced the representation in Congress of states that did not allow blacks to vote.

This amendment was a giant step in the struggle for democracy. It overturned the Supreme Court's *Dred Scott* decision of 1857, which said that blacks were not, and could never become, American citizens. It placed into the Constitution abolitionist William Lloyd Garrison's prewar vision of black membership in American society. It proclaimed that freedom for America's slaves was a national right, to be protected by the power of federal law.

For a handful of Republican legislators, the 14th Amendment was not enough. These men, many of whom had been abolitionists before the war, were called "Radicals" because of their strong hostility toward slavery and their uncompromising support of black citizenship and rights. Thaddeus Stevens, a representative from Pennsylvania, was the leading Radical. Stevens walked with a limp and wore a brown wig, and he could deliver terrible tongue-lashings to people who angered him. Break up the big plantations,

Who shall govern now? At last black freedmen had a say as they flocked to ballot boxes all over the South. They cast their votes in New Orleans in 1867 (right) while white citizens glower. Black votes swept many former slaves into office—a far cry from days when a slave was counted as three-fifths of a person in deciding how many congressmen a state would send to Washington.

President Andrew Johnson pampers the "Southern Dragon" in this 1866 cartoon (left). His mild policies toward the South angered Washington lawmakers who wanted to punish the rebels. Many Union veterans chose to stay in the South to farm, teach, or enter professions or politics. Other Northerners joined them, some toting bags (below) that gave them all a nickname: carpetbaggers.

Hiding under hoods, terrorists of the Ku Klux Klan fight ballots with bullets as they gun down a black voter in his home. Two Klansmen posed proudly in 1868 (below) for a portrait as chilling as their purpose: to keep blacks from the polls. Other secret societies sprang up all over the South. One called itself the Shotgun Club, another the Pale Faces. But they did their work as the Klansmen did. "We're born of the night and we vanish by day," crowed a Klan poet. To blacks and their white friends, the poem began and ended with a grim warning: "Get out of the way!"

Stevens told Congress, and give the land to the poor people, both black *and* white; don't leave it in the hands of tyrants and traitors. If you do not do this, he said, "all our blood and treasure have been spent in vain." Few congressmen listened to his message.

Andrew Johnson at once attacked the 14th Amendment. Blacks, he said, were not fit to receive "the coveted prize" of citizenship. Reject the amendment, he told the South. By the summer of 1866 a war of words had broken out between President and Congress. The two sides took their case to the electors in the congressional election campaign that fall—a vote for the Democrats would be a vote for Johnson's policy, a vote for the Republicans would be a vote for the amendment. The Republicans won by a landslide.

Congress Takes Charge

Congress returned to Washington in March 1867 in an angry and determined mood. It wiped out the state governments that Johnson had permitted to be set up in the South and divided the region into five districts under military control. Army commanders drew up new lists of voters that included former slaves and excluded certain former Confederates. Under the Army's protection, political power in the South shifted for the first time away from the wealthy planter class to a new base: the masses of male voters, both black *and* white. Three new groups now held the reins of government. First were Northerners who had moved South during and after the war, some to help rebuild the region, some to make their own fortunes. These men were called "carpetbaggers" because they often carried suitcases made of carpet material. The second group were Southerners who had opposed secession and who now voted Republican. They were called "scalawags," after the Scottish island of Scalloway, which was said to grow puny cattle. The third group were the blacks, who, just two years out of slavery, were being elected to public offices. A majority of white Southerners opposed all three groups.

By 1870 this "Congressional Reconstruction" was complete. All the southern states had agreed to the 14th Amendment. The 15th Amendment had also been adopted. It said that no citizen could be denied the vote simply because he had been a slave.

For the first time in the country's history, black people voted in large numbers, sat in state legislatures side by side with white colleagues, ran for local office, and went to Washington, D. C., as representatives and senators. Hiram Revels, a minister from Mississippi, became the first black ever to sit in the U. S. Senate.

All of this spelled defeat and humiliation for Andrew Johnson. But he was still a formidable enemy to the Republicans in Congress, for as Chief Executive, he had the legal power to hinder and stall the Reconstruction. The Republicans decided that they must rid themselves of the President and put a man in the White House who would work with Congress, not against it. Johnson was impeached in March 1868—that is, he was officially accused of wrongdoing and brought to trial before the Senate. He was charged with

In this 1895 cartoon the textile industry turns from old New England to a young upstart: the South. For many years Yankee mills had ruled the industry, running on waterpower from swift rivers that the South could not match. Then the steam engine tipped the balance. Hissing away on cheap coal from the Appalachians, steam could run a factory anywhere. The industry gradually moved south, where labor too was cheap. There paddle-wheeled steamboats bumped wharves piled with cotton (opposite, upper).

War brought freedom to the slaves. But peace brought few of them the "40 acres and a mule" promised by land-reform plans. Like these cotton pickers of about 1870 (left), many former slaves stayed on their old plantations because they could not afford to leave.

Northern know-how helped start up southern industries such as this tobacco factory in Virginia (opposite, lower). But cheap labor kept them going. Before the war a slave could be rented from his owner for up to $140 a year. After the war, factory owners paid a freedman half as much. "They say we will starve through laziness. That is not so," wrote one worker. "But it is true we will starve at our present wages."

Southern cotton pickers, about 1870

Bales of cotton on a southern wharf

Workers at a Richmond tobacco factory, late 1800s

the "high crime" of firing Secretary of War Edwin Stanton, an ally of the Radical Republicans, in defiance of a federal law called the Tenure of Office Act. The charge was a weak one, but the trial was the focus of a bitter political battle between Johnson's supporters and enemies. When the vote to convict Johnson was taken before a packed and tense Senate chamber on May 16, 1868, it fell one short of the two-thirds majority needed for conviction.

The KKK Terrorizes the South

The enemies of the new Reconstruction governments began planning how to overthrow them the moment that they came into being. In late 1865 champions of white man's rule had come together in Pulaski, Tennessee, and organized the Ku Klux Klan (taking its name from a Greek word meaning "circle"). This was the most notorious of several terrorist gangs backed by Confederate veterans. Now the KKK resolved to drive blacks from the voting booths and destroy black support for the new governments through threats, beatings, and murder.

In 1868 violence flamed across the South. Only a minority of whites were responsible, but everywhere blacks had reason to fear for their lives. James H. Alston, a black member of the Alabama legislature, was one of hundreds of black leaders attacked. "I was shot . . . by a band of men who were against my politics," he told a committee of Congress in 1871. "Two hundred and sixty-five shots were counted in the weatherboarding of my house . . . five through the headboard of the bed I was sitting on . . . and two in my body."

So effective was the terrorism that, little by little, the Reconstruction governments began to crumble. Northerners were getting tired of hearing repeated pleas for military protection by southern blacks and their supporters. By 1877 the old white ruling class had regained power in all the southern states. They called themselves "Redeemers" because they claimed to have "redeemed" their states from what they condemned as "Negro rule," although in no state had blacks ever controlled the government.

Besides driving out the Reconstruction governments, the Redeemers loudly accused them of having been enormously corrupt. In fact, these governments of blacks, carpetbaggers, and scalawags had tried hard to restore the South to prosperity by rebuilding roads, establishing school systems, and attracting northern industry. They were no more honest or dishonest than other local and state governments. Nevertheless, the myth of their total corruption worked its way into history books for decades to come.

Not relying solely on violence to maintain power, the white ruling class began to figure out ways to keep blacks from the polls permanently, without openly defying the 15th Amendment. During the 1890s southern states set up conditions that a man must meet before his name could be listed on the voter's register. (No women—black or white—were allowed to vote at this time.) A voter might be required to be able to read a paragraph of the state or federal Constitution and explain what it meant. He might have to own

193

a certain amount of property. He might have to be on record as a taxpayer. Many states had a "grandfather clause," which gave the vote to anyone who had an ancestor who could vote before 1867. Despite this and other efforts to make the voting restrictions apply to blacks only, the restrictions kept tens of thousands of poor and illiterate whites from the polls too.

In one of its last major efforts on behalf of the freedmen, Congress in 1875 passed a Civil Rights Act banning segregation—the practice, that is, of keeping blacks apart simply because of the color of their skin. Some Reconstruction governments had passed similar laws between 1867 and 1870. Black people, these laws said, had the right to ride in the same railroad coaches and streetcars, to sleep in the same inns, and to dine in the same restaurants. But white Southerners usually defied or ignored the laws.

The U. S. Supreme Court declared most of the Civil Rights Act of 1875 unconstitutional in 1883, and no new federal civil rights laws were passed until 1957. During the 1890s all the southern states passed laws, called "Jim Crow" laws, requiring the segregation of black people. Jim Crow, a shuffling clown figure, was an insulting term for a black person coined during slavery days. Jim Crow laws spelled out in detail how blacks must live apart from whites and not mingle with them anywhere. They must not "contaminate" with their presence the inns, churches, waiting rooms, schools, or steamboat cabins that white people used. They must not drink from the same water fountains or read at the same libraries.

By 1900 southern blacks were again a people apart; those on plantations worked from sunup to sundown as they always had. In some ways their situation was better than it had been during slavery: They were free to move about and to own land if they had money to buy it. And they had gained a measure of simple dignity as legally free people. But without the vote and without rights, the black people continued to be exploited and abused.

From an 1896 Supreme Court case known as Plessy versus Ferguson *came the phrase that set the stage for decades of racial segregation: "separate but equal." By the mid-1900s blacks still had to endure drinking fountains, rest rooms, even waiting rooms (below) that were plainly separate but seldom equal. Under "Jim Crow" laws of the late 1800s, a black riding a train might have to sit behind a screen or in a separate car.*

History class at Tuskegee Institute, 1902

In 1881 a freedman named Booker T. Washington founded a school in Alabama to teach unskilled blacks "to do a common thing in an uncommon manner." To Tuskegee Institute came eager students. In exercise classes (opposite, lower) they toned their bodies; in history classes (left) they stretched their minds. In a laboratory (below) a student learns from George Washington Carver, brilliant botanist and pioneer in plant research.

George Washington Carver (right), 1902

195

The minister comes to call (left) on a Virginia family in this 1881 painting. In him they see a pastor tending a church run not by whites but by blacks. And in them he sees a family free from the fear of separation that tore at many a slave family when a parent or child was sold.

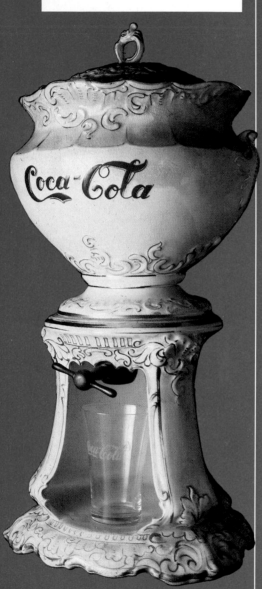

A Coca-Cola urn spouted the syrup created in Atlanta, Georgia, in 1886 to cure "Headache or Tired Feeling." Druggists added fizzy water for a soda-fountain drink.

Children of Confederate leader Jefferson Davis sit for a portrait. One boy holds a hoop and a stick for rolling it, the other a spool, which he probably twirled on a string between the two long poles.

Pull toys like this one (right) rang a bell with youngsters. As it rolls, the black man clangs the bell—perhaps to celebrate the 15th Amendment that gave him his voting rights in 1870.

Black dolls probably made northern white children smile. Who wouldn't smile at a topsy-turvy doll that changes color at a flip?

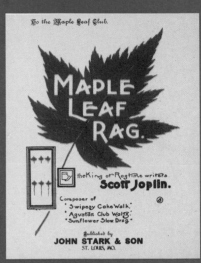

To the music for his ragtime hit (above), black composer Scott Joplin later added lyrics: "I can hypnotize this nation . . . with the Maple Leaf Rag." And he did; ragtime is still popular today.

A poster from 1894 beckons crowds to a minstrel show. "Gentlemen, be seated!" barked a host called Mr. Interlocutor—and then the fun began. Songs and dances kept audiences clapping as "Negroes"—usually white actors with blackened faces—poked fun at everyone.

An advertisement for Ayer's Sarsaparilla, "The Strongest-Best-Cheapest Blood Medicine," promised it would cure a long list of ills. Most patent medicines of the late 1800s cured little except the patient's trust in the salesmen who sold them.

197

CLOSING THE FRONTIER 1865-1900

Spaniards were the first people in America to raise cattle. Columbus brought over a small herd on his second voyage to the New World in 1493, and when Spanish conquerors marched into New Spain (later to be called Mexico) in the early 1500s, they brought cattle and other livestock with them. Some of the cattle escaped and became as wild as bears or wolves. Over the years these *cimarrones* (wild ones) mixed with other domesticated cattle, creating a new breed with long spreading horns and coats of earthy browns and grays and reds. As early as 1690 Mexican *vaqueros* (herders—from the Spanish *vaca*, cow) were raising these long-horned cattle in the thickets and prairies on both sides of the Rio Grande, in what were then the vast Spanish provinces of Coahuila and Texas.

During the 1830s English-speaking colonists migrated to the coastal regions of Texas and began to raise cattle. But they lacked skills to herd the animals and had to learn from the Mexican vaqueros. The vaqueros wielded the lasso to herd, catch, and control range cattle. Basil Hall, an English traveler visiting the Americas in 1821, wrote that Spanish cowhands could twirl a lasso over any part of the animal they wished, "over the horns or the neck, or round the body; or they can include all four legs, or two, or any one of the four." The secret? Years of practice. "I have often seen little boys . . . lassoing cats, and entangling the legs of every dog that was unfortunate enough to pass within reach," Hall wrote.

As the years went by and Texas sought to break away from Mexican rule, many of the English-speaking settlers stole Mexican cattle from the borderland between the Nueces River and the Rio Grande. The newcomers built up their herds by breeding their own eastern cattle with the wild Mexican ones. The result was the Texas longhorn, a tough, rangy animal with long legs and a spread of horns up to eight feet wide. As historian J. Frank Dobie described them, these Texas longhorns "could walk the roughest ground, cross the widest deserts, climb the highest mountains, swim the widest rivers, fight off the fiercest band of wolves, endure hunger, cold, thirst and punishment as few beasts of the earth have ever shown themselves capable of enduring."

The Texans raised their cattle along the many rivers that flowed southward into the Gulf of Mexico. But the cradle of the Texas

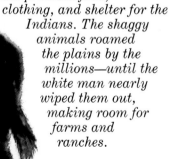

Vaqueros, *America's earliest cowboys, rope a horse on a California ranch during the 1870s. These mounted herdsmen of Spanish and Indian descent took great pride in their riding and roping abilities—skills they later taught to English-speaking settlers of the Southwest.*

Buffalo provided food, clothing, and shelter for the Indians. The shaggy animals roamed the plains by the millions—until the white man nearly wiped them out, making room for farms and ranches.

199

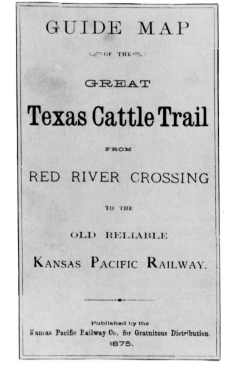

GUIDE MAP

OF THE

GREAT

Texas Cattle Trail

FROM

RED RIVER CROSSING

TO THE

OLD RELIABLE

KANSAS PACIFIC RAILWAY.

Published by the
Kansas Pacific Railway Co. for Gratuitous Distribution.
1875.

cattle kingdom was a vast diamond-shaped area at the southernmost part of the state. A mild climate, plentiful grass, and clumps of timber to give shade made cattle-raising conditions perfect. Far from the Great Plains, the area was also spared most of the Comanche raids that had plagued generations of settlers in New Mexico and upper Texas.

The Texas cattle business began to prosper in the 20 years before the Civil War. Herders drove some 200,000 longhorns over the Shawnee Trail to Missouri. Steamboats carried other longhorns across the Gulf to New Orleans. One herd even arrived in New York City—driven on foot to Illinois and then shipped east by train and ferryboat. But when the war came, these drives ended. Ranchers and their hands went to fight the Yankees and left the cattle to take care of themselves. During the four years of war the longhorns grazed on the prairies and multiplied. When the veterans came back home, they found their stock, much of it unbranded, roaming the plains and thickets. The herds had doubled in size.

There was opportunity in these cattle for their owners. With the war over, immigrants from Europe once more swarmed into the United States, lured by the promise of mill and factory jobs in the booming industrial cities of the North. Many also came to build the railroad lines that were beginning to thrust westward across the continent. These workers needed meat to keep them going; money, clearly enough, was to be made out of the Texas herds if they could be rounded up and shipped north.

But how could the Texans transport large numbers of cattle across the thousand miles that separated them from their markets? By 1866 the Missouri Pacific Railroad had pushed its rails from St. Louis to Sedalia, Missouri. Perhaps the cattle could be driven north to Sedalia, then shipped to St. Louis. At St. Louis the animals could be slaughtered and the meat sent east, again by rail.

A crackle of lightning, a crash of thunder, and the stampede is on. "One jump to their feet and another jump to hell," is how one old trail hand described the sudden panic that could transform a herd of slumbering longhorns into a rampaging horde. Almost anything could trigger a stampede: A flash of lightning— as in this painting by Frederic Remington—the snap of a twig, even the flare of a match or the click of a gate latch.

Here, trail riders lunge after a fleeing herd to head off the leaders and start them running in a broad circle. And woe to the cowboy whose horse stumbled. Sometimes the herd would part, leaving the man unharmed. But one cowboy on the trail in Nebraska was not so lucky. All that could be found of him after a stampede pounded past was the butt of his revolver.

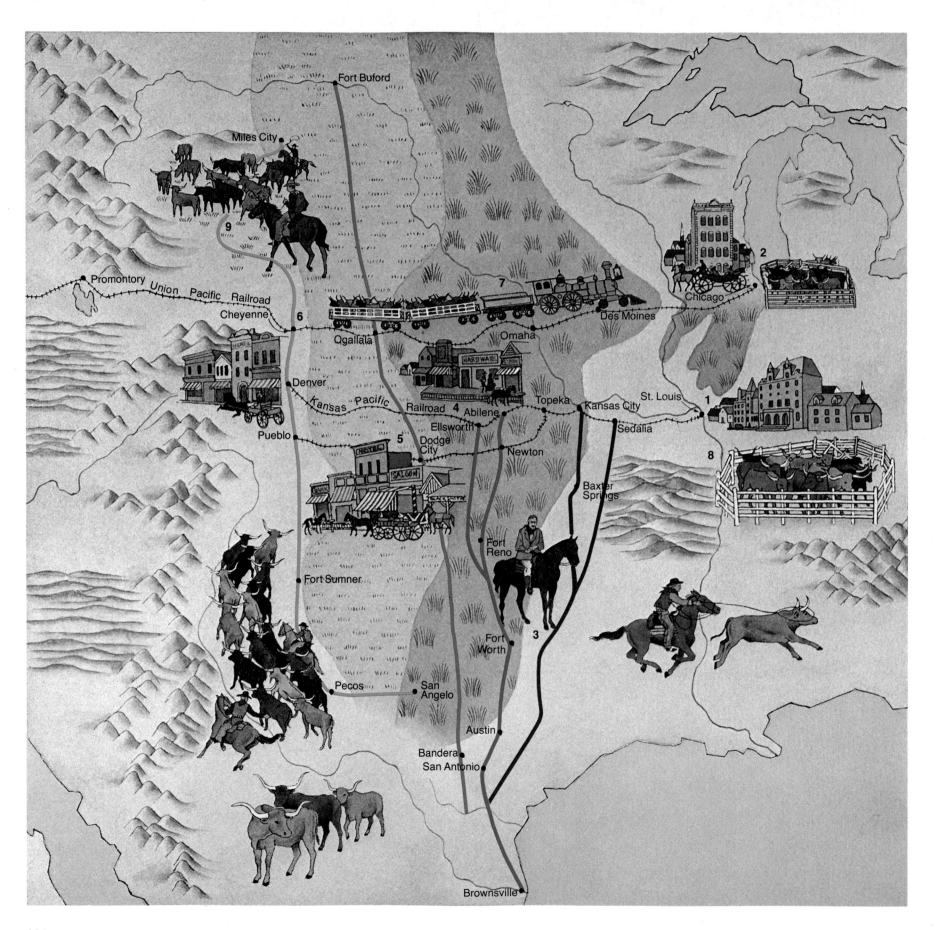

Fort Buford

Miles City

9

Promontory

Union Pacific Railroad

Cheyenne

6

Ogallala

Omaha

7

Des Moines

Chicago

2

Denver

Kansas Pacific Railroad

4

Abilene

Topeka

Kansas City

St. Louis

1

Pueblo

Ellsworth

Dodge City

Newton

Sedalia

5

Baxter Springs

8

Fort Sumner

Fort Reno

Fort Worth

3

Pecos

San Angelo

Austin

Bandera

San Antonio

Brownsville

Cow Towns and Cattle Trails

➡ Goodnight-Loving Trail
➡ Western Trail
➡ Chisholm Trail
➡ Shawnee Trail
➡ Sedalia Trail

The cattle empire of the Old West spanned a quarter of the continent—from the dry, short-grass plains along the eastern edge of the Rockies to the taller prairie grasses of the central lowlands.

Before the Civil War Texas cattlemen drove their herds to northern markets along the Shawnee Trail toward Sedalia, Missouri. After the war Missouri farmers objected to the tick-infested herds trampling their fields. Railroad lines also began to extend across the plains from St. Louis (1) and Chicago (2). So the Texans gave up their old route and tried a new one farther west—the Chisholm Trail, named after Jesse Chisholm (3), a trader who had driven his wagons over an ancient buffalo trail.

As the railroads reached westward, towns sprang up along the tracks. Some, such as Abilene (4), Dodge City (5), and Cheyenne (6), prospered as cow towns, where cattle were sold and held until they could be shipped out by train (7). Stockyards (8) near the slaughterhouses of Kansas City and Chicago held the cattle until they could be butchered; other herds fattened on the northern ranges of Montana (9).

But the system couldn't last. Overstocking, falling prices, barbed-wire fences, and the disastrous winters of 1886 and 1887, in which tens of thousands of cattle starved or froze to death, doomed the great cattle empires—and ended the era of the open-range cowboy.

Milling and mooing in a Montana stockyard, a herd of cattle waits to board an eastbound train in the early 1900s. Getting the cows into the cars—16 or 18 to a car—was no easy job. The cattle had to be prodded up ramps with poles, a chore that earned cowboys a lasting nickname—"cowpokes."

In the year 1866 some 200,000 longhorns started north across Indian territory toward Missouri. But the herders ran into trouble. First, the Indians demanded payment for the grass the longhorns ate along the way. Then angry Missouri farmers, rifles in hand, blocked the path and insisted that the cattle turn back because they were infested with disease-carrying ticks. If this wasn't trouble enough, the herders also had to defend the herds from rustlers. As a result, few longhorns made it to Sedalia that year, and the northern market seemed farther away than ever.

The following year a young stock dealer from Illinois named Joseph G. McCoy solved the problem of angry farmers. By then the railroad stretched from Missouri to the open prairies of central Kansas. Why not establish a market center far to the west of the Missouri farmlands? Then the Texans could drive their cattle over the grassland trails without interference from Missouri farmers. Buyers at the railhead could ship the steers in cattle cars to Chicago and the East.

Choosing Abilene, Kansas, as a gathering place for the Texas cattle, McCoy set to work building an elaborate complex of pens

The Cowboy: Suiting the Man to the Task

Every bit of a cowboy's equipment reflected his active life under open skies. His small, tough, surefooted horse, a descendant of Spanish stock, could carry him 30 to 40 miles a day. The wide-brimmed hat protected him against the sun—and doubled as a pillow or water bucket. The red bandana, worn as a mask, kept him from choking when riding dusty trails. Heavy leather chaps protected his legs in brushy country; gloves and cuffs helped prevent rope burns when working with the lasso. The vest provided handy pockets; the slicker, carried behind the saddle, kept him dry in the rain—and was useful at night as a ground cloth. High-heeled boots held the stirrups. The six-shooter could be used to signal—or to blast rattlesnakes and rustlers.

Foiled getaway: Dropping a loop over the horns of a fleeing steer, a cowboy catches its hind legs with the slackened rope. He then veers his horse and cinches the rope tight, violently and abruptly ending the steer's attempt to escape. Such ropework, learned originally from Spanish and Mexican cowherders—*vaqueros*—enabled a few skilled hands to control large herds of cattle. The rope itself, called a lariat, from *la reata*, was made of twisted grass or braided rawhide. When thrown, it kept a flat, open loop. Many other Spanish terms found their way into cowboy lingo: *Chaparreras* became the "chaps" a cowboy wore, *estampida* became "stampede," and the vaquero himself became the "buckaroo."

Brand marks—burned on with a hot iron—told at a glance who owned which cattle, especially important information in the days when a cow or steer could wander freely over the unfenced range. Each rancher had his own mark registered in a "brand book." This steer shows some of the places a brand might be placed—on hip or side or jaw. Typical marks (above) included the "lazy B," "flying A," "rocking R," and "crazy S."

where the ranchers might keep their cattle until they were sold and shipped out. He then sent word to Texas that if the cattlemen drove their herds to Abilene, they would find fine corrals and eager buyers for them.

The Texans responded eagerly to the good news. That year 35,000 longhorns arrived in Abilene; they were sold and shipped to the slaughterhouses of Chicago. The trail from Texas which the cattle now began to tread lay far to the west of the old trail to Sedalia. The new route had been used by the buffalo and their Indian hunters for countless years. Texans named it the Chisholm Trail, after Jesse Chisholm, a trader who had driven his wagons over part of it near the end of the Civil War. The trail led from the Rio Grande, north across Texas and the Indian territory, until it hit the railheads in Kansas.

Abilene became the first of the new cattle towns, and the Chisholm Trail the first of the postwar prairie trails. For nearly 25 years millions of longhorns threaded their way along these trails to Kansas in one of the greatest animal movements on record. Some of the cowboys who worked for Texas ranchers were Mexican. Their feelings about the long cattle drives found expression in a famous trail song:

> *Cuando salimos pa' Kiansis con una grande partida*
> *¡Ah, que camino tan largo! no contaba con mi vida.*

(When we left for Kansas with a great herd,
Ah, what a long a trail it was! I never thought I'd make it.)

One after the other prairie cow towns began to spring up along Kansas railroad lines—Ellsworth, Dodge City, Salina, Wichita. Villages with a few huts became bustling cow towns where stockyards spread, where cattle bawled, where cowboys milled in the streets.

Chowtime at the chuck wagons (above) gives the cowhands a welcome break during a roundup in the Dakota Territory.
Stagecoaches (below) carried passengers, mail, and freight until the railroads arrived.

Wells, Fargo & Co. opens for business in Guthrie, Oklahoma. The freight and parcel shipping company carried everything from sacks of mail to miners' gold.

*Town! A
cowboy's
dream after months
on the trail called for a bath,
shave, haircut, new clothes—and
a real celebration, often with
guns blazing and rebel war yells.
Dancing, drinking, gambling
(sometimes with marked cards—
notice the notched upper borders
of these cards) usually lasted
until the carousing cowpoke was
dead broke again and ready to hit
the trail for home.*

What was a cowboy's life really like? No one has left a more vivid record than Andy Adams, whose book *The Log of a Cowboy* was published in 1903. Born in Indiana, Andy moved to Texas with his family as a youngster and at the age of 22 joined a cattle drive that took him from the Rio Grande to Montana—a distance of 1,700 miles.

Andy's outfit, the Circle Dot, hit the trail in April 1882, strung out like a winding snake for about a mile. Cowboys rode the lead, both flanks, and the rear. Everybody moved along at an easy pace. The trail boss told Andy and the other men, "the secret of trailing cattle is never to let your herd know that they are under restraint." The cattle moved at their own pace, grazing as they went. Andy and the other cowboys made sure that none strayed and that not too many other range cattle slipped into the column.

A drive of this sort usually numbered between one and three thousand head of cattle. Any more and the herd might become too strung out to control easily—and downright dangerous in a stampede. A trail boss oversaw a crew of ten to twenty men, which included a cook and a horse wrangler. The cook took charge of the chuck wagon and supplies, and the wrangler took care of the horses—seven or eight for each man. Cowboys always needed lots of horses, fresh ones to ride and spares in case of loss, theft, or accident. On the plains, nobody was more useless to himself or to his companions than a cowboy without a horse.

211

A bone depot in Saskatchewan, Canada, 1884

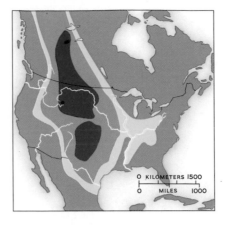

**The Shrinking Range of the
North American Buffalo**

- 1600
- 1800
- 1870
- 1890

Shortly before dawn each day the men broke camp, roused the cattle, and got them moving. A cowboy sat in his saddle all day—whether under a broiling sun or in driving wind or drenching rain. When evening came, the cattle bedded down at a site chosen in advance. The men ate their supper, sat around the fire, and unrolled their blankets. Even then a cowboy's tasks were not done. At night he also had to guard against hostile Indians, rustlers, and horse thieves. Through the hours of dark each man served a two-hour watch, with at least one other companion. A storm or a stampede kept everybody up all night. The cowboys told Andy that he was expected to get his sleep during the winter. This was supposed to be a joke, but it was also true.

During night duty the guards rode in opposite directions in a huge circle round the sleeping herd. "The guards," wrote Andy, "usually sing or whistle continuously, so that the sleeping herd may know that a friend and not an enemy is keeping vigil over their dreams." The songs which most soothed the cattle were lullabies, ballads, and hymns. Some of the most beautiful songs in the English language were sung to sleeping cattle, ballads such as "The Night Herding Song," "The Cowboy's Lament," and, one of the most widely sung of all, "The Colorado Trail":

> *Eyes like the morning star, cheeks like a rose,*
> *Laura was a pretty girl, God almighty knows.*
> *Weep all you little rains, wail, winds, wail,*
> *All along, along, along the Colorado Trail.*

Life on the trail was mostly dull, dirty, and exhausting. It was also dangerous. Lightning killed many men. Swift-flowing rivers had to be forded, and they often swept away cattle, horses, and men. Once while crossing a river with the Circle Dot herd, Andy heard a cry above the shouting voices and rushing waters. "It

Passengers and train crew blaze away at a buffalo herd along the Kansas Pacific line during the 1870s. Such hunting excursions drew hundreds of "sportsmen" from the East and from as far away as Europe. A three-day trip through Kansas cost $10 and promised "buffaloes . . . so numerous . . . that they are shot from cars every day."

But the real slaughter began a few years later with the discovery that buffalo hides could be converted into shoes and drive belts for machinery. Soon, professional hunters and hide skinners swarmed across the plains. One hunter boasted of shooting 263 buffalo a day— at a rate of three a minute. By 1883 the great herds that had once roamed as far as New York and Pennsylvania had all but vanished. Their skeletons, gathered into heaps by bone hunters, were shipped east to be ground into fertilizer.

dawned on my mind," he wrote, "that someone had lost his seat, and that terrified cry was for help." Sure enough, one of the trail riders was missing, sucked down to death in the swirling waters.

A stampede was worst of all. Longhorn cattle were extremely nervous. The least thing—a stranger's voice, a sudden shout, a flicker of lightning—could throw them into a panic. The cattle might be lying quietly on the ground when suddenly some instinct would bring them all to their feet. Off they would go, rushing headlong into the darkness, in a frantic, plunging mass with bluish sparks dancing from the tips of their horns—a display of static electricity caused by the friction of hundreds of hairy bodies jammed together.

When cattle stampeded, there was little the cowboys could do except to ride with the herd. Their one hope was to turn the cattle and let them run in a wide circle until they tired. A rampaging herd generated heat so fierce it almost blistered the faces of men riding nearby. Sometimes the cattle scattered over a huge area, and it took several days to round them up again. Some animals were injured so badly they had to be killed; others were crushed by

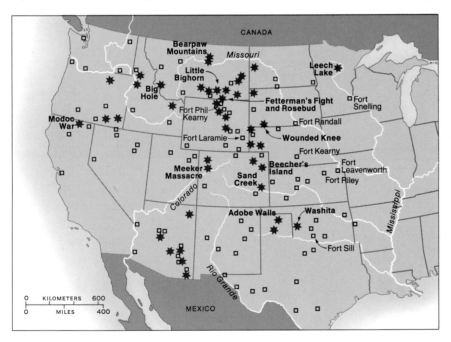

Army vs. Indians 1864-1898
- Army forts
- ✳ Battles and skirmishes

Barely visible through the smoke and dust of battle, Gen. George Custer and his troops make their last stand on a rise near the Little Bighorn River in Montana. The 1876 engagement—one of the few won decisively by the Indians—pitted 3,000 Sioux and Cheyenne warriors against the

215 men of Custer's command. The battle lasted less than an hour. When it was over, Custer and his men lay dead. "The blood of the people was hot," an Indian brave later recalled, "and they took no prisoners that day."

Though the Indians won the battle, they lost the war. Custer's fate so enraged the nation that the full force of the U. S. Army was brought to bear against the Indians in a series of bloody engagements (map).

214

The Nez Perce: A Valiant Last Stand

Chief Joseph had not wanted to fight at all. For years his tribe, the Nez Perce Indians of the Pacific Northwest, coexisted peacefully with white settlers who came to carve out farms and ranches among the beautiful mountains and valleys of the Nez Perce homelands. Land had been given to some of the early settlers. Many tribesmen—including Joseph's father—embraced Christianity and even adopted a life of farming and raising fine horses and cattle.

Meriwether Lewis of the Lewis and Clark expedition encountered tribe members in 1805 and described them as "among the most amiable men we have seen."

So it went for many years, until it became a tribal boast that no white man had ever been killed by a Nez Perce.

But trouble brewed as more and more settlers arrived—especially after 1860, when prospectors found gold on Nez Perce lands.

And now, in 1877, the year after Custer's defeat, the U. S. government gave Joseph's branch of the tribe 30 days to move from their ancestral lands in Oregon's Wallowa Valley to a reservation at Lapwai, Idaho, or face war.

Chief Joseph counseled peace, as he always had during these difficult years. But during the move to Idaho rebellious warriors went on a rampage that left several miners and settlers dead.

Expecting retaliation and realizing the hopelessness of his situation, Chief Joseph gathered his group and began one of the most remarkable feats in U. S. military history—a 15-week fighting retreat through some of the wildest mountains of the West.

About 200 warriors commanded by White Bird, Looking Glass, and other war chiefs fought more than a dozen engagements and dodged or outfought four Army columns (map). They did this while

Route of the Nez Perce Indians

Chief Joseph in 1900, age 60

Chief Joseph's surrender, Snake Creek, Montana, October 5, 1877

Chief Joseph's encampment on the Colville Reservation, Nespelem, Washington

shepherding some 500 women and children across towering passes and raging rivers.

While cutting through Yellowstone National Park (established only five years earlier), the Indians came upon sightseeing parties. A few of the visitors were killed or wounded in these encounters but most escaped—or were released unharmed.

Despite overwhelming odds, Chief Joseph's little band fought gallantly and bravely: no wanton killing, no scalping, no butchering fallen foes. When supplies ran short in Montana, the Nez Perce didn't raid or steal; instead they paid for what they needed with gold dust and horses.

But the 1,500-mile trek had taken a fearsome toll, and now the winds of autumn blew cold. The old and the wounded could not go on. After a bitter, five-day siege just 40 miles short of the Canadian border—and safety— Chief Joseph surrendered his tattered and weary band: "My heart is sick and sad," he said. "From where the sun now stands, I will fight no more forever."

Sitting Bull at Fort Randall, Dakota Territory, 1882

Arapaho Indian Ghost Dance in Oklahoma Territory, 1893

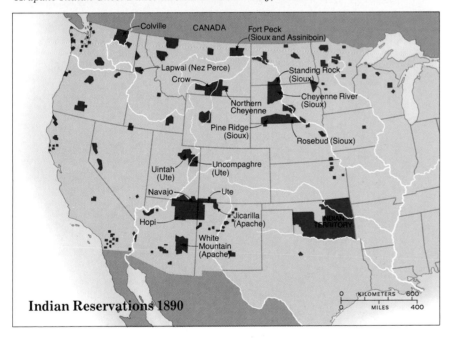

Indian Reservations 1890

Tatanka Iyotake—Sitting Bull —a powerful Sioux leader and medicine man, sits glumly with his family and white visitors after his return from Canadian exile in 1881. To escape the roundup that followed Custer's defeat at Little Bighorn, Sitting Bull led 2,000 of his people into Canada. But hunger and homesickness eventually brought them home—and onto reservations set aside for them in Dakota Territory.

Demoralized by the growing power of the U. S. Army after 1876, most Plains Indians surrendered and moved onto reservations (map).

At Ghost Dances, such as the one shown above, they turned from guns to the ancient gods to bring back long-dead warriors and old times.

pounding hooves; still others plunged over cliffs or river bluffs. Once in a while a cowboy might be thrown from his horse—and found with a broken neck or lying crushed at the foot of a precipice.

After months on the trail, cattle and cowboys reached their destination. The boss paid the men and sold off the horses. In the railhead towns millions of cattle were sold, packed into cattle cars, and shipped to Chicago. But money was made in these towns from cowboys as well as from cattle. After months in the saddle the cowboys had money to jingle in their pockets; they craved amusement, whiskey, and women. Lots of people were ready to help a cowboy spend his cash—storekeepers, saloon keepers, gamblers, swindlers, and prostitutes. Men died in the gunfights and duels that took place in the brawling cow towns. Such incidents later made thrilling novels, movies, and television shows, but were only a small part of the dangers cowboys faced. The perils of the trail were infinitely greater—as could be seen from the nameless graves scattered along the Chisholm Trail.

During the 1870s the entire Great Plains area became a grazing ground for the Texas longhorns, a turn of events made possible by the relentless destruction of the buffalo. Until then buffaloes beyond counting roamed the plains—perhaps 60 million or more. To the Indians who lived on the plains, the buffalo was the source of life, a sacred animal. Traditionally, when Indians killed a buffalo, they wasted nothing. Buffalo skins made robes, tents, lariats, saddles, boats. The horns were shaped into ladles and spoons. Buffalo bones became war clubs. Sinews and tendons made string for Indian bows. Even the tail was used—to swat flies and mosquitoes. Indian hunters took only what they needed. Even though they killed many buffalo, the herds did not grow smaller.

The Great Buffalo Slaughter

In the early 1870s Americans began to slaughter the buffalo herds in appalling numbers. Railroad crews building new lines across the plains needed meat; so did the soldiers who manned the forts that now began to dot the plains. Buffalo hunting became a fashionable sport among the wealthy. Luxurious railroad coaches hauled European aristocrats and their servants out onto the plains. All day they enjoyed the shoot; at dusk they retired to the coaches for an evening of wining, dining, and cardplaying. Professional buffalo hunters took advantage of a rising demand for buffalo hides back East. The strong, elastic hides made, among other things, admirable belts to drive the machines used in factories. During these years hundreds of hunters moved out onto the prairies for the kill. Most took only the hides and left the flesh to rot. By Indian standards the slaughter of the buffalo was pure waste. The white men "did not kill them in order to eat," wrote Black Elk, a leader of the Oglala Sioux, "they took only the hides to sell. Sometimes they did not even take the hides, only the tongues." Chief Seattle was even more eloquent in his lament: "What is man without the beasts?" asked the leader of Washington Territory's Dwamish

Huddled against murderous cold and driving snow, range hands keep their charges drifting with the wind to avoid freezing. Such heroism was mostly in vain. The great blizzards of 1886 and 1887 virtually destroyed the once proud cattle empires of the West.

The sheet music (below) recalls a plucky teacher who roped her pupils together and guided them to safety after a similar blizzard blew the roof off their schoolhouse in 1888.

tribe. "If all the beasts were gone, men would die from great loneliness of spirit, for whatever happens to the beasts also happens to man. All things are connected. Whatever befalls the earth befalls the sons of the earth."

Why didn't the federal government stop the slaughter? Because the United States was then at war against the Plains Indians. The Army had a single objective in these campaigns: to end the Indians' resistance to the advance of white settlers in the West by forcing them onto reservations. Destruction of the buffalo herds fitted in well with these plans. As Gen. Philip Sheridan told the Texas legislature, buffalo hunters deserved the nation's thanks. "It is a well-known fact," said the general, "that an army losing its base of supplies is placed at a great disadvantage . . . for the sake of a lasting peace, let them [the hunters] kill, skin and sell until the buffaloes are exterminated. Then your prairies can be covered with speckled cattle and the festive cowboy."

Angry warriors fought back, raiding farms and settlements and attacking wagon trains. But they fought a losing war. The U. S. brought against them hundreds of soldiers, armed with guns, ammunition, and plentiful supplies. Faced with such overwhelming power, many tribes accepted defeat. They gave up their freedom and became prisoners on the reservations set aside for them by the government. Some Indians refused to go onto the reservations, and some fled from them. The Army looked upon these Indians as outlaws to be hunted down.

The Tribes Strike Back

Sioux warriors under Crazy Horse and Sitting Bull defeated Gen. George Custer on the Little Bighorn River in 1876. But 14 years later the Seventh U. S. Cavalry took a terrible revenge when they massacred 300 Sioux at the Wounded Knee campsite on the Pine Ridge Reservation in South Dakota. Black Elk saw it with his own eyes. "Dead and wounded women," he said, "and children and little babies were scattered all along there where they had been trying to run away. The soldiers had followed along the gulch, as they ran, and murdered them in there."

Even more extraordinary was the struggle of Chief Joseph and the Nez Perce, whose tragic and remarkable flight to freedom fell just 40 miles short of success.

From the Canadian border to the Rio Grande the great buffalo herds were gone by 1884, and the power of the Plains Indians was broken. Longhorns grazed freely on the open range not only in Texas and Kansas but in Nebraska, Wyoming, Colorado, the Dakotas, and Montana as well. The cattle flooded like water onto the northern plains, and the cowboys came with them. The early 1880s were boom times for the cattle business. Investors began to dream of easy riches. As one of them exulted, "The profits of stock-raising have been large. For this reason, men have endured hardships and dangers, dwelling apart from friends and civilized society. The prospect of speedy fortunes reconciled them to privations for the time being." Dozens of cattle companies were formed by businessmen and bankers who rarely went West themselves but who hired managers to run their ranches for them.

By 1885 the market was glutted with cattle; the big companies were in trouble with their heavy investments and falling prices. Thousands of homesteaders were settling the open plains, fencing off the rangelands with a new invention—barbed wire. The final knockout came in the two winter months of January 1886 and January 1887. Terrible blizzards howled across the Great Plains and brought death to millions of longhorns. "The cattle," one rancher wrote, "turn their heads from the blast, and huddle close like a flock of sheep. . . . drifting with the cruel storm. . . . guided only by the

course of the freezing gale." Some cattle found shelter in ravines where they slowly starved to death. Others stumbled on until they fell, froze, and died. Some cowboys followed the herds and died with them. "They are lost," wrote one, "all lost together, out here upon the pitiless plains." In the spring the snows melted. Rivers flooding across the prairies bore countless carcasses, tumbling slowly as they floated.

The disastrous winters spelled the end of the open-range cattle business. Ranchers began to fence in with barbed wire and supply feed and shelter to the cattle in winter. The romance of the trail came to an end. Ranch hands raised and harvested hay in the summer, fed hay to their beasts in the winter, built cattle sheds, strung fences, and repaired buildings and machines.

What happened to the trail riders after 1890? Some, broken in mind and body by the blizzards, never worked again. Others quit the cattle business and went on to other jobs. Few among them had grown rich. The sum total of one typical old trail hand's possessions after some 20 years as a cowboy were "the high-heeled boots, the striped pants and about $4.80 of other clothes. . . ."

Barbed wire, invented by an Illinois farmer in 1874, was both blessed and cursed by cowboys. It kept cattle from straying vast distances and enabled choice herds to be kept apart for selective breeding. But it also brought homesteaders swarming onto the plains—and allowed them to fence off pastures and water holes the cattlemen regarded as rightfully theirs. Such conflict led to years of bitterness and bloodshed across the plains.

Nebraska pioneer Sylvester Rawding and his family pose for an itinerant photographer in front of their sod home in 1886. The house, partly dug into the hillside, was made of the only building materials readily available to settlers—sod strips chopped into three-foot lengths and laid row upon row like bricks. Wooden doors, glass windows, and livestock in the yard testify to the family's prosperity. Though cool in

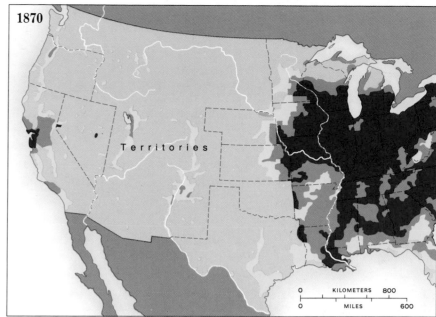

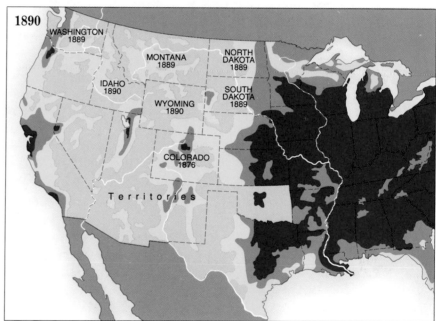

summer and warm in winter, such houses were muddy and uncomfortable when it rained—and often infested with insects, rodents, snakes, and other vermin. As one song put it:
  "My house is constructed of natural soil;
  The walls are erected according to Hoyle;
  The roof has no pitch but is level and plain
  And I never get wet till it happens to rain."

Vanishing Frontier 1870-1890
Settlers per square mile

	Fewer than 2
	2-6
	6-18
	More than 18

These maps show an explosion of people that in two decades brought millions of settlers fanning out across the West and saw the addition of seven new states for a total of 44. The

Homestead Act, signed into law by President Lincoln in 1862, and the removal of the Indians after the Civil War, set the stage for settling the western plains. But technology really made it work: Railroads opened distant markets to farmers; barbed wire provided cheap, effective fences; windmills pumped water from deep below ground; and improved farm machinery made cultivating the dry plains possible—even profitable.

Hearty midday meal
of fresh bread and homegrown
corn and beef keeps body and soul
together at the Parmenter ranch
near Denver, Colorado, in 1889.

Pull the trigger
and kick the Chinaman—whose
mouth snaps shut on a cap.
Anti-Chinese feelings ran high
in the late 1800s, when this toy
pistol found favor.

Girl and pickle
boost Heinz baked beans in the
1880s. Canning became an
important way to preserve food
before widespread refrigeration.

A stereoscope amused
viewers in the 1860s with three-
dimensional effects. One saloon
keeper paid a $25 fine for showing
"obscene and lascivious pictures."

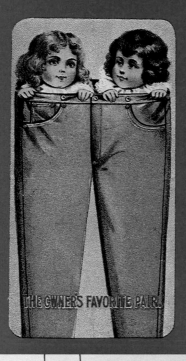

Advertising postcard
for the copper-riveted jeans made by Levi Strauss & Co. The company, founded in San Francisco in 1853, at first sold its pants to gold miners.

A gasoline-powered motor
helps to banish washday blues on the prairie. This lady of leisure reads the *Breeders' Gazette* on an Indiana farm in 1914.

A metal "match safe"
of the early 1900s kept old-fashioned friction matches from catching fire in a pocket.

To open a can
with this 1896 device, simply punch through the lid and turn. If the can slips—aargh!

The "choker trap"
of the 1890s strangled any unwary mouse that poked its head into a side hole.

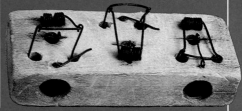

Mail order catalogs
such as this enabled farm families to order anything from sunbonnets to saddles.

The sodbusting steel plow
invented by John Deere came into use on the prairies in the 1850s. Its rolling cutter sliced thickly tangled roots.

THE AMERICAN COLOSSUS

INDUSTRY AND EMPIRE 1865-1914

"**G**o West, young man, and grow up with the country," New York journalist Horace Greeley advised in 1850. All across the East, men and women began to take his advice, for beyond the Mississippi a vast undeveloped region stretched from the Canadian border to the Rio Grande, from the Great Plains to the Pacific Ocean. Here was land to settle and to farm. Here also were immense resources for industry—coal, timber, and iron. But an efficient means of transportation was needed. The answer lay in building railroads in the West to join existing lines back East.

On July 1, 1862, President Lincoln signed the Pacific Railroad Act, which authorized two companies to build the nation's first transcontinental railroad. The Central Pacific Railroad Company started work in California and moved east across the rugged mountains of the Sierra Nevada. The Union Pacific Railroad Company began work in Nebraska, moving west across the gently sloping Great Plains to the Rocky Mountains.

The two companies raced to see which could lay more track. There was good reason for their haste. The federal government was lending them money by the mile, and the company that laid more track would get more money. Equally important, the government gave each company ten square miles of land for every mile of track laid. This meant that the railroad builders could make a fortune selling this land to new settlers.

The Union Pacific brought in more than 10,000 men to lay its line. Most were Irish immigrants, some of them Union and Confederate Civil War veterans. In California the Central Pacific recruited more than 10,000 Chinese immigrants to build its part of the line. Some of these men had come to California because of the discovery of gold there in 1848, but many had come to find jobs, planning to return home in a year or two with the wages they earned.

Armed with picks, shovels, and sledgehammers, the railroad workers cleared and leveled land for the track. Then, working as quickly as they could, they positioned pieces of lumber called crossties, laid the rails on top, and spiked the rails into place. "Two men seize the end of a rail and start forward, the rest of the gang taking hold by twos . . . ," one witness wrote. "They come forward at a run. At the word of command the rail is dropped in its place. . . . Less than thirty seconds to a rail for each gang, and so four rails go down to the minute. . . . Close behind the first gang come the gaugers, spikers and bolters, and a lively time they make of it."

The Central Pacific could not move nearly as fast as its rival. Crossing the craggy Sierra meant snaking the rails up and down steep hills and bridging treacherous river gorges. Sometimes it was impossible to go over or around the mountains; instead the workers had to bore tunnels through them.

Ceremony at Promontory, Utah (above), in 1869 marks the finish of the first rail line to span America. Head-to-head engines represent the two companies that raced from opposite directions to lay the track. Chinese (left) and Irish immigrants provided much of the muscle that built the early railroads.

227

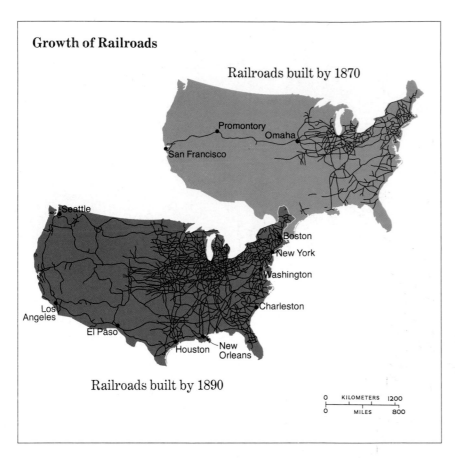

Growth of Railroads

Railroads built by 1870

Promontory
Omaha
San Francisco

Railroads built by 1890

Seattle
Boston
New York
Washington
Los Angeles
Charleston
El Paso
Houston
New Orleans

KILOMETERS 1200
MILES 800

Between 1870 and 1890 the miles of railroad line in the United States (above) increased threefold. More than 160,000 miles of rail linked America's cities by 1890. Factories needed the lines to ship their goods to buyers; farmers needed them to send crops and livestock to market. The federal government encouraged the building of new lines by granting to the railroad companies ten square miles of land—and later twenty square miles—for each mile of track laid by the company.

Two wheels keep a boxcar from toppling onto other wreckage of a Union Pacific train (above, right). Brittle iron rails or a rotted bridge frame may have caused this disaster in the early 1900s. Trains also faced danger from exploding boilers and overturned heating stoves. Engineers crossing the prairie sometimes had to cope with hostile Indians and with herds of buffalo crossing the tracks.

But rail journeys could be pleasant as well as hazardous. The pampered passengers shown opposite enjoy a meal in an elegant dining car.

The men who built the transcontinental railroad suffered great hardships. In the summer some dropped dead from heat exhaustion; in winter men froze or were buried by avalanches. Hundreds were killed by explosives and landslides and in falls off bridges; many others died fighting the Indians whose hunting grounds lay in the path of the "iron horse."

On May 10, 1869, the exciting news was telegraphed to the East and West from a place in Utah called Promontory, where the two lines met: The first transcontinental railroad line was complete. The Union Pacific had laid 1,085 miles of track, while the Central Pacific had put down 690 miles.

For the first time, large numbers of people and huge amounts of freight could be hauled rapidly and cheaply across nearly 2,000 miles of western mountains, plains, and deserts. Trips that once took months in covered wagons could now be completed in a week. The rails that took settlers westward also brought wheat and livestock from the West to feed the growing number of workers in eastern factories.

The first transcontinental line and the four that soon followed helped to transform America from a country of farmers into an industrial giant—a colossus with muscles of iron and steel. Because so much iron and steel was needed to build the railroads, the United States—which had made little steel before the Civil War—quickly became the world's leading producer. By 1900 more than 11 million tons a year were coming out of America's mighty mills.

Spouting flames and smoke, Bessemer converters, like the one at right, turned iron into steel, a stronger form of that metal. Invented in 1855 by Englishman Henry Bessemer, the converter blasted air through molten iron to remove impurities. This and other inventions and improvements made steel production quick and cheap. Steel soon began to be used instead of iron to build railroads, buildings, and machinery.

Fortunes soared with the oil tapped at Beaumont, Texas, in 1901 (above). A Texas oil boom began early that year when a well gushed at nearby Spindletop. The state's vast supply surprised oil drillers, who quickly dug more and more wells for the "black gold." Some lucky Texans who owned oil-rich land became millionaires almost overnight.

Smart tycoon or shifty tyrant? A cartoon from 1900 (right) takes a harsh view of oil magnate John D. Rockefeller, shown with the White House in his hand. Behind him, government buildings appear as a part of Rockefeller's huge Standard Oil Company. The cartoonist was saying that Rockefeller controlled the oil market by controlling Washington lawmakers and the President.

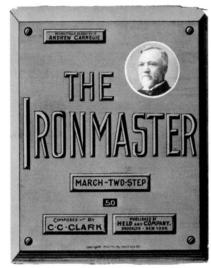

Music dedicated to steel millionaire Andrew Carnegie (above) was an expression of gratitude for his generosity. Early in his career, Carnegie felt that he should "cast aside business forever, except for others." He finally did so in 1901, at the age of 66. For the next 18 years, Carnegie shared his wealth with others by building libraries, art galleries, parks, and university facilities.

Attracted by the promise of land, millions of settlers journeyed west on the new railroads. These pioneers needed guns, axes, barbed wire to fence their land, windmills to draw water from their wells, and steam-powered tractors for farming. To produce these things, eastern businessmen built bigger factories, bought more machinery, and hired more workers. People in the East began to leave their farms and small towns for factory jobs in the cities.

All this meant that just 100 years after the Declaration of Independence, America was changing with breathless speed. At the same time, inventors were devising wonderful new machines— typewriters, telephones, high-speed printing presses, and harvesters—that made life easier and work more efficient and also created whole new industries.

In 1876 the nation celebrated its 100th birthday. Ten million people went to the huge Centennial Exposition in Philadelphia to see exhibits of art, agriculture, and—most of all—industry. Among the marvels displayed were the newly invented telephone, the luxurious Pullman Palace Car, the world's biggest steam engine, and a cylindrical press that printed 25,000 sheets of paper in one hour.

As America's economy boomed in the years after the Civil War, many a hardworking man dreamed of making a fortune. A 13-year-old Scottish immigrant named Andrew Carnegie began work in a textile factory, earning $1.20 a week. Andrew educated himself and was able to get better and better jobs, ending up in the iron industry. By the time he was 33, he was earning $50,000 a year. Before he was 50, he owned a steel mill and had become a millionaire.

During this period America produced many other self-made millionaires (people who grew rich by their own efforts instead of inheriting wealth). John D. Rockefeller made millions from refining crude oil. Philip Armour and Gustavus Swift, who began as small-town butchers, grew rich by using mass-production methods and refrigeration in their Chicago slaughterhouses.

231

Thomas A. Edison
1847-1931

Young Tom Edison played with fire and burned the family barn to the ground. He played with chemicals and set fire to a railroad car. Growing up, he lost job after job because he seemed lazy or absentminded, and he lost friend after friend because he annoyed them with practical jokes or borrowed money he did not pay back. To one friend Tom complained of bad luck. But, he wrote, "I'll never give up. . . ."

Eventually, Tom would have his name on 1,093 patents and become a wealthy man. It was not luck. The patents flowed from his faith in himself and from a restless mind that could keep him busy in his workshop for 22 hours a day. "My business," he said, "is thinking," and his thoughts became the electric light, the phonograph, the movies—the sights and sounds of the modern world.

When he was about 12 years old, Tom began to lose his hearing. Eventually he became almost completely deaf. But he said that he didn't mind, because his deafness enabled him to concentrate harder.

Tom never spent much time with his wife and children. Inventing always came first. One day, at work on a new phonograph, Tom wanted to record a baby's cries. He had his infant daughter brought to his laboratory, and when she did not cry on cue, he pinched her.

During World War I, he offered the Navy more than 40 ideas. They were all rejected, he said, because the Navy lacked "creative minds." When he died in 1931 at the age of 84, two of those ideas—sonar and the helicopter—still were ahead on the path that Edison had blazed with light and wired for sound.

THOMAS B. ALLEN

Thomas Edison in his laboratory, 1893

These new millionaires were hard-driving, sometimes unscrupulous, men. Most of them lived in a style unlike anything that had ever before existed in America. They built grand town houses and filled them with fine furniture and priceless paintings. They imported Italian gardeners to lay out exotic gardens. They hired armies of servants. To escape the summer heat, they built "cottages" in the cool mountains or at the seashore. Cornelius Vanderbilt II's summer home at Newport, Rhode Island, had 70 rooms.

Some millionaires were troubled by the fact that they enjoyed so much when many people had so little. Andrew Carnegie, for one, thought that rich men should spend some of their money to benefit others. So Carnegie and other millionaires built public libraries, museums, art galleries, and parks. "No more useful or more beautiful monument can be left by any man," said Carnegie, "than a park for the city in which he was born or in which he has long lived. . . ."

These public institutions enriched the lives of millions of people, but they could not compensate for the misery that poor people endured when they moved to the cities to find jobs.

The Miserable Hordes

Because public transportation was expensive, if available at all, most people lived close to their work. But many could not afford decent housing. Instead they had to pack their families into dark, crowded buildings known as tenements.

Built in the shadows of smoke-belching factories, the tenements had little light or air; many rooms had no windows. Several families had to share a single water faucet and a single toilet. Halls and stairways were dark and filthy. One report described the tenements of the Lower East Side in New York as "containing, but sheltering not, the miserable hordes that crowded beneath mouldering, water-rotted roofs or burrowed among the rats of clammy cellars."

Under such conditions many people died from diseases like consumption (tuberculosis) and smallpox. In many tenement districts, one out of every five babies did not survive the first year of life.

Many children abandoned these dwellings and took to the streets, surviving by doing odd jobs or begging, sleeping in doorways, in stairwells, or under docks. Appalled by the situation, several organizations tried to provide meals, shelter, and education for these homeless children, many of whom were orphans. They even sent groups of children west on "orphan trains," to be taken in by families on farms and ranches.

The nation's cities were growing rapidly and changing in many ways. Above the shacks and tenements rose skyscrapers as high as 20 stories; electric street lighting began to replace gas lamps; great bridges were built. On May 24, 1883, the Brooklyn Bridge was opened, linking Manhattan with Brooklyn. With its steel supporting cables and tall stone towers, this bridge was hailed as the eighth wonder of the world and regarded as a symbol of the greatness of America's cities.

Electrical wiring raised grisly fears among some people in the 1880s as this mysterious new power began to replace gas for lighting. Many other inventions fascinated the nation in these exciting times. Typewriters brought an end to the time-consuming chore of writing business letters by hand. The telephone opened a new age of easy communication.

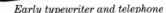

Early typewriter and telephone

Birthday of a Nation

The Main Hall was 1,876 feet long.

"The hour of the opening has arrived.... The moment we have dreamed of ... has come." With these words a reporter expressed the excitement and pride felt throughout America on May 10, 1876, when the nation's long-awaited birthday party began. America was now 100 years old, and it was celebrating by holding its first world's fair.

The Centennial Exposition ("centennial" means 100th anniversary) was spread across 450 acres of Fairmount Park in Philadelphia, the city where America's founders had signed the Declaration of Independence.

Exhibits from more than 35 nations filled the fair's 200 buildings. But the spotlight was on America as the young nation proudly displayed its industrial might and inventive skill. In Machinery Hall, visitors marveled at devices and gadgets that spun cotton, folded paper into envelopes, made shoes, sawed logs, and printed wallpaper. All these machines were powered by the hissing boilers and 56-ton flywheel of an enormous Corliss steam engine.

Other wonders awaited the fairgoers. Alexander Graham Bell exhibited his curious new invention, the telephone. Many visitors saw for the first time lamps lit not by gas or oil but by the power called electricity.

Crowds in the huge Main Hall gazed at furs from Norway, saddles from Egypt, and the newest designs in artificial teeth and silver jewelry made in

Agricultural Hall

Crowds head for the fair.

America. Tropical gardens grew in Horticultural Hall, which one visitor described as a palace of enchantment.

Paintings and sculpture from around the world filled the Art Gallery. So did the visitors; one woman complained bitterly about the "pushing, jamming, seething" crowd.

A coat, vest, and breeches worn by George Washington were displayed in Government Hall. Exhibits in the Women's Pavilion ranged from fancy needlework to an interesting new machine that washed dishes. In Agricultural Hall were sugar-cured hams from Ohio, cotton from India, tobacco from Kentucky, wines from California, France, and Germany, and row upon row of reaping and mowing machines.

A narrow-gauge railroad line transported visitors around the fairgrounds. More than a hundred restaurants fed them.

"Come at all events," the *Chicago Tribune* advised, "if you have to live six months on bread and water to make up for the expense." And come they did. A Japanese visitor described the opening-day scene: "Crowds come like sheep, run here, run there, run everywhere." By the time the Exposition was closed in early November, some ten million people had come to see the fair.

Right: A Liberty Bell made of tobacco

Tools of the dentist

Huddled on the deck of the S.S. Pennland (right), European families cross the Atlantic in 1893 to a new life in America. Most of the immigrants could only afford tickets for steerage—crowded quarters below the decks, so stuffy that many passengers preferred the cold but fresh air on deck. Between 1890 and 1914, nearly 16 million European immigrants poured into America.

Most immigrants spent their first hours in America at the Ellis Island reception center in New York harbor, shown in the postcard above. There, doctors examined them for illnesses. Other officials judged their ability to care for themselves in a strange, new land.

By 1914 nearly half of America's 99 million people lived in cities and large towns. Many of those who streamed into the cities to find work were native-born Americans who left their farms for better opportunities; but many more came from overseas. Before 1890 most immigrants had come from western Europe and Scandinavia. Now a new wave of immigrants also began to arrive from eastern and southern European countries, such as Poland, Russia, Italy, and Greece. This "new immigration," as it was called, brought nearly 16 million Europeans to America between 1890 and 1914.

Ships carrying the immigrants landed at various ports, but many of them came to New York. In 1892 the federal government opened a reception center for them on Ellis Island in New York harbor, in the shadow of the Statue of Liberty. This statue, a gift to the United States from the people of France, had been dedicated in 1886. For many immigrants the torch held high by Liberty was their first glimpse of America. Emma Lazarus, a famous young Jewish poet, won a contest for the poem to be inscribed on the statue's pedestal. It says, in part:

> *Give me your tired, your poor,*
> *Your huddled masses yearning to breathe free,*
> *The wretched refuse of your teeming shore,*
> *Send these, the homeless, tempest-tost to me,*
> *I lift my lamp beside the golden door.*

To Go to America

Most of the immigrants were poor peasants and villagers who came to America with the dream that one day they would have land of their own. Others came to escape forced military service or religious persecution. All came because they believed that America was a land where they could better themselves. "Those days everybody's dream in the old country was to go to America," recalled one immigrant. "We heard people were free and we heard about better living."

But most of the millions who reached Ellis Island after 1890 did not travel much farther. About a third of them stayed in New York City. Many others ended up working in the mines and mills of New York, New England, Ohio, and Pennsylvania or in the packing-houses of Chicago. Most immigrants simply could not afford to travel out to the West or to buy land; they had spent all of their money just to reach America. Hunger forced them to take the first job they could find.

America's cities became places where many nationalities mingled and many European languages were spoken. Life in America was hard for the newcomers. Few spoke English, and they were bewildered by the number of people, the noise, and the fast pace. "Buses and trolleys rushed through the streets with devilish force," recalled one immigrant. "It was all wild, all inconceivable."

Between 1865 and 1914 city workers usually toiled for at least ten to twelve hours a day, six or even seven days a week, in factories,

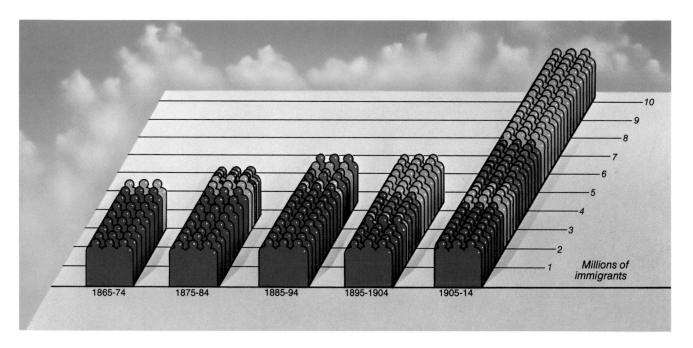

Immigrants to the U.S.A. 1865-1914

From:
- ⬛ Northwest Europe
- ⬜ Central Europe
- ⬛ Southern Europe
- ⬜ Eastern Europe
- ⬜ Other continents

With the ever-rising tide of immigrants came a dramatic change in America's ethnic mix (right). Until the 1890s most new Americans came from such western European countries as England, Ireland, and Germany. But in the 1890s millions of people began to arrive from countries in southern and eastern Europe, such as Italy, Greece, Poland, and Russia.

1865-74 · 1875-84 · 1885-94 · 1895-1904 · 1905-14

Millions of immigrants — 1 · 2 · 3 · 4 · 5 · 6 · 7 · 8 · 9 · 10

Newly arrived in America, weary youngsters (opposite) undergo a health checkup. If the official suspected a problem, he would chalk a symbol onto the immigrant's coat and send him on to a doctor. A large E, for example, meant possible eye trouble. An H stood for heart problems. About 2 percent of the immigrants were declared to be unfit and sent back to Europe.

A rooftop playground (above) was established at Ellis Island in 1904 for children whose parents were delayed for tests or questioning. During the busiest years, as many as 5,000 people passed through Ellis Island each day. Immigration officials often had to work seven days a week. One examiner said, "I thought it was a stream that would never end."

mills, and "sweatshops"—small, crowded workrooms where such products as clothing, cigars, and artificial flowers were made by hand. Men earned about ten cents an hour; women got even less.

Even when husband and wife both worked, they often could not earn enough money to pay for food, clothing, and rent. Thus they had to send their children to work. In 1900, for example, almost two million children under the age of 16 worked in the United States. Some were employed in glassmaking factories, working a ten-hour shift, often at night. Many boys, some of them as young as 9, worked in coal mines. They led the mules that hauled carts loaded with coal. Or they sat hour after hour in the cold, dark tunnels opening and closing the doors between different sections of the mine.

Many boys were employed to sort coal as it rolled down a chute, or coal breaker. "Work in the coal breakers is exceedingly hard and dangerous," wrote one observer. "Crouched over the chutes, the boys sit hour after hour, picking out the pieces of slate and other refuse from the coal as it rushes past to the washers. From the cramped position they have to assume, most of them become more or less deformed and bent-backed like old men. . . ."

Girls worked in textile factories. Some tied up threads when they broke on the spinning wheels; others—called "spoolers"—put new spools of thread on the looms. Both boys and girls, some not more than six or seven years old, were put to work sweeping factory floors. Marie Van Vorst, one of the first women to investigate child labor, told of seeing a little boy in a South Carolina cotton mill who "sweeps the cotton and lint from the mill aisles from 6 p.m. to 6 a.m. without a break in the night's routine." Bosses threw cold water on the children's faces to keep them awake.

Reports of such scenes worried and angered many people. America was becoming richer almost daily, chiefly because of the tremendous rate of production its working people achieved. And yet the workers themselves received few, if any, benefits from this

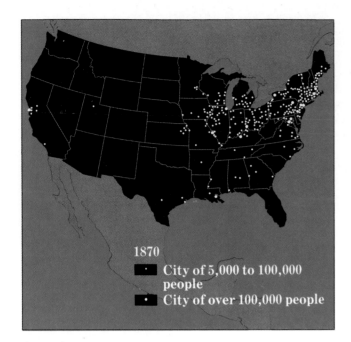

1870
■ City of 5,000 to 100,000 people
□ City of over 100,000 people

1900
KILOMETERS 1000
STATUTE MILES 500
■ City of 5,000 to 100,000 people
□ City of over 100,000 people

increasing wealth. There were so many people who lived in wretched poverty. So many children had to go to jobs instead of school. And their numbers were growing. Finally, misery and anger led to action. Workers began to form unions.

"An injury to one is the concern of all," was the rallying cry of the Knights of Labor. One of the first large unions, it was organized in 1869. The Knights and other unions wanted an eight-hour working day, higher pay for the workers, an end to child labor, and the passage of safety and health laws. They backed up their demands by threatening to strike—that is, shutting down a business by refusing to work.

Organizing a union was dangerous. Many organizers were fired from their jobs and "blacklisted." This means that their names were put on a list that was sent around to other employers so that the organizers would have trouble finding another job. Even so, many remarkable people organized unions during the closing years of the 19th century.

"Big Bill" Haywood, a miner from the West, organized workers across the whole country, from the textile mills of New England to the lumber mills of Washington State. His national organization was called the Industrial Workers of the World and nicknamed "Wobblies." Mary Jones, a fiery Irish immigrant known as "Mother Jones," began attending meetings of the Knights of Labor in 1871, when she was 41 years old and a widow. Soon she was organizing unions and leading strikes, especially among the coal miners. She was still at work at the age of 87, "a little old lady in a black bonnet," rallying the coal miners in West Virginia.

English immigrant Samuel Gompers, a cigar maker, was an important organizer of skilled workers. He founded the

Growth of Cities 1870-1900
New and expanding cities changed the face of America between 1870 and 1900 (above). Clustered mostly in the industrial Northeast, these cities bulged with immigrants.

Jam-packed Broadway (left) in New York City reflects the rapid growth of America's cities at the turn of the century, as millions of job-seeking immigrants poured into them. By 1900 four-fifths of the people in New York City were either immigrants or the children of immigrants.

Many immigrants made their new homes in the crowded neighborhoods of Manhattan's East Side, usually living in shabby tenements. Cart-pushing vendors (opposite) turned East Side streets into noisy market-places. The streets also served as playgrounds for children (above). For friendship and protection some boys formed clubs or gangs—that sometimes got into trouble with the law. One East Side youth explained, "It is hard for a boy who has just come over here to start right."

American Federation of Labor (AFL) in 1886. The AFL helped unions to get started and to stand together in their negotiations with business owners.

Businessmen did not give in easily to the unions' demands; often the workers carried out their threat to strike. In 1894 alone there were nearly 1,400 strikes, involving half a million workers.

When workers went on strike, they picketed the factory, marching in lines in front of its doors and carrying signs that told about their complaints. This discouraged other workers—called strikebreakers—from taking the strikers' jobs. Such picket lines kept the factory closed until the boss agreed to negotiate. Then leaders chosen by the workers would sit down with the employers to discuss their demands.

"We Had to Teach Our Employees a Lesson"

Many strikes failed. Employers simply waited until the workers ran out of money and food and had no choice but to return to work. Or the employer hired new immigrants to take the place of striking workers. "All I want in my business is muscle," said one California employer. "I don't care whether it be obtained from a Chinaman or a white man, from a mule or a horse!"

Sometimes violence erupted during a strike. In 1892, for instance, Andrew Carnegie's manager, Henry Frick, used a private army and the state militia against union steelworkers in Homestead, Pennsylvania. Sixteen men were killed; many more were wounded. When it was all over, Frick wrote to Carnegie, who was vacationing in Scotland, "We had to teach our employees a lesson and we have taught them one they will never forget." Carnegie sent congratulations back to Frick.

Many strikes ended peacefully and successfully, with workers winning larger paychecks and shorter working hours, but progress was slow and difficult.

While industrial workers were taking union action, farmers were also organizing. So much new land was being farmed after the Civil War that prices for produce fell rapidly. But railroads charged more and more for delivering produce. Farmers could not earn enough money to pay their mortgages and buy new machinery. The farmers began to form small, local groups called alliances, which then merged into larger and larger alliances. These organizations, like the industrial unions, tried to help the farmers by getting new laws passed. Americans must remember, they said, that the farmer is the man who feeds them all.

In July 1892 a group of reformers and political radicals met in Omaha, Nebraska, to form a new political party they called the People's, or Populist, Party. Among them were farmers, union leaders, women's-rights crusaders, and socialists. Federal control of the railroads was one of the reforms sought by the Populists. Another goal was a graduated income tax. This means that the more money a person earns, the more tax he or she must pay.

Mine workers in Pennsylvania, about 1900

Girl laborer in a Georgia mill, 1908

Grim poverty often meant that every family member, including young children, had to find a job. Like their parents, children labored long hours for little pay. The somber boys at left worked in coal mines. The girl at bottom left tends spools in a spinning mill. Below, a boy carries garment pieces off to be sewn.

The children at right lived in the Carnegie Steel Mill town of Homestead, Pennsylvania. There, in 1892, company action against the workers' union ended in bloodshed and drew national attention to the plight of the poor.

Left: Garment worker in New York City, about 1912. Above: Carnegie Steel Mill, Homestead, Pennsylvania, 1907

A cartoon from 1883 (lower) charges that the wealthy railroad industry kept its workers poor and powerless. The knight represents the bosses. Horselike armor stands for "monopoly," the control over the sale of a product by one company, or several companies acting together. Lack of competition allowed the big company to charge high prices—and keep the workers' pay low. The worker's hammer represents his only weapon: the strike.

In 1894 federal troops (upper) went into battle against members of the railroad workers' union in Chicago, Illinois. The trouble began when the owner of the Pullman Company cut his workers' wages.

The Populists believed that a graduated tax would help narrow the immense gap between rich and poor people.

The new party's candidate got almost 10 percent of the popular votes in the 1892 presidential election. Three Populist senators and eleven representatives were elected, along with several governors. The strength of the Populists surprised other political parties, who now began to take the reform movement more seriously.

Although the Populist Party survived for only a few years, many of the reforms it sought did eventually become law. Important social changes were beginning to occur during these years, which became known as the Progressive Era. Some city and state governments enacted laws banning child labor and requiring safe working conditions in factories and mines. The federal government, under the leadership of President Theodore Roosevelt, also began taking action to improve the lives of working people and to control business monopolies. The Pure Food and Drug Act of 1906, for example, set the first standards for preparing and labeling foods and medicines. In 1913, Congress passed a graduated income tax law supported by President Woodrow Wilson.

Rapid population growth and industrial development raised another concern—the uncontrolled use of natural resources. In 1891, Congress authorized a system of forest preserves. Fifty million acres were set aside during the next ten years. President Roosevelt added nearly 150 million acres and established the National Forest Service. John Muir and other conservationists founded the Sierra Club in 1892 to help protect the country's wild places.

An Empire for the United States

At this same time people called expansionists were arguing about another subject. They believed that the United States was ready to become a world power. They had seen the great nations of Europe—Great Britain, Germany, and France—divide much of Africa and Asia into colonies, and they argued that America should have its own overseas territories. Among the leading expansionists were Assistant Secretary of the Navy Theodore Roosevelt; Senator Henry Cabot Lodge, an influential Republican from Massachusetts; and Commodore George Dewey. Within a short time expansionism would lead to war with Spain.

Spain had once been one of the most powerful nations on earth; its vast overseas holdings included much of Central and South America and several islands in the Caribbean. At the beginning of the 19th century, however, Spain's empire shrank as, one by one, the countries of Central and South America rebelled and became independent. By the end of the century, all that remained of the Spanish Empire were Cuba and Puerto Rico in the Caribbean Sea and the Philippines and a few other islands in the Pacific. But these islands yielded rich profits to Spain. Cuba, for example, was a leading producer of the world's sugar.

In 1895, American eyes turned sympathetically toward Cuba— less than 100 miles from the United States—where rebels were

Holding signs in their native languages, members of a garment workers' union join together in a strike in New York City around 1912. Shorter hours and higher pay were the chief goals of unions, but they were also concerned about worker safety. At the Triangle Shirtwaist Company in New York, the foremen kept the exit doors locked. In March 1911 a fire raged through the building; 154 workers, mostly young women, jumped to their deaths or died in the flames. This tragedy enraged union organizers like Eugene V. Debs (left). Debs led the union action against the Pullman Company in 1894—and ended up with a jail sentence.

LOCATION OF THE MAINE—HAVANA HARBOR

RECOVERING THE DEAD BODIES.

Cries for war against Spain arose after the battleship Maine blew up in the Havana harbor of Spanish-ruled Cuba on February 15, 1898, killing 260 men. The explosion was probably an accident, but Americans and Spanish blamed each other. For years American newspapers had been printing grim—and often false—stories of Spanish cruelty toward the Cuban people in their struggle for independence.

The United States had been pressuring Spain to free Cuba. But now, with the sinking of the Maine, Americans demanded action. President William McKinley (left) had hoped to avoid a war but finally gave in. War was declared in April. The war ended less than four months later, with the United States an easy victor.

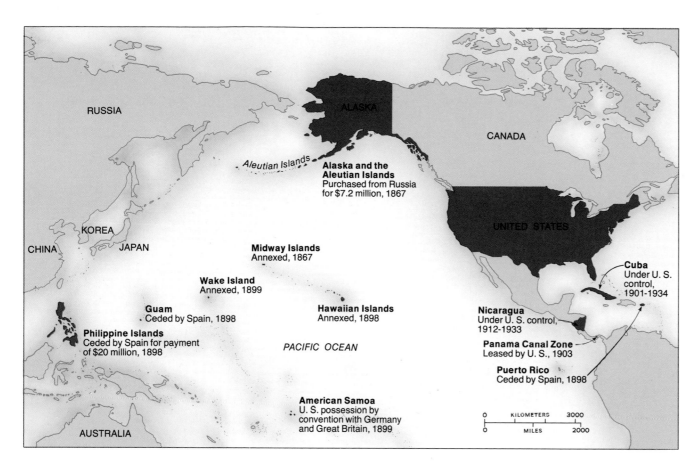

Growth of Empire

■ U. S. possession, protection, or control

Military action and shrewd bargaining spread American influence far beyond the mainland states (left). By the early 1900s the United States had bought Alaska from Russia and gained control of islands scattered across the Pacific and Caribbean. This expansion opened new avenues for global trade. The government also built military bases abroad to boost the nation's power. For the first time, America ruled an empire.

RUSSIA

ALASKA

CANADA

Alaska and the Aleutian Islands
Purchased from Russia for $7.2 million, 1867

Aleutian Islands

KOREA

CHINA   JAPAN

UNITED STATES

Midway Islands
Annexed, 1867

Cuba
Under U. S. control, 1901-1934

Wake Island
Annexed, 1899

Guam
Ceded by Spain, 1898

Hawaiian Islands
Annexed, 1898

Nicaragua
Under U. S. control, 1912-1933

Philippine Islands
Ceded by Spain for payment of $20 million, 1898

PACIFIC OCEAN

Panama Canal Zone
Leased by U. S., 1903

Puerto Rico
Ceded by Spain, 1898

American Samoa
U. S. possession by convention with Germany and Great Britain, 1899

0   KILOMETERS   3000
0   MILES   2000

AUSTRALIA

---

fighting for independence from Spanish rule. Spain had sent an especially brutal general to Cuba to put down the rebellion. Shocking stories of Spanish cruelty soon reached the United States. These reports pleased the expansionists, who wanted to arouse popular sentiment for seizing Spain's colonies.

The expansionist cause was also helped by two men who owned competing newspapers in New York City. William Randolph Hearst's *New York Journal* and Joseph Pulitzer's New York *World* tried to attract new readers by publishing sensational—and often false—stories of Spanish atrocities. Americans were angered by what they read. Then on February 15, 1898, the U. S. battleship *Maine*, which had been sent to Cuba to guard American lives and property, exploded and sank in Havana harbor, killing 260 men. The United States government claimed that a mine had destroyed the ship. The Spanish denied responsibility for the tragedy. The cause of the explosion was never established; it may have been an accident. But a wave of anger spread across the United States. Finally, in April, Congress declared war.

The Spanish-American War lasted less than four months. The first American victory came on May 1, when a U. S. Navy squadron commanded by Commodore Dewey easily defeated the Spanish fleet in the Philippines. Six weeks later, 17,000 U. S. Army troops landed in Cuba and quickly overwhelmed the Spanish forces.

The victory in Cuba gave America a new hero, Theodore Roosevelt. Colonel Roosevelt had organized a cavalry regiment called the

Opponents of expansionism offer Uncle Sam (the United States) a dose of anti-fat medicine in this cartoon from 1900. Labels on Uncle Sam's pants list the territorial gains made through the years. President McKinley appears as a tailor, happily outfitting a growing nation. Americans were deeply divided *on the subject of overseas expansion. Some felt that America was seeking power at the price of other people's freedom. Some believed it was the nation's duty and destiny to spread its civilization to other lands.*

The United States became a world power under the energetic leadership of Theodore Roosevelt (below), who was President from 1901 to 1909. Roosevelt built up America's Navy so that rival countries would hesitate to invade. In 1907 he sent 16 battleships—the Great White Fleet—on a tour of the world to show off America's might. At right, the ships steam past well-wishers off San Francisco.

Rough Riders. Newspaper reports of their stirring charge—on foot—during the Battle of San Juan Hill made Roosevelt a hero to the nation. Roosevelt was elected governor of New York in 1899 and eventually became President of the United States.

Spain's defeat in the Spanish-American War gave the United States its empire: Puerto Rico, Guam, and the Philippines. The U. S. Army quickly took control of Guam and Puerto Rico but not the Philippines. Over the years the Filipinos had been fighting as fiercely as the Cubans for freedom from Spanish rule. Now they learned that control of their land had been shifted to the United States. In February 1899 the Filipinos launched a war of independence against the Americans. Once again the United States was fighting a war of conquest.

The anti-expansionists were appalled. They called it a war against liberty and a betrayal of the ideals expressed in the Declaration of Independence. Leaders such as Samuel Gompers and Andrew Carnegie traveled around the country trying to persuade the people that the war was wrong.

But expansionists had a different view. Control of the Philippines meant control of the Pacific, they said. And the islands were rich in minerals, timber, and fertile farmland.

In 1901 the Philippine leader, Emilio Aguinaldo, was captured, and in 1902 the patriots surrendered. The Philippines became a colony of the United States.

The Panama Canal

Now the expansionists directed their efforts toward the Isthmus of Panama, the narrow strip of land in Central America that separates the Atlantic and Pacific Oceans. The idea of a canal across Central America was not new. When the *Maine* blew up, two months passed before another ship, the *Oregon*, could reach Cuba, sailing from San Francisco around the tip of South America. The expansionists argued that the *Oregon*'s 12,000-mile journey would have been 8,000 miles shorter if there had been a canal across Panama. Such a canal was even more important now that America had a widespread empire to control.

In March 1903, Congress approved a treaty paying ten million dollars to Colombia, which controlled Panama, for the right to dig a canal across the isthmus. But the Colombian Senate voted to hold out for more money. In November rebels gained control of Panama and declared independence from Colombia. The new Panamanian government soon approved a canal treaty. Work began the next year. Tens of thousands of men and an army of machinery worked for more than ten years to finish the 51-mile-long canal, at a cost of about 387 million dollars.

But there was little fanfare when the Panama Canal finally opened in 1914. The world's attention had shifted to Europe, where a terrible war was under way. The years from 1865 to 1914 had seen America transform itself into a rich industrial nation. Now it was emerging as a world power as well.

249

Pieces of Our Past
1865-1914

Smartly dressed children (left) pose at a summer house in New Hampshire in the 1880s. Wealthy families built summer "cottages" as elaborate as their houses in the city.

A toy locomotive (below) made of tin clanged its bell as the wheels were turned. The new age of machinery inspired new toys—and provided the machinery for making them.

The early vacuum cleaner (above) gave its owner more status than service. This one from 1911 worked by being pumped continuously by hand.

A little slugger (above) comes to bat in the 1880s. Based on an old English game called rounders, baseball evolved in America. The sport quickly became a national passion.

Phonographs like this early 1900s model (right) brought music to the home. A hand crank wound the spring that turned the turntable. The flaring oak horn boosted the sound volume.

Cuddly teddy bears like this one from the early 1900s owe their name and fame to President Theodore Roosevelt, who refused to shoot a trapped bear.

Steam radiators replaced room stoves when central-heating furnaces began to be used during the last half of the 19th century.

Bathing shoes (below) protected a lady's feet both on the beach and in the water. This pair, from about 1910, was made of black satin.

Fancy circus wagons brought wild animals and wild excitement to small towns across America. Sometimes school was closed for the circus parade.

BECOMING A WORLD POWER

WARS AND A TROUBLED PEACE 1914-1945

On August 4, 1914, World War I broke out. By the time it ended four years later, nearly 15 million people had been killed by bullets or shells, starvation, or disease. Most of the victims were Europeans, for the deadliest fighting took place in Europe. Still, it was truly a world war, because at stake were not only European lands, but also European-owned colonies around the world. How did such a bloody war happen?

The countries of Europe had been relatively peaceful for a century. But national rivalries had recently created an atmosphere of bitter tension. Then on June 28, 1914, a young Serbian nationalist shot and killed Archduke Francis Ferdinand, the heir to Austria-Hungary's throne, in the city of Sarajevo (see map on page 254). The assassination triggered the war.

Austria-Hungary, with Germany's backing, prepared to punish little Serbia for the crime. Russia came to Serbia's aid to protect its own interests in the region. France, bound by treaty, joined the Russians; Britain allied itself with France; and soon armies all across Europe were on the move. One by one, in early August of 1914, the great powers followed each other into World War I.

The Germans launched a massive attack of more than a million men in Western Europe, fighting their way west through Belgium against stiff resistance and eventually reaching the Marne River near Paris. There the French rallied with the help of the British and drove them back. The two sides dug in, facing each other in a double line of trenches 400 miles long. They settled down to almost four years of attack and counterattack that cost millions of lives.

In Eastern Europe the huge Russian Army moved into action against Germany faster than expected. But after the Russians made a few gains, smaller and better-led German forces began to outmaneuver them. By late 1914 Germany had expelled the Russians from its own territory for good. But the fighting continued along an ever shifting front from the Baltic Sea to the Black Sea.

When the war started, U. S. President Woodrow Wilson, a Democrat, was busy putting into effect his domestic program, including a Federal Reserve Act to create a government-controlled banking system. The last thing Wilson wanted was to involve the United States in a foreign war. On August 19, 1914, he told the American people that "the United States must be neutral in fact as well as in name." But it was hard to stay neutral. The British set up a naval blockade to keep countries from trading with Germany. In response Germany decided to use its new weapon, the submarine, to sink without warning all enemy merchant ships found in the waters around Britain. This new kind of warfare outraged the American public, especially after a German torpedo sank the British passenger ship *Lusitania* in May 1915, killing almost 1,200 people, including 128 Americans.

Despite his desire to stay out of the conflict, President Wilson made it clear that if the Germans sank any American ships, they would risk war with the United States. The German government decided to hold off attacking the unarmed merchant ships.

HALT the HUN!

BUY U.S. GOVERNMENT BONDS
THIRD LIBERTY LOAN

An American soldier kisses his girl good-bye (above) before leaving home for the war in Europe, a struggle later called World War I. In 1917 and 1918 nearly two million Americans were shipped off to fight in Europe. Americans at home, stirred by patriotic posters (left), helped pay for the war by buying government bonds to halt the "Hun"—a scornful nickname for a German soldier.

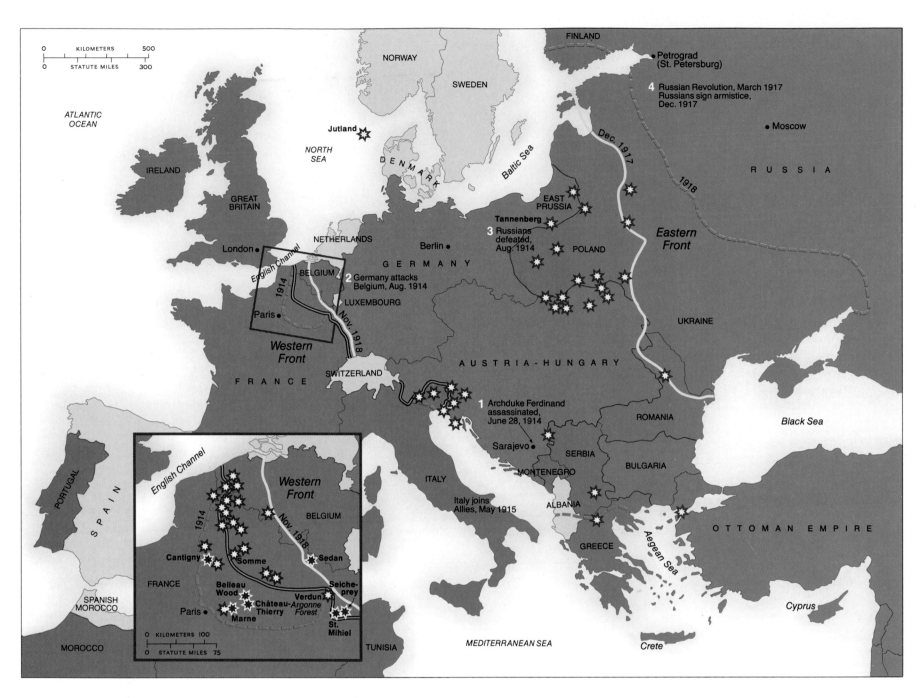

World War I: Alliances and Areas of Conflict

Allied powers
Central powers
Neutral nations
Farthest advance of Central powers
Trench lines
Armistice lines
⭐ Major battles
✹ Battles involving American troops

In 1914 a Serbian nationalist touched off World War I when he shot Archduke Francis Ferdinand, heir to the Austro-Hungarian throne (1). Austria-Hungary attacked Serbia. Russia rallied to Serbia's aid. A pact tied France to Russia—and left Germany trapped between them.

The Germans decided to strike first. Linked with Austria-Hungary to form the Central powers, they stormed through Belgium (2) into France. Allies England and France joined forces and dug in opposite the foe. For more than three years the two sides fired at each other from trenches. On the eastern front the Germans beat back the Russians at Tannenberg (3), then struck deep into Russian territory. Russia, reeling from an internal revolution (4), made peace with Germany in 1917. The harsh treaty signed in 1918 forced Russia to give up a large portion of its western borderlands. With peace in the east, Germany was free to move its troops to the western front.

In April 1917 the United States stepped in on the Allied side. Its first victory came at Cantigny (inset). The Second Battle of the Marne halted the German advances. As the Americans drove into the Argonne Forest, the German center gave way. With the Allies closing in, Germany signed an armistice in 1918.

In the fall of 1916 the war entered its third year. Both sides had suffered terribly, but because British ships had cut off supplies to Germany and Austria, their people were beginning to starve. Early in 1917 the desperate Germans resumed the submarine attacks, even though they knew this might bring the United States into the war. They hoped to knock out Britain and France before the Americans had time to train soldiers and send them into battle.

On March 1, 1917, the Zimmermann telegram was made public. This was a message from Germany promising the Mexican government the return of Texas, New Mexico, and Arizona if Mexico would join the German side against the United States. The British intercepted the telegram and relayed it to President Wilson. American anger at Germany increased.

Two weeks later, on March 15, Nicholas II, the tsar of Russia, was forced to give up his throne. The Russian people, goaded by hunger, ineffectual leadership, and unending bloodshed, had risen up and swept away the ancient monarchy. The new government, a democracy, promised to continue the war, but soldiers and civilians alike wanted nothing more than to get out. It was becoming more and more likely that Russia's war effort would soon collapse.

The Americans Declare War

The day after Tsar Nicholas's fall, German submarines sank three American merchant ships. In early April, at a special session of Congress, President Wilson asked for and got a declaration of war against the Germans. The nation began to mobilize its resources for war. Camps all over the country were set up to train American soldiers. The government started regulating private businesses—railroads, telephone companies, and factories—and telling people what they could buy, what they could eat, and how much fuel they could use.

Meanwhile, amid growing unrest in Russia, a group of Bolshevik, or Communist, revolutionaries led by V. I. Lenin took control of the government. One of the new government's first acts was to ask the Germans for peace. Agreeing to Germany's harsh demands, Russia withdrew from the war. With peace in the east, the Germans could now transfer thousands of troops west to wage all-out war against the French and British.

By spring of 1918 troopships were carrying nearly 100,000 American soldiers a month across the Atlantic Ocean to help the Allies fend off the Germans. They reached the battlefields of France in time to help block the last great German offensive in early June of 1918. The exhausted Germans had lost their race to win in the west. Germany's government collapsed, and Kaiser Wilhelm, the German ruler, went into exile. The German leaders who replaced the kaiser accepted a peace offer from the Allies, and all fighting ended at 11 a.m. on November 11, 1918.

War seemed a lark to American recruits who had yet to taste its horrors. Many rode through Issoudun in central France (above). There they spilled from troop trains to gulp coffee and sandwiches served by American Red Cross volunteers while a band tooted a welcome.

Back home, a sign (below) foretold a grim fate for many: "We Will Die For The U.S.A.— What Will You Do?" Volunteers posing under it sold savings stamps during this fund drive in 1918. Children bought 25-cent stamps to stick on a "thrift" card that could be traded in for a $5 war savings certificate when full.

Volunteer workers near the front in 1918

A cannon firing near Saint-Mihiel, France, in 1918

American gun crew, Argonne Forest, France, 1918

British soldiers in a trench in France, January 1917

Along battle lines that barely budged in three years, soldiers dug vast webs of trenches. There they hid in mud and dampness, peering across "no-man's-land" with periscopes (above). Cannons fired shell after shell at the foe in his trenches (opposite, lower). Even volunteer workers took to the trenches to make pies and other supplies for the troops (upper). Often infantry swarmed "over the top" in bloody attacks. Most were futile, but this one in 1918 (left) succeeded. Here in the Argonne Forest in France, a gun crew inches ahead. Nearly 120,000 Americans fell in this costly battle—but so, at last, did the German strongholds.

Harlem "Hell-fighter" on Fifth Avenue, New York City, February 1919

One soldier who will march no more (opposite) pauses to accept an admirer's gratitude during the victory parade of the 369th Regiment, the famed Harlem "Hell-fighters." This unit of blacks, led by officers both black and white, returned in glory to New York City in 1919. "From under their battered tin hats," said a parade spectator, "eyes that had looked straight at death were kept to the front." Two years earlier the new regiment had drilled in the streets of Harlem without uniforms, weapons, or seasoned leaders.

James Reese Europe (below), first black bandleader known nationwide, poses with his Clef Club Band in 1914. Later he would go to war as leader of the Hell-fighters' Band. Europe outlived the war by only three months, but the "Jazz Age" he helped to start had just begun.

In December 1918, Woodrow Wilson went to Paris to help the Allies prepare a peace treaty. He hoped the treaty would lead to limits on arms, fairer colonial policies, and a "League of Nations"—an assembly where all member countries would meet regularly to discuss how to settle their quarrels and protect the peace. On his arrival in Paris with his wife Edith he was greeted as a hero. "Paris," Mrs. Wilson wrote, "was wild with celebration. Every inch was covered with cheering, shouting humanity.... Flowers rained upon us until we were nearly buried."

Despite Wilson's promise of a just peace that would leave no hard feelings, the treaty signed at the Versailles Palace on June 28, 1919, was a bitter blow to the Germans. Germany was forced to give back a large territory it had taken from France 48 years earlier, as well as lands to the east. It had to disband most of its armed forces, admit that Germany alone was to blame for starting the war, and pay billions of dollars in reparations.

Wilson hoped that the U. S. Senate would approve the Versailles Treaty. But many senators, mostly Republicans, did not favor the League of Nations proposal as it was written into the treaty. Some were angry that Wilson had not allowed them to participate in drafting the League proposal, and many opposed connecting the United States to an international organization that would further entangle it in European affairs. After much debate the Senate refused to ratify the Versailles Treaty or let the United States join the League. Congress, by joint resolution, ended the war with Germany and Austria-Hungary on July 2, 1921, and ratified separate treaties with each country a few months later.

After the war, fear that Communism would spread to the U. S. caused a panic in 1919-1920 known as the "Red Scare"—so-called because Russian Communists used a red flag as their national symbol. American workers who preached socialism or went on strike, as many were doing because of low wages, were accused of being Russian agents. Many Americans, including high government officials, believed that foreigners, especially Russians, should be carefully watched or forced to leave the country. In violation of the Constitution, more than 4,000 citizens were arrested and jailed for their political activities.

After 1920, Americans slowly began to pick up the threads of peacetime life. In a period that came to be called the "Roaring Twenties," changing conditions created new attitudes, new amusements, and new problems.

Before World War I, most people could not afford cars. Then Henry Ford, a Michigan farmer's son, began to use a new, efficient

259

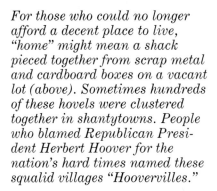

Men without jobs—and some without hope—line up for a handout of bread or a can of soup (left) as the Great Depression of the 1930s grips a somber nation. Wealthy women help run this New York City bread line, their elegant furs reminding the down-and-out that some people still prospered. The Roaring Twenties had ended as farms and firms went bankrupt, and millions lost their jobs.

For those who could no longer afford a decent place to live, "home" might mean a shack pieced together from scrap metal and cardboard boxes on a vacant lot (above). Sometimes hundreds of these hovels were clustered together in shantytowns. People who blamed Republican President Herbert Hoover for the nation's hard times named these squalid villages "Hoovervilles."

method of production called the assembly line to manufacture them. His factory could put together one of his Model T's in an hour and a half. Ford and other manufacturers sold cars at low prices; by 1926 nearly four million a year were rolling off the lines.

Cars gave people a freedom to move about that they had never had before—freedom to live far from their jobs and to travel into town for shopping and entertainment. Some drove to "speakeasies," secret nightclubs where people went for music, dancing, and—especially—alcoholic drinks. In 1919 the making and selling of alcoholic drinks had been prohibited by law. Because so many people were eager to drink during "Prohibition," speakeasies popped up in cities across the nation. Criminals organized into mobs and made immense profits producing and selling illegal whiskey, gin, and beer.

Movie-going became a popular American amusement. By 1929 some 80 to 100 million people a week were paying 10 or 15 cents to visit a movie palace and laugh at the antics of Charlie Chaplin and Buster Keaton or thrill to the heroics of cowboy star Tom Mix.

The Roaring Twenties brought radios into millions of households. People listened to comedy programs, music, and news, and followed the exploits of sports heroes like Babe Ruth, Jack Dempsey, and Red Grange. From the radio came news of an even greater American hero, Charles Lindbergh, who in 1927 became the first person to fly alone across the Atlantic Ocean. Radio advertisements told about the new time- and laborsaving devices that were hitting the market—refrigerators, washing machines, toasters. Many Americans began to buy these and other goods on credit: "Buy now, pay later!" urged the radio announcers.

From Prosperity to Panic

Factories were humming in the 1920s, and most people enjoyed secure jobs. But problems began to show up in the economy. During World War I, farmers had borrowed money to buy more machinery and land to meet the high demand for food in Europe. When the war ended, their foreign markets collapsed. Now, with too many crops and falling prices, most farmers could not afford to pay their debts.

In the cities, too, problems arose. Factories were producing mountains of goods but paying low wages to workers. People couldn't afford to buy all the goods produced, even on credit, so inventories piled up.

Meanwhile more and more Americans began to risk their money in the New York stock market. People bought stocks, or "shares," in large corporations, hoping to make a profit by selling them at higher prices. During the late twenties, stock prices went up and up. Then in 1929 the market began a slow decline. On Thursday, October 24, 1929, since known as "Black Thursday," a panic hit Wall Street, the nation's financial center in New York City. Millions of people rushed to sell their stocks. But buyers were scarce, and within a few days millions of shares became almost worthless.

261

A Blanket of Dust

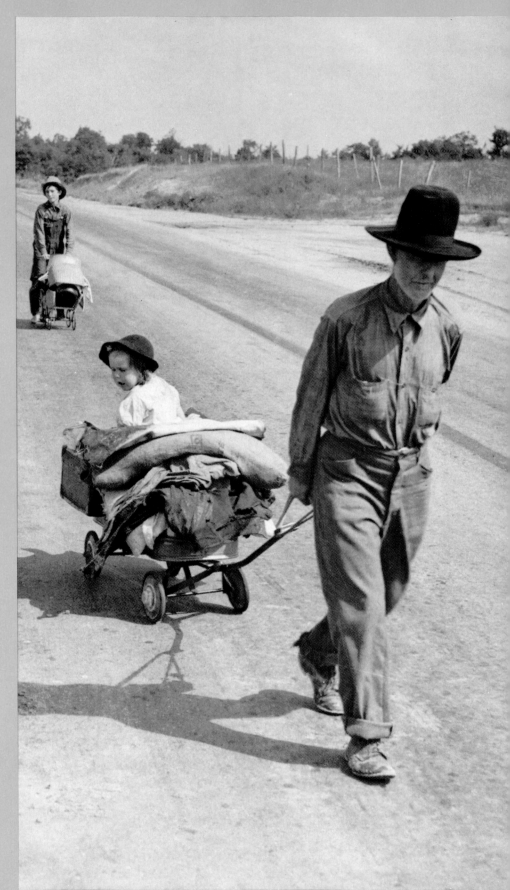

"**I** hope it'll rain before the kids grow up," one farmer joked. "They ain't never seen none." And, to this farmer in the Dust Bowl of the 1930s, it must have seemed that they never would. In 1932 a drought had settled over the Southwest; not until 1940 would normal rains return. By then the southern Great Plains region looked like a wasteland, its crops shriveled, its soil blowing in the wind, its families clinging to hope and government aid or trudging away in defeat.

How could it happen? For centuries, dense prairie grasses had carpeted the plains despite dry spells that parched the region for years at a time. Then in the late 1800s herds of ranchers' cattle chewed the short grass and chopped up roots and soil with their hooves, leaving less and less grass to hold the soil in place. Wheat farmers moved in, tearing up the sod with plows hitched to tractors that could work many acres a day. After a good harvest, confident farmers plowed up thousands of new acres to grow more crops the next year. In 1932 the drought shriveled the wheat, leaving the soil bare and unprotected over millions of acres. The misery of the Dust Bowl had begun.

Parched into powder, the soil billowed up with the wind, swirling into awesome dust storms that traveled hundreds of miles. Some of the dust even settled as far away as New York City or sifted down on ships 500 miles out in the Atlantic Ocean.

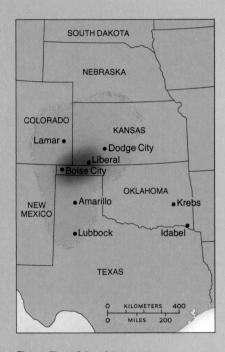

Dust Bowl in the 1930s
- ◼ Worst-hit area
- ◻ General Dust Bowl area

Spawned by wind, bad farming methods, and drought that struck the whole mid-continent, dust storms called "black blizzards" turned the southern Great Plains into the Dust Bowl of the 1930s. The "bowl" stretched over the Texas and Oklahoma panhandles, the eastern edges of Colorado and New Mexico, and the western half of Kansas. Hard times spurred farmers and government conservationists toward wiser use of the land. Even so, erosion and periodic droughts still plague the area.

A homeless family walks from Idabel to Krebs, Oklahoma, 1939.

Great Plains motorists caught in a dust storm often had to stop, unable to see the road even with their headlights on. Train engineers had to back into railroad stations after chugging right past them in the blinding murk.

Home owners taped up their window frames, stuffed rags under doors, hung wet bed sheets by the windows to catch the invading dust—and then found a pile by the door where it had blown through the keyhole. "All we could do about it," said one sufferer, "was just sit in our dusty chairs, gaze at each other through the fog that filled the room and watch that fog settle slowly and silently, covering everything including ourselves in a thick, brownish gray blanket."

Jokes spread like dust storms—about farmers planting seeds by tossing them in the air as the soil blew by . . . hunters shooting gophers overhead as the rodents burrowed through the dust . . . birds flying backward so grit wouldn't get in their eyes. But it was no joke when a farmer had to shovel drifts that often rose head-high, or lost his farm and had to move into a shack.

Government aid helped many farmers—and the businesses that depended on them—to hold on. Conservation programs taught better ways to farm; soon plowmen were following the contours of the land and piling the soil in ridges to slow wind erosion. By 1940 the rains had returned, and the dust settled at last on a grim chapter of history.

An Oklahoma farmer digs out a dust-covered fence, April 1936.

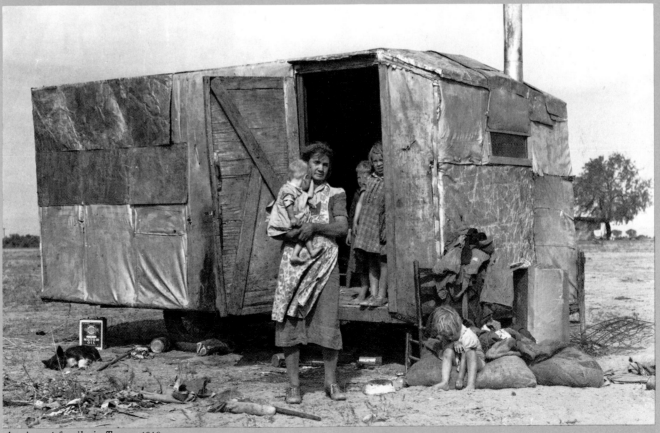

A migrant family in Texas, 1940

"My friends," began President Franklin Delano Roosevelt—and millions leaned closer to their radio sets for another of his "fireside chats" (left). Elected in 1932, FDR often used the talks to win support for government programs that put jobless people to work again. Some programs hired workers to build dams; others hired artists to paint murals (below). Under the "New Deal" the economy slowly began to revive.

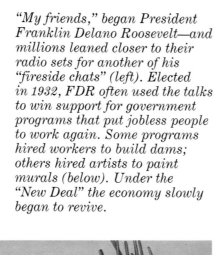

By the end of the year, Americans were losing confidence in the economy. Factories began to slash production and lay off workers. Streets became crowded with jobless and hungry men and women. The era known as the "Great Depression" had begun.

Jobless and Homeless

By 1932 about 12 million people were unemployed. This was nearly one out of every four American workers. Some cities had money to help them, but it soon ran out. No federal welfare programs existed. Millions of people had no place to turn except to charity. They went to church soup kitchens and Salvation Army shelters. Mayors and governors were flooded with appeals for help. "I have six little children," wrote a jobless Pennsylvanian to his governor in 1931. His wife was in the hospital, and he faced losing his home because he had no money for rent. "Where am I to go in the cold winter with my children?"

Thousands, like this worker, lost their homes. They sought shelter on vacant lots, by riverside swamps, and in public parks; they crammed into abandoned shacks; they pitched tents; they made sheds from packing crates, corrugated iron sheets, and cardboard boxes. Many other jobless people took off across the country, hopping freight trains, hitchhiking, or walking. They often slept on park benches and begged or scrounged for food. A song called "Wandering" told how it was:

I've been wandering far and wide,
I come with the wind, I drift with the tide,
And it looks like I'm never going to cease my wandering.

American farmers, too, were on the move in the early 1930s. A huge area of the southern Great Plains came to be called the Dust Bowl as high winds blew away fertile topsoil dried up by severe drought. Thousands of small farmers lost everything. Many abandoned their land, loaded their belongings onto jalopies, and joined the homeless bands trekking across the country. Some headed toward California, following rumors of jobs that weren't there.

Even Americans who had been able to hang on to their jobs were hit by the ailing economy. Their salaries got smaller, and many had to get used to a lower standard of living. The spirits of the American people were very low as the presidential election of 1932 approached. The Democratic Party chose Franklin Delano Roosevelt as its candidate. FDR, as he was called, was a distant cousin of former Republican President Theodore Roosevelt. FDR had started a promising political career in 1910 when he was elected to the New York State Senate and then was made assistant secretary of the Navy. In 1920 he ran for Vice President. A year later it looked as if Roosevelt's public life was at an end: Polio struck, and he lost the use of his legs. But Roosevelt, with the help of his wife, Eleanor, fought his handicap and made a comeback to public life; in 1928 he was elected governor of New York.

In his 1932 campaign for President, Roosevelt promised that if he were elected, the federal government would step in to end the Depression. "I pledge myself," he said, "to a new deal for the American people." Roosevelt was elected by a landslide. Nearly 23 million people voted for him while only 16 million voted for the incumbent President, Herbert Hoover. Roosevelt's efforts to put the country on the road to recovery were named the "New Deal."

Back to Work

Roosevelt and Congress created programs that put people to work building hospitals and highways, repairing school buildings, draining swamps, fixing public playgrounds, and constructing huge dams to control floods and to generate electric power for the countryside. A special program for young men, called the Civilian Conservation Corps, or CCC, gave hundreds of thousands of jobless, out-of-school youths a chance to leave the city and work in rural or wilderness areas caring for forests, cutting trails, building shelters and conservation facilities, and fighting forest fires.

Artists, musicians, and writers went to work, too. Inspired by Mexican art, the artists painted murals on the walls of government office buildings, high schools, hospitals, zoos, libraries, and post offices all over the country.

By the mid-thirties businesses were slowly beginning to recover and to hire more workers. Workers with a craft, such as carpentry or plumbing, could join a union belonging to an old, established association of craft unions, the American Federation of Labor, which would work to improve their wages. But the vast majority of workers in the nation's mass-production industries had no one to represent them. They were forced to accept low wages for long hours of hard work. In 1935, Congress passed one of the New Deal's most important laws, the National Labor Relations Act. Also known as the Wagner Act, after the New York senator who sponsored it, this law guaranteed the right of workers to organize and to bargain as a group with their bosses.

The act sparked a nationwide membership drive by a new kind of union organized by industry instead of by worker's craft. The Congress of Industrial Organizations, or CIO, enrolled thousands of auto workers, steelworkers, coal miners, longshoremen, and other industrial workers and began to conduct strikes for higher wages and better working conditions. Even with the law on their side, union leaders and members were sometimes harassed and beaten by factory owners and their strong-arm deputies. But the unions finally won recognition as the workers' representatives in bargaining with management.

With each passing year the Roosevelt Administration and Congress made the federal government more responsible for helping Americans recover from the Depression.

Factory workers organized into unions during the Depression and struck plant after plant for higher pay and better working conditions. When nonstrikers tried to drive through a picket line in Ohio in 1939, enraged strikers overturned one car. They would have flipped the one above, but for the clubs and tear gas of the police.

Farmers, too, were hit hard. With more food to sell than people could buy, they faced ruin. Dairymen like the one at right poured their milk on the ground, hoping a shortage would push the price up. Herdsmen killed their own animals; planters let fruit and vegetables rot in the fields, while jobless millions went hungry. The plight of some farmers improved in 1933 when Congress passed an agricultural-aid bill.

Eleanor Roosevelt
1884-1962

In the 1930s and 1940s, she appears in many snapshots, a tall, busy woman with a radiantly homely smile. In one, she is in a coal mine; in another, in the cabin of a sharecropper's family; and in another, in the White House opening thousands of letters. Her husband was the President, but Mrs. Franklin D. Roosevelt, who called herself the "ugly duckling" of a beautiful family, had her own kind of fame. She earned it by giving hope to a nation in Depression and a nation at war.

More snapshots: In her Red Cross uniform by a warplane named "Our Eleanor." Bent over the bed of a wounded soldier. On one trip to the war fronts, she traveled 25,000 miles in five weeks and went home to make hundreds of surprise phone calls to the mothers and girl friends of the soldiers she had seen.

When her husband died in 1945, Eleanor Roosevelt remained America's First Lady. The snapshots show her busier than ever: As a U.S. delegate to the new United Nations, she gently lectures the Soviet Union on peace and freedom. She helps to write the Universal Declaration of Human Rights. At 75, three years before her death, she teaches at a university, hosts a television show, still lectures all over the country, writes a newspaper and a magazine column. Her writing, like Eleanor herself, was plain with an honest beauty: "You have to accept whatever comes and the only important thing is that you meet it with courage and with the best that you have to give." The last snapshot: Borne to what will be her deathbed, she asks someone to thank the stretcher-bearers for doing "a magnificent job."

THOMAS B. ALLEN

Eleanor Roosevelt visiting a coal mine in Bellaire, Ohio, May 21, 1935

Nazi rally at Nuremberg, Germany, September 1937

Adolf Hitler salutes from his car (left) as Germany readies again for war. Playing on Germany's humiliation in World War I and the economic chaos that followed, der Führer—the Leader—led his National Socialist, or Nazi, Party to power. Under its swastika symbol his State Labor Service marches past in a stiff strut called the goose step. At this rally in Nuremberg in 1937, the marchers carry shovels to build a stronger fatherland. But soon Hitler's armies will take up guns and plunge much of the world into war.

An American cartoon (below) ridiculed Hitler's second-in-command—the bulging, medal-heavy Hermann Goering, chief of the Luftwaffe, *or air force. Italy's dictator, Benito Mussolini, and Japan's Prime Minister Hideki Tojo—Germany's Axis partners —follow him on chains. Death follows, too, its scythe poised for the bloodshed to come.*

They created programs to help homeowners keep their homes, to help farmers earn more money, to help young people, old people, small businesses, bankers. In so doing, they began to expand the size of the government and involve it in new activities. Some Americans, mainly Republicans, fiercely opposed the growth of the government and accused the President of trying to become a dictator. But during most of the thirties FDR had overwhelming support in Congress for his programs.

As bad as the Depression was for Americans, it was worse in many foreign countries and perhaps worst of all in Germany. In the decade following World War I, the Germans suffered widespread unemployment. Their money lost its value. People were bitter about the outcome of the war and especially about the harsh terms of the Versailles Treaty. Political unrest turned to violence as the private army of the National Socialist, or Nazi, Party battled in the streets with German Communists. The breakdown of the social order created ideal conditions for a politician who was willing to play on the fears and suspicions of the German people. Such a person was Adolf Hitler, the leader of the Nazis.

In 1933, Hitler seized power in Germany. Half genius, half madman, he applied his talents to the creation of a vast German empire. His plan was to conquer all of Europe. Hitler was a racist: He taught the Germans that they were a "Master Race." He believed that many of the world's peoples were inferior beings, whom the Germans had the right to conquer and to enslave or slaughter. Hitler and most Nazi officials were consumed with a special hatred for the Jewish people. Nazi propaganda blamed the Jews for Germany's defeat in World War I and for the present economic troubles.

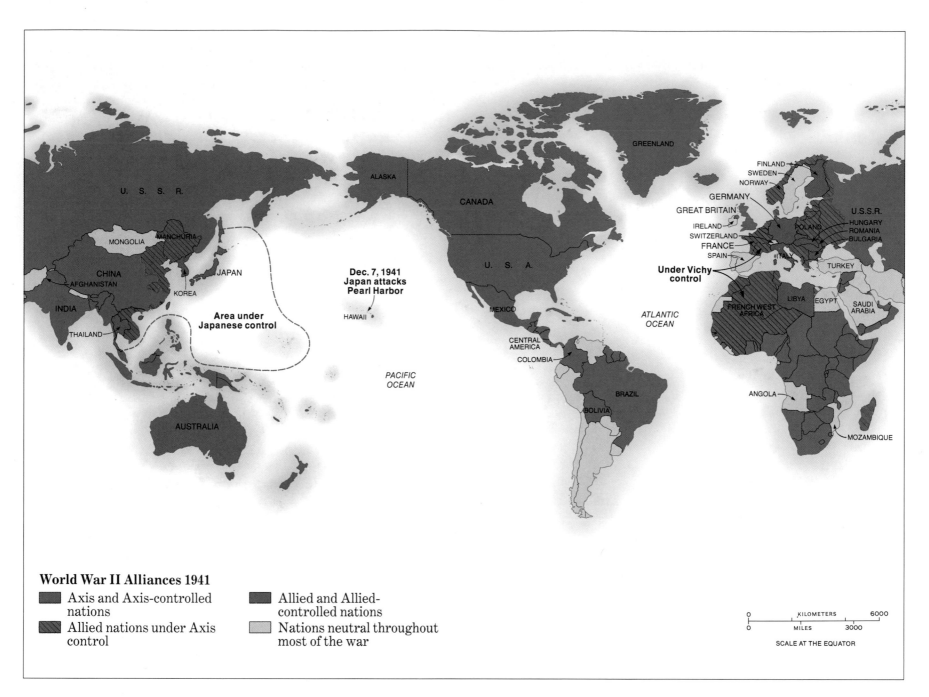

World War II Alliances 1941

- ■ Axis and Axis-controlled nations
- ▨ Allied nations under Axis control
- ■ Allied and Allied-controlled nations
- □ Nations neutral throughout most of the war

Dec. 7, 1941
Japan attacks
Pearl Harbor

Area under
Japanese control

Under Vichy
control

KILOMETERS
0   6000
0   3000
MILES
SCALE AT THE EQUATOR

A world again at war left few nations neutral in 1941, when Japan attacked Pearl Harbor and drew the United States into the conflict. The alliances that bound the warring nations had been taking shape for decades.

When Japan seized Manchuria from rebellion-torn China in 1931, some leaders spoke out, but none chose to act. While Hitler armed his new Germany, the allies who had beaten the old Germany watched, nervous but disunited. Many wanted to appease the aggressors, allowing them a few conquests in hopes they would not seek more.

But they did. Japan sought to rule "Greater East Asia." Italy claimed Ethiopia in 1935 and Albania in 1939. Germany and Italy, linked to form the Axis powers, grew bolder. Germany seized Austria, Czechoslovakia, Poland, Denmark, Norway, the Netherlands, Belgium—and in 1940, France. The Nazis ruled half of France; their French collaborators at Vichy, the other half.

As Europe exploded into war, Japan joined the Axis alliance and seized more European-held lands in Asia and the Pacific Ocean. The world took sides. From Denmark's 15,000 troops to America's 12 million, the Allies mustered a mighty force to face the Axis nations in fighting that spanned the globe.

Millions of ordinary Germans—soldiers and civilians—came to believe whatever Hitler told them. In obedience to Hitler's doctrines and commands, his armies embarked on a rampage of conquest and murder in which millions of innocent people became the victims of racist fury.

In the late 1930s, Hitler seized Austria and Czechoslovakia and made plans to invade Poland. Then in August 1939 he signed a non-aggression treaty with Joseph Stalin, the dictator of Russia. (Under Communism Russia became known as the Soviet Union). A secret part of this treaty said that after Hitler invaded Poland the two dictators would divide that country between them.

The Nazis Charge West

On September 1, Hitler's forces charged into Poland. They easily defeated the Polish Army, which sometimes faced German tanks, planes, and machine guns with troops mounted on horseback. Two days later Britain and France, which had pledged to come to Poland's defense, declared war on Germany. Then, on September 17, Stalin's armies marched into Poland and soon occupied the eastern half of the country. The Polish nation ceased to exist. Hitler, secure from attack by the Soviet Union, turned his full attention to the west. In the spring of 1940, the Germans overran Denmark, Norway, Holland, Belgium, Luxembourg, and even much of France.

After the fall of France, Hitler hoped that the British would realize the hopelessness of their cause. Instead British leader Winston Churchill rallied his people and vowed to keep fighting until Nazism was destroyed.

President Roosevelt watched the war in Europe with growing concern. For years he had felt that the Nazis posed a serious threat to democracy in Europe and throughout the world. But as a master politician, he had been careful not to state this view in public, for he knew that the majority of Americans strongly opposed getting involved in another European war. In the presidential election campaign of 1940, Roosevelt declared, "I have said this before, but I shall say it again and again and again: Your boys are not going to be sent into any foreign wars."

But the President hoped to change American public opinion in favor of helping the victims of aggression. This became more urgent after the German conquest of Western Europe. Roosevelt feared that the British would be unable to hold off the Germans alone.

Slowly he managed to persuade more and more Americans that Hitler's growing strength was a danger not only to Europe but also to the United States. He won the permission of Congress to send ships, planes, and weapons to the British under an agreement called "Lend-Lease."

On June 22, 1941, Hitler violated his treaty with Stalin by launching a massive attack against the Soviet Union. His aim was to destroy the Soviet Communist government and give the country's land to German settlers. As a result the Soviet Union joined Great

Youngsters take to the trenches as warplanes blaze across the skies of England in 1940. Children of crop pickers, they found refuge in these crude shelters dug right into the fields for handy access when the Germans raided. And raid they did: first the British seaports, then the air bases, and finally London and other civilian targets in a vain attempt to weaken Britain so Axis troops could invade. But Britain's Royal Air Force beat back the savage air attacks in several months of aerial combat known as the Battle of Britain. Said Prime Minister Winston Churchill of Britain's debt to its heroic pilots: "Never . . . was so much owed by so many to so few."

Britain as an ally. America, too, began to help the Russians fight Germany, by extending Lend-Lease aid to them. At first the German assault progressed well. But in October desperate Russian resistance and fierce weather brought it to a halt. German soldiers spent a long, bitter Russian winter with no warm clothing.

Germany and its ally, Italy, were not the only countries in the world following an aggressive policy. In East Asia, Japan had for many years cast eyes on China's rice and on the oil, rubber, and tin of Southeast Asia.

Japan had begun its expansion in 1931 by occupying Manchuria, in northern China. The Japanese invaded China's other northern provinces in 1937. In 1941 it looked like it would be easy for them to scoop up the Dutch and French colonies in Asia, now that Holland and France had come under the control of Japan's friend, Germany. The Asian possessions of Britain also would be easy pickings; the British were too involved in the European war to protect them. The only obstacle to further Japanese expansion was the United States.

President Roosevelt was determined to resist Japan's takeover of East Asia. He decided to pressure Japan to withdraw from the conquered territories by imposing an economic embargo. The U. S. stopped selling crucial war materials like oil, scrap iron, and steel to Japan. But instead of withdrawing, the Japanese planned new conquests. Relations between the U. S. and Japan grew very tense in the summer and fall of 1941. And when the United States cut off all trade with Japan and locked up, or "froze," the millions of dollars in Japanese funds deposited in this country, Japan decided on war. Some of FDR's critics accused him of deliberately provoking a Japanese attack to get the United States into the war.

The Japanese Attack

The Japanese decided to try to knock out the U. S. Pacific Fleet—the strength of American forces in the Far East—by launching a surprise attack. Early on the morning of Sunday, December 7, 1941, hundreds of Japanese planes took off from aircraft carriers and bombed the large American naval base at Pearl Harbor in Hawaii.

Within two hours the Pacific Fleet was crippled; more than 2,400 Americans died. Shortly after, Japan launched a devastating attack on the Philippines, which was under U. S. protection. On December 8, Congress declared war on Japan. Three days later Germany and Italy, Japan's Axis allies, declared war on the U. S.

During the wartime years, 1942 to 1945, American factories turned out tanks, trucks, planes, ships, and other military equipment in enormous quantities. Large numbers of women and black people came to work in the factories. Unemployment nearly disappeared. Many children spent these years with both parents away for much of the time—Dad in the Army, Mom in the war plant.

Almost every American family felt the war directly. To make sure that the armed forces had all the food, supplies, and vehicles they needed, the government put strict limits on how much of

"AIR RAID ON PEARL HARBOR," said the message that shocked America—"THIS IS NO DRILL." At the big U. S. naval base in Hawaii, Americans awoke to a surprise attack on Sunday, December 7, 1941, as Japanese planes attacked ships of the Pacific Fleet at their moorings. Sailors in a launch at left rescue a comrade from burning oil around the sinking battleship West Virginia.

Survivors honored the dead with garlands of flowers (above, lower) and resolved to avenge the worst military disaster in American history. Meanwhile, Japanese fighter planes called Zeros (top)—depicted by a Japanese artist—lined up to take off from a carrier deck for fresh targets in the Pacific Ocean.

273

certain items civilians could buy. Americans received coupons for a share of these goods. This program, called rationing, meant that families might have to do without meat once or twice a week. They might not have enough sugar for their coffee, or perhaps no coffee to put the sugar in. If the refrigerator broke, there might be no replacement parts until the war was over, and the family might have to start buying ice. Shoes had to last much longer than before. Auto tires were in short supply.

Young people helped the war effort in many ways. They grew vegetables for the family in "victory gardens." They collected scrap paper, tin cans, foil from chewing-gum wrappers, and other materials to be used in making planes, tanks, and weapons. They loaned part of their allowance to the government to help pay for the war. Each week, millions of schoolchildren bought a 25-cent stamp to paste in a special book. When the book was filled, it would be traded for a $25 Defense Savings Bond.

By calling on everyone to make sacrifices, the government hoped to instill a sense of solidarity and confidence in the American people. One sorry exception to this policy hurt Americans of Japanese descent. Shortly after the attack on Pearl Harbor, the U. S. War Department ordered the Army to round up almost every Japanese-American living on the West Coast—about 110,000 men, women, and children—and ship them off to spend the war in bleak, miserable camps in the interior of the country. Regardless of how long their families had held American citizenship, regardless of

Riveter at work, Nashville, Tennessee, 1942

V is for Victory, say the upraised fingers of youngsters on a mound of metal they collected in 1942. Children gathered scrap metal, paper, rubber, rags, even nylon stockings for use in making the goods of war. Women and blacks in large numbers filled a need for labor in the factories. One woman works on a bomber engine housing (opposite). Another drives rivets in a dive-bomber (above).

Schoolchildren in Butte, Montana, on a 1942 scrap drive

274

Worker at a California aircraft plant, 1942

America's Fast-Moving Fighting Men

Fighting men slug it out in gear designed for armies on the move. All of it is government issue, or "GI"—a term that soon came to mean the soldier himself. A GI battling in Europe in 1944 (left) fires a Garand rifle; in an instant it would reload itself for the next shot—firing eight shots before needing another eight-bullet "clip." His M1 helmet has an inner shell that stayed clean when he used the outer shell to wash up or dig a hole. In its netting he'd stick leaves for camouflage.

Green and brown blotches camouflage the helmet cover of a Marine (right) as he crouches to fire a Thompson submachine gun on a Pacific island in 1943. Along with a pistol, ammunition, and canteens, he carries a first-aid bandage in a packet to guard wounds from infection in the humid islands. Both men serve in the fastest-moving fighting force in history. Reporter Ernie Pyle witnessed firsthand "the constant roar of engines and the perpetual moving and the never settling down and the go, go, go, night and day."

Battlefields could be almost anywhere—and so could the jeep, named perhaps for the initials G. P. that stood for "general purpose" vehicle. This one jounces a howitzer to the front lines. Next it might carry wounded to the rear, serve a general as a mobile command post, pull planes around an airstrip, or even haul railroad cars. It seemed all but indestructible as it clawed through swamps and up slopes.

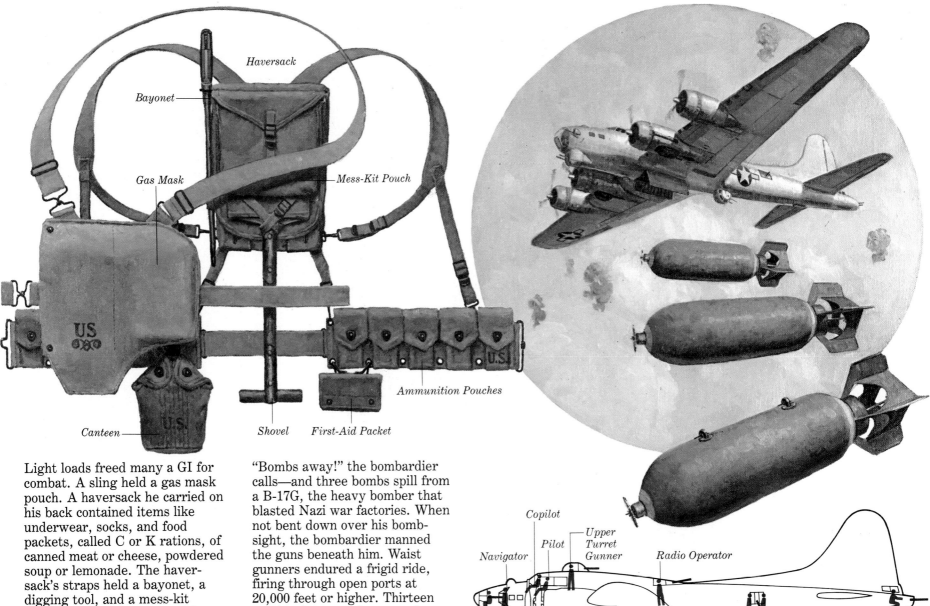

Haversack

Bayonet

Gas Mask

Mess-Kit Pouch

US

Ammunition Pouches

Canteen

Shovel   First-Aid Packet

Light loads freed many a GI for combat. A sling held a gas mask pouch. A haversack he carried on his back contained items like underwear, socks, and food packets, called C or K rations, of canned meat or cheese, powdered soup or lemonade. The haversack's straps held a bayonet, a digging tool, and a mess-kit pouch. A belt with ammunition pouches also held the canteen and first-aid packet.

"Bombs away!" the bombardier calls—and three bombs spill from a B-17G, the heavy bomber that blasted Nazi war factories. When not bent down over his bombsight, the bombardier manned the guns beneath him. Waist gunners endured a frigid ride, firing through open ports at 20,000 feet or higher. Thirteen guns and a rugged, armored frame earned this tough plane a name: Flying Fortress—yet one in three was shot down.

Copilot

Pilot

Upper Turret Gunner

Navigator

Radio Operator

Bombardier

"Belly" Gunner

Waist Gunners

Tail Gunner

World War II European Theater

- ■ Allied and allied-controlled nations
- ■ Axis and axis-controlled nations
- □ Greatest area under Axis military occupation
- □ Neutral nations
- → Allied advances
- ✪ Major battles

The highly mobile fighting forces of World War II swept through Europe as had no other armies in history. By 1942 the Axis powers, dominated by Germany, had overrun most of Western Europe and were headed east toward Stalingrad in the Soviet Union (1) and across North Africa toward the Suez Canal (2). But in November 1942 the Russians lashed back. In early 1943 they captured a German army and swept toward Romania (3); in 1944 they plunged into Poland (4). Meanwhile British troops in 1942 stopped Germany's Afrika Korps at El Alamein in Egypt (5); then British and American soldiers landed in western North Africa (6) and captured the Axis forces in 1943. Using Africa as a springboard, the Allies invaded Sicily (7) and battled their way up the Italian peninsula.

Allied invasions at Normandy (8) and southern France (9) opened new fronts in 1944. Soon Hitler's troops had retreated to their own soil. They struck back in the Ardennes region (10), but this "Battle of the Bulge" was the Germans' last offensive. American and Russian forces met near the town of Torgau (11). With Russian troops fighting in Berlin (12), Hitler chose suicide in April 1945, leaving aides to surrender in May.

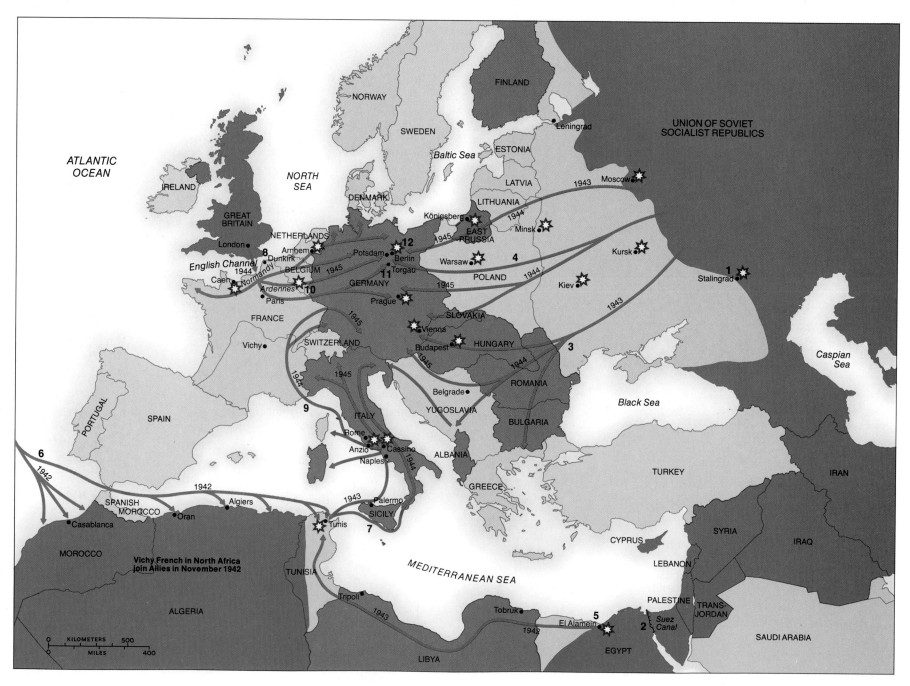

278

whether they had husbands or sons in the armed forces, they were considered potential traitors simply because of their Japanese ancestry. Most were forced to pack up and leave on only a few days' notice. They had to sell their homes and businesses to their non-Japanese fellow citizens for any price offered.

In early summer of 1942, Hitler returned to the attack on the Russian front, advancing as far as the city of Stalingrad (today called Volgograd). Hitler now controlled most of Europe. He also controlled part of North Africa. The Japanese ruled the Netherlands East Indies, French Indochina, the Philippine Islands, much of China, and a large portion of the Pacific Ocean.

But 1942 was the year that the Allies moved to counterattack. In

Events weigh heavily on British Prime Minister Winston Churchill in 1944 (below, right), as he and American Gen. Dwight D. Eisenhower inspect troops that will invade France on D-Day. Eisenhower commanded a huge force from many nations assembled for the invasion. Churchill doubted its chances. "My dear General," he said, "... liberate Paris by Christmas and none of us can ask for more." He got much more. Eisenhower's

forces freed Paris in August and by mid-December were fighting on the German border. In early spring they battled their way deep into enemy territory.

American infantrymen mop up enemy resistance in a small German town (left) as Allied forces bear down on Berlin.

U. S. infantrymen in a German town

early June the U. S. Navy sank four important Japanese aircraft carriers near Midway Island. That summer the U. S. Army Air Force joined Britain in a bombing campaign against the cities and factories of Germany.

In November 1942 a joint British-American invasion force landed in North Africa. The American general, Dwight D. Eisenhower, and British Gen. Bernard Montgomery cooperated in an offensive that swept the Germans out of North Africa six months later.

On November 19 the Russians moved from defense to attack at Stalingrad, then fought their way westward in 1943 and 1944, toward the borders of Germany.

On June 6, 1944, after months of preparation, the United States

D-Day—June 6, 1944

Months of training ended in hours of chaos as American and British troops struggled ashore on D-Day. German strategists had long expected this Allied invasion of France. For months their troops had been watching the English Channel, guns ready.

During the nighttime Channel crossing, balloons floated over the ships to thwart dive-bombers. P-51 Mustangs (1) and other Allied fighter-planes protected the ships, then zoomed inland to strafe German forces.

In a gray dawn at Normandy the attack roars in at last—the largest amphibious invasion in history. Its numbers seem overwhelming: nearly 5,000 ships and landing craft . . . 11,000 planes . . . 176,000 soldiers. But the attack covers nearly 60 miles of coastline. Here at a section of Omaha Beach with the code name "Dog Green," the American soldiers meet fierce resistance.

From the U.S.S. Thomas Jefferson (2) and other transports pours the invasion force itself—boxy landing craft (3) crammed with weapons and men. As support craft (4) lob shells and rockets at the defenders, the open boats churn toward the beach.

Many won't make it. A mortar shell shatters one (5). Another sinks far offshore (6), where soldiers laden with perhaps 50 pounds of equipment struggle to stay afloat. Tanks lumber ashore, brought in on big LCTs (Landing Craft, Tank) (7) that now back away. One is beached and takes a hit (8). Behind the wrecks, behind the enemy's log and steel obstacles, even behind the waves, soldiers find what shelter they can. Some dash to a seawall (9) across about 200 yards of beach under heavy fire from guns in the bluffs (10). Still the soldiers stream ashore. "The Americans barely held on by their eyelids," said British Gen. Bernard Montgomery. For the day's survivors, the Allied drive to Berlin had begun.

American tanks in Palermo, Italy, July 1943

and Great Britain launched a massive invasion of German-occupied Western Europe. More than 176,000 men in a great fleet of ships stormed the French coast at Normandy, supported by thousands of planes and paratroops. After a few days of heavy fighting, the Allies secured a shaky foothold, and within seven weeks over a million men had landed, along with an endless stream of jeeps, tanks, and guns. Through the rest of the year the Allied troops advanced, liberating Paris and then sweeping the Germans out of France.

By September the Allied forces had freed Belgium and Luxembourg. They were pushed back briefly in mid-December by a savage German counterattack, but in the spring of 1945 the offensive went forward again. Everything was going well for the Americans when tragic news rocked the country. President Franklin D. Roosevelt had died suddenly of a cerebral hemorrhage on the morning of April 12. FDR had spent more time in office than any other President. The man who had been elected President four times and had led the country out of its worst economic depression and through most of its worst war was gone. A grieving Vice President Harry Truman took the oath of office as President that same day. While the nation mourned, the war went on.

On April 25, American soldiers advancing eastward and Russian soldiers fighting their way west met near the German town of Torgau. On April 30, with Russians fighting in the streets of Berlin, Hitler committed suicide in his bunker. A week later the war in Europe was over.

Victory! Crowds jam New York's Times Square (left) on May 7, 1945, to await the official announcement of Germany's surrender. A replica of the Statue of Liberty raises her torch as people in the crowd raise two fingers for the victory sign. The celebration was a day early. Not until the next morning did President Harry Truman confirm the news: "The flags of freedom fly all over Europe." Thus the U.S. finally celebrated the victory in Europe—V-E Day —on May 8, and turned its full attention to the war against Japan.

In July 1943, American soldiers liberated Palermo (opposite), largest city on the Italian island of Sicily. Citizens spilled into the streets to watch and welcome. German defenders had left the city, but many Italian soldiers stayed behind to surrender to the Americans.

On July 25, Mussolini fell from power. The Italians surrendered in September 1943, but German troops in Italy kept fighting the Allies. From Sicily, the Allied armies pushed north, driving the stubborn enemy up the Italian peninsula in some of the bloodiest fighting of the war. It took eight months to advance only 100 miles from Naples to Rome.

Japanese planes fall out of a smoke-filled sky as the American aircraft carrier U.S.S. Hornet fights for its life near the Santa Cruz Islands in the South Pacific. There planes roared off the flattop decks of aircraft carriers to attack enemy vessels beyond the horizon.

One pilot in this picture makes a fateful choice: With a final effort he rams his crippled dive-bomber into the doomed Hornet's signal bridge. By late 1944 desperate Japanese forces turned such suicide attacks into missions of honor. Volunteer pilots, called kamikaze— *"divine wind," took off in planes loaded with bombs and gasoline. By the war's end their dives had sent 34 ships to the bottom; more than 300 vessels bore scars from the "divine wind."*

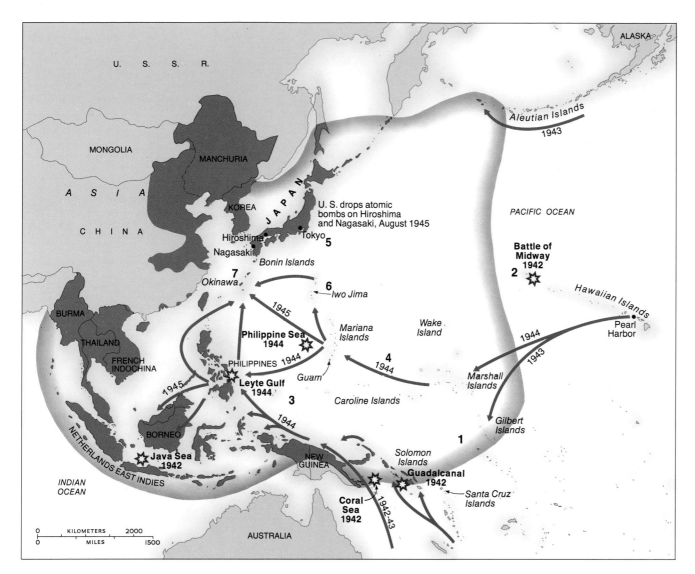

**World War II
Pacific Theater 1942-45**

☆ Major naval battle
→ Allied advance
▇ Land taken by
Japanese, 1931-42
▇ Limit of Japanese
control in the Pacific,
1942

*Japan held much of the Pacific
Ocean in 1942; its rule reached
some 4,500 miles from mainland
Asia to the Solomon and Gilbert
Islands (1). Americans needed a
victory to turn the tide—and got
one near Midway Island (2) as
carrier-based planes defeated a
Japanese fleet sent to seize the
island as a base. Before long
Americans were fighting from
island to island—one thrust
headed toward the Philippines
(3), another, through the central
Pacific (4)—to bring troops and
bombers within range of Tokyo
(5). Islands like Iwo Jima (6)
and Okinawa (7) saw bloody
battles as the Allies drove by
land, sea, and air toward Japan
and victory in 1945.*

*Gen. Douglas MacArthur (below)
walks with Allied officers
on Borneo Island. His strategy
guided Allied troops as they
battled for island bases.*

General MacArthur (right of center) and Allied officers, Borneo, 1945

As the Allied forces drove deep into Germany, they liberated
hundreds of thousands of prisoners of war and slave laborers. Now
the German concentration camps revealed the awful truth of the
Holocaust, as Hitler's campaign of human destruction came to be
called. Into stockades equipped with guards, savage dogs, machine
guns, and electrified fences, Hitler had dragged millions of people—Jews, gypsies, Communists, anti-Nazi Germans, and others
—to work as slaves or simply to be slaughtered. Here the Nazis
carried out much of their plan to murder every Jew in Europe.
They killed thousands of men, women, and children a day—a total
of nearly six million victims—using mostly poison gas and then
burned their bodies in specially designed ovens. R. W. Thompson,
correspondent for the *London Sunday Times*, was with British soldiers when they captured the camp of Bergen-Belsen and began to
bury the bodies they found: "Stand with me," he wrote, "at the
brink of this death pit. . . . It is about 30 feet deep . . . nearly filled
now with human bodies. . . . Here are girls, boys, men, women,
naked, half-naked, upside down . . . some staring up to the sky,
others with their heads buried in human remains."

285

A city died as an atomic bomb nicknamed "Little Boy" leveled Hiroshima, Japan (right), on August 6, 1945. "We had seen the city when we went in," said B-29 pilot Paul W. Tibbets, Jr., "and there was nothing to see when we came back." The blast, which equaled 12,500 tons of high explosive, came from an atomic charge about the size of a grapefruit. About 78,000 people were killed outright; thousands more died later. A victim told of "the intolerable pain of their burns. . . . Every living thing was petrified in . . . indescribable suffering."

The grim cloud below recalls pilot Tibbets's words, "There was the mushroom cloud growing up, and we watched it blossom . . . black and boiling underneath." Facing ruin, Japan surrendered on August 14. Ceremonies aboard the battleship Missouri on September 2 (opposite) ended history's most destructive war.

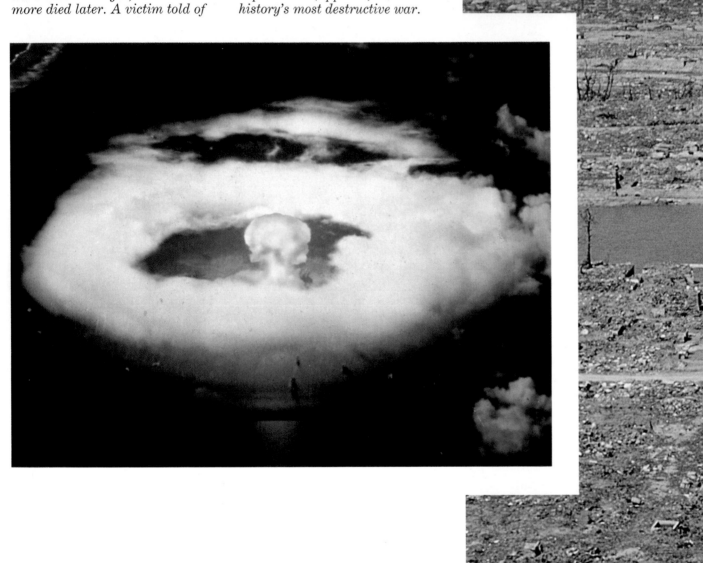

Hiroshima, Japan, eight months after the atomic bomb attack

General MacArthur accepts Japanese surrender, Tokyo Bay, September 2, 1945.

In the war against Japan, American military leaders wanted to bomb the enemy as they did in Europe. But at first the Japanese home islands were beyond the reach of planes from the nearest American air bases. The U. S. forces, therefore, started a campaign of recapturing Pacific Ocean islands from Japan, working their way closer to the enemy's home base.

Island after island fell to the Americans, and at the same time the U. S. Navy won a string of victories over the Japanese Navy, sinking aircraft carriers, battleships, cruisers, and other warships. By the summer of 1944 the Americans had advanced close enough to reach Japan with bombers, and Japanese cities began to go up in flames. Over the following months Japan's situation became hopeless, but the country's military leaders wanted to fight to the end to resist an invasion of their homeland.

The United States now faced an awesome decision. A team of engineers and scientists had spent three years creating a new, unbelievably powerful weapon, the atomic bomb. Should the United States now use this terrible new weapon against Japan? Some scientists who had worked on the bomb said, *No.* But the President's military advisers warned that if the United States were to invade Japan, hundreds of thousands of Americans and Japanese would be killed. They urged President Truman to use the bomb and knock the Japanese out of the war.

On August 6 an American bomber, the *Enola Gay,* dropped an atomic bomb on the city of Hiroshima. The bomb blotted out the city in a blinding flash. About 78,000 people died at once. Tens of thousands more would die in the months and years after from wounds and radiation sickness. On August 9 the U. S. dropped its only other atomic bomb—this time on the city of Nagasaki. Five days later Japan surrendered. World War II was over. A new era was about to begin—one haunted by the knowledge that in another such war atomic weapons could destroy the world.

Pieces of Our Past
1914-1945

Gathered by the radio, a farm family of 1925 tunes in a show. Broadcasting was just five years old; soon it spellbound millions with newscasts, concerts, dramas, sermons, even exercises.

Born in 1928, Mickey Mouse starred in the first movie cartoon to use sound: *Steamboat Willie*. Cartoonist Walt Disney spoke his lines—and rose to fame with the mouse beloved around the world.

Kewpie dolls sprang from 1909 sketches of chubby Cupids. Beloved by children and adults alike, they rose to worldwide fame in the 1910s and 1920s.

Marbles have filled pockets for generations. Comic-strip characters—Betty Boop and Little Orphan Annie—smile from two of these, as they did from newspapers of the 1920s.

Luxury on wheels, a Packard phaeton made any trip a joyride in 1929. Cars, plain and fancy, turned Americans into travelers, whether on a cross-country tour or just out for a Sunday drive.

Jukebox (opposite) played 1940s hits: show tunes, country music, swing. This one plays 24 records at a nickel a song. Dancers called "hepcats" did the jitterbug to big-band swing tunes.

Diners like the "Palace" dotted roadsides in the 1920s. Cooks served "hounds on an island" (franks and beans) and "Adam and Eve on a raft" (two poached eggs on toast).

A 1924 electric mixer named the "cyclone" frothed up milkshakes at a soda fountain. A growing craze for kitchen appliances in the 1930s sent customers after home-model mixers.

Shirley Temple became the nation's darling as she danced and sang in 1930s films. Little girls wished for Shirley Temple dolls, books, soap, ribbons, and hairdos with 56 curls.

In late April 1945, even before World War II had ended, representatives from 50 nations gathered in San Francisco, California, to draw up a charter for a new organization called the United Nations. Like the unsuccessful League of Nations that followed World War I, the United Nations was created to help countries find ways to avoid war, to solve conflicts by peaceful means. The United States was a founder of the UN. Another powerful member was the United States' World War II ally, the Soviet Union.

Would the United Nations succeed? A big part of the answer lay with these two countries. During the war they had set aside distrust from earlier years to fight Nazi Germany. Would they, through the United Nations, promote world peace?

The prospects looked poor. Each side's prewar suspicion of the other soon reappeared. The U. S. government was unhappy about Russian actions in Eastern Europe. Soviet dictator Joseph Stalin refused to withdraw his Red Army from the Eastern European countries it had overrun in pushing back the Germans during World War II. Stalin had promised to allow these countries to choose their own forms of government through free elections. Instead, within four years after the war, the Russians forced Poland, Czechoslovakia, Bulgaria, Romania, and Hungary to adopt Communist governments that took their orders from Moscow. In Germany, which the allied powers had occupied at the end of the war, the Russian-occupied eastern part became Communist. Communists also took over Yugoslavia and Albania. Outrage at these events turned the United States bitterly against the Soviet Union.

President Truman guided the U. S. transition from wartime to peace. He proposed many social reform measures under a new, "Fair Deal." He took a firm stand against the spread of Communism abroad and asked Congress for a massive aid plan to help Europe recover from the war. Beginning in 1948 this plan, named for Secretary of State George C. Marshall, sent billions of dollars in money and materials to Western Europe.

For its part, the Soviet Union feared America's military power—above all, the atomic bomb. The Soviet Union charged that the Marshall Plan was meant as a hostile act. And it resented American protests against Soviet policies in Eastern Europe. The Russians had suffered horribly during the war from German aggression—some 15 to 20 million of them had died. Stalin felt fully justified in seeking to defend the Soviet Union against future attack by controlling the small countries that lay between it and Germany.

The distrust and dislike, so strong on both sides, came to be called the "Cold War." Each side contested for allies in this non-shooting war. In the late 1940s, the contest centered in war-torn Western Europe, where strong and popular Communist parties—especially in Italy—threatened for a time to win power through free elections. In later decades, as scores of new countries around the world gained independence from colonial rule, the contest shifted to them. Political commentators lumped these developing nations together in a so-called "Third World" to distinguish them from the two other "Worlds," one "Free" and one Communist.

Happiness is a new pair of shoes, sent to this Austrian orphan by the children of the American Junior Red Cross. The havoc of World War II left Europeans in desperate need of food, clothing, and medicine. The American Red Cross distributed tons of supplies to them. Between 1948 and 1951, the U. S.-sponsored Marshall Plan sent some 12 billion dollars to help rebuild Western Europe.

Post-World War II Alliances

North Atlantic Treaty Organization (NATO) countries

Warsaw Pact countries

By 1949 a number of countries were aligned in two opposing groups (above). The United States and the Soviet Union, leaders of the two sides, had been allies during World War II and had worked together to form the United Nations (right) in 1945. But mutual distrust began to change allies into enemies. As the war ended, the Soviet Union began to take control of the Eastern European countries its armies occupied. It set up Communist governments in each country, creating a political boundary that Great Britain's Winston Churchill called the Iron Curtain. Soviet expansion alarmed the Western allies, and thus the "Cold War" began —a tense but nonviolent relationship between countries.

Germany—including the city of Berlin—had been divided into four zones, controlled by the U.S., France, Great Britain, and the Soviet Union. The Soviet zone surrounded Berlin. In June 1948 the Soviet Union cut off all land traffic into and out of the zones of Berlin occupied by the Western allies, hoping to force them to leave. But the allies responded with a gigantic airlift (far right), delivering food and supplies to stranded Berliners. After 11 months, the Soviet Union ended its blockade. In 1949 the U.S. and 11 other countries formed the North Atlantic Treaty Organization (NATO) to protect each other from Communist aggression. In 1955, when West Germany was admitted to NATO, Soviet-dominated countries banded together under the Warsaw Pact.

The United Nations

An allied plane brings supplies to Berlin in 1948.

In 1949 most Western European countries, the United States, and Canada formed a military alliance, the North Atlantic Treaty Organization, called NATO for short. It created a united front to guard against the possibility of a Communist attack.

Two other events in 1949 stepped up the tension between the United States and the Soviet Union. In September the Soviet Union exploded its first atomic bomb. The second event was the success of the Communist revolution in China. After years of civil war, the Chinese Communist armies swept the Nationalist government of Chiang Kai-shek off the Chinese mainland. Chiang took what was left of his army and fled to the island of Taiwan.

With China's vast population now under the Red flag, some American officials feared that many other countries would, like dominoes, fall to Communism. The string of Communist successes left the American people wondering what was happening and why. There were no simple answers; situations differed in different parts of the world. But some American politicians thought they knew the answer—or at least had an answer, true or not, that the public might accept. The Communists were making so many gains, they said, because American traitors were helping them.

In February 1950, Republican Senator Joseph McCarthy of Wisconsin gave a speech in Wheeling, West Virginia. He claimed that the U. S. government was full of secret Communists who were carrying out the orders of the Russians. He accused these people, most of whom he did not and would not name, of being spies and

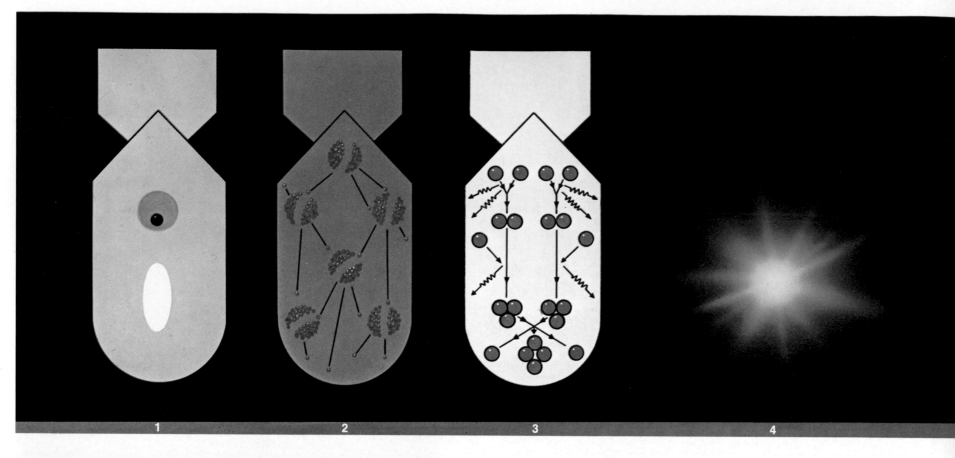

1   2   3   4

North American Aerospace Defense Command (NORAD), Colorado

saboteurs and of belonging to a Communist conspiracy to take over the United States. McCarthy's astonishing claims made headline news. He said Communists were also in colleges and universities, in the movie business, in labor, in industry—even in the new television business. All these enemies of America, said McCarthy, must be tracked down, investigated, exposed, and fired from their jobs, if the United States was to be safe.

A few months after McCarthy's speech, Communist North Korean forces, with Soviet support, invaded South Korea, an ally of the United States. At the request of the U. S., the United Nations condemned the invasion and asked its members to help South Korea. Over the next three years, troops under a United Nations command (but mostly provided by the U. S.) fought a bitter, bloody war against the North Koreans, who were assisted by hundreds of thousands of Communist Chinese soldiers. A truce stopped the war in 1953, leaving the border between the two Koreas just about where it had been before the war.

Senator McCarthy's warnings were made to seem more real by the actual face-to-face warfare between Americans and Communists in Korea. He became the leader of an anti-Communist crusade that obsessed the United States. But McCarthy's way of opposing Communism was to make wild accusations that everybody read in the papers. He ordered people to appear before his investigating subcommittee to answer questions about their beliefs, their friends, their activities. Some people answered the questions,

Washington, D.C., area

American scientists were the first to create a hydrogen bomb. The drawings above show its stages of explosion. The bomb (1) consists of a trigger (black), and three kinds of explosives: chemical (purple), atomic (gray), and hydrogen (yellow). The trigger and the chemical explosive touch off the atomic explosive, ripping apart its nuclei (2). Searing heat results, which sets off the hydrogen explosive. Particles called protons collide and stick together (3), producing lethal radiation, shown as wavy lines. The bomb becomes a blinding flash (4). Then crushing air and ground waves fan out (5). A column of scorching air sweeps upward (6), carrying disintegrated earth and other matter. Finally, a mushroom cloud forms (7); deadly radioactive particles rain down from it.

Computers at NORAD (far left)—the North American Aerospace Defense Command— inside a Colorado mountain would give early warning of an enemy nuclear attack. An aerial photo of the Washington, D.C., area (left) helps show the effects of a hydrogen explosion. If a small bomb were dropped on the Pentagon, America's military headquarters (center circle), the building would vaporize instantly. Everyone within 0.7 miles of the blast would be roasted by a fireball. About 98 percent of the people within the next mile would die at once from radiation, fire, and fierce wind. Buildings would be crushed or tossed skyward. Half the people living three miles from the Pentagon would die instantly; another 40 percent would die soon afterward from burns or radiation poisoning. Five miles out, half the population would be injured or die. If many bombs were dropped, drifting radioactive dust could block the sunlight, causing all plant and animal life to freeze.

The Korean War

On June 25, 1950, troops from Communist North Korea suddenly invaded South Korea. United Nations forces, mostly Americans, rushed to South Korea's defense. The first Communist surge pushed the UN defense line (1) to the country's southeast corner. U. S. Marines landed at Inch'ŏn to launch a counterattack that pushed far to the north (2). Then, in October, China sent troops to aid North Korea, forcing a UN retreat below Seoul (3), the South's capital. After three years of war, a truce was signed at P'anmunjŏm. South Korea remained free of Communist rule. The cease-fire line (4) became the new border dividing the two Koreas.

Their country and their lives torn apart by war, Korean children (left) huddle in trenches with U. S. Marines. More than 54,000 Americans and 522,000 South Koreans died in the war.

some didn't; in most cases it didn't make much difference. To many Americans, McCarthy, as a Senator, was one of the most respectable, patriotic men in the country. If he suspected someone of being a Communist, people thought, there must be something to it. In this kind of atmosphere, just being called up before McCarthy's questioners was usually enough to ruin a person's good name and often cost people their jobs. McCarthy's tactics disturbed many of his fellow politicians, but most of them feared to criticize him. If they made him angry, he might accuse *them* of being Communists.

After four years of such attacks, McCarthy finally went too far. In his search for new and more sensational "exposures," he finally forced Congress to stand up to him. The Senate held hearings on McCarthy's attack on the U. S. Army, and the whole country got a chance to watch on television. For the first time McCarthy was shown to the public as the fraud and bully he really was. Late in 1954 the Senate voted to condemn McCarthy for his behavior. His power to terrorize innocent Americans was ended.

New Tensions in the Cold War

The hostility between the United States and the Soviet Union took a more dangerous turn in 1952 and 1953, when each country successfully tested a hydrogen bomb, a far more powerful bomb than those used against Hiroshima and Nagasaki. These nuclear tests and the others that followed spurred an arms race that continues to this day.

As the fifties wore on, the degree of bad feeling between the United States and the Soviet Union varied from incident to incident. In 1959 relations relaxed enough for the Russian leader, Nikita Khrushchev, to visit the United States. But in 1960 the Soviet Union detected an American U-2 spy plane flying over its territory and shot it down. Premier Khrushchev used the incident to boycott a planned meeting of the leaders of major nations in Paris. The same year the new revolutionary leader of nearby Cuba, Fidel Castro, began to accept aid from the Soviet Union and to sound more and more like a Communist himself.

In 1961, Khrushchev and the new American President, John F. Kennedy, did meet. Kennedy was young, handsome, intelligent, and witty. He was tremendously popular, especially with young people. He offered vigorous leadership, and he encouraged all Americans to participate in public life. One of Kennedy's most inspiring new programs was the Peace Corps; many dedicated men and women signed up to help developing countries improve their farms, schools, and medical care.

Unfortunately, Kennedy's meeting with Khrushchev produced no improvement in relations between the United States and the Soviet Union. Shortly after the meeting the Russians built a high, ugly wall across the heart of Berlin, Germany's capital, which the Allies had divided after the war into four zones of military occupation. The Berlin Wall was to stop people from leaving Communist East Berlin for the city's democratic western zones.

Early in 1950 Wisconsin Senator Joseph McCarthy (below) began a stormy crusade against Communism in America. He claimed that the United States government employed people who were known to be Communists. McCarthy had no proof for his charges, but many people believed him. Americans had become afraid of Communism, worried by stories about spies and by news that the Soviet Union had exploded its first atomic bomb. In 1954 the Senate held hearings about McCarthy's charges against the U. S. Army. Americans watched on television and saw for themselves McCarthy's reckless and irresponsible behavior. In one hearing, an outraged lawyer said to McCarthy, "Have you . . . no sense of decency?" McCarthy's influence ended after the Senate later voted to condemn his behavior.

Seen from West Berlin, the lights of Communist-controlled East Berlin glow beyond the Berlin Wall (left). A guard (below) peers over the Wall. Barbed wire and more walls surround the rest of West Berlin, making it an island of democracy in the middle of Communist East Germany.

With such barricades the Soviet Union hoped to halt the flow of refugees from East Berlin into the democratic zones of the city. In 1961 a meeting was held between Soviet Premier Nikita Khrushchev and U. S. President John F. Kennedy (opposite). Khrushchev insisted that all allied troops must leave West Berlin. Kennedy refused, believing that the Soviets would take control if the allies departed. Two months later, the Soviet Union shocked the people of both Berlins—and the world—by building the Berlin Wall.

Some sections of the Wall, such as the one shown at left, consist of three parts: the concrete wall itself, barely visible at the bottom of the picture; a central "death strip" lined with mines and tank traps; and an inner fence. Today, in spite of great danger, East Germans are still escaping to the West. In one daring feat, a circus performer, aided by a relative in West Berlin, walked a tightrope strung above the Wall.

Relations reached their most dangerous point in October 1962 when the United States discovered that the Russians were secretly installing nuclear missiles in Cuba, less than 100 miles from Florida. President Kennedy ordered a naval blockade, threatening to stop any Soviet ship trying to bring more weapons to Cuba. For about a week the world faced the direct threat of nuclear war as several Russian freighters neared the blockade line. Then Khrushchev backed down and began to remove the missiles from Cuba. After that terrifying episode, the two sides came together in 1963 and agreed to limit the testing of nuclear weapons to under the ground. They also set up a direct telephone "hot line" between the White House and the Kremlin for use in times of crisis.

While the Cold War and the threat of Communism captured the attention of most Americans in the postwar period, one group of citizens was launching a movement for social reform. These were black Americans, especially those living in the South. Life for southern blacks was much the same after World War II as it had been since the end of Reconstruction. They did the hardest, dirtiest

The Soviet Union's Premier Khrushchev (left) with President Kennedy in Vienna, Austria, 1961

American corn pours into a barge (above) for shipment to the world's hungry. As a goodwill measure—and to open new export markets—the United States began in the 1950s to offer surplus food to poor nations. Help also went abroad in the form of Peace Corps volunteers. Established in 1961, the Peace Corps sent teachers, nurses, and technicians to Third World lands. By 1966 some 15,500 volunteers were serving in 51 countries. At right, a Peace Corps worker teaches farming methods to people of the Pacific island of Borneo.

work for the lowest wages. And state and local segregation laws, known as "Jim Crow" laws, kept black people apart from the rest of society simply because of their race.

Black children were segregated into separate schools that were usually old, crowded, and shabby. Black people could not use most public libraries, beaches, or swimming pools. They often could not attend the same movie theaters as whites or drink from the same water fountains. When traveling by train, they had to ride in separate coaches; in city buses they had to sit in the back.

Segregated schools existed not just in the South, but in other parts of the country too. Linda Brown, for example, went to an all-black elementary school in Topeka, Kansas, even though she lived in a racially mixed neighborhood. One day in 1950, Linda's father asked the principal of the all-white school in the neighborhood to admit her. The principal refused. So Mr. Brown, along with other black parents, went to court to challenge school segregation. The National Association for the Advancement of Colored People (NAACP), which had for years been battling in the courts for fair treatment for black people, sent lawyers to help Mr. Brown and the other parents.

The federal court in Kansas judged in favor of the white school principal—in favor of segregation—so the NAACP lawyers appealed the decision all the way to the U. S. Supreme Court. Linda's case became famous as *Brown* versus *Board of Education*. On Monday, May 17, 1954, Chief Justice Earl Warren read the Court's decision in Linda's case. The state of Kansas and the city of Topeka were violating the Constitution when they sent black children off to a separate school just because their skin was dark. Equal treatment of all American schoolchildren regardless of their race or color, said the Court, wasn't just somebody's dream; it was the law of the land.

The next big event in what was to become the "Civil Rights Movement" involved Mrs. Rosa Parks, a black woman who lived in Montgomery, Alabama. On December 1, 1955, Mrs. Parks finished her working day at a Montgomery department store, caught the bus home, and took a seat at the front of the black section. As more whites boarded the bus, the driver ordered Mrs. Parks to get up and give her seat to a white passenger. But Rosa Parks was tired from a hard day's work, and she didn't see why she should have to let someone else have her seat. She refused to get up. The driver called the police, who arrested her.

Outraged by the incident, Montgomery's black community organized the Montgomery Improvement Association (MIA) and elected a 26-year-old minister named Martin Luther King, Jr., as

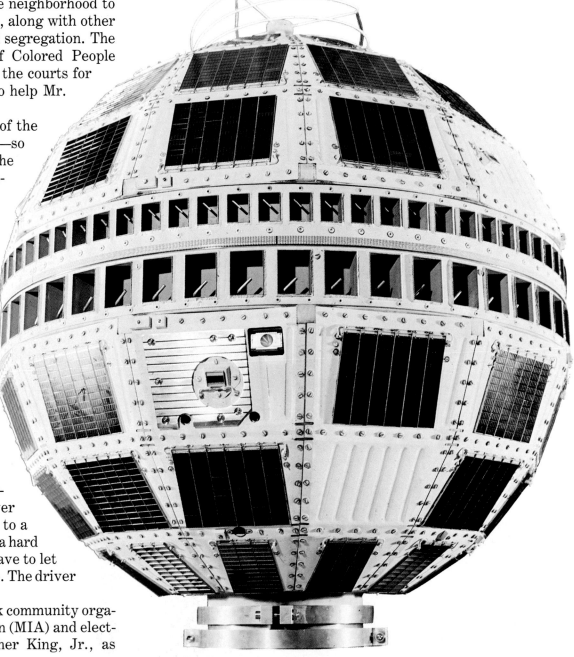

The United States launched a new era of communications when it rocketed the experimental Telstar satellite (below) into Earth orbit in 1962. The 30-inch sun-powered sphere relayed the first live telecast from the U. S. to Europe. It also relayed telephone and telegraph signals. Telstar, and the many other communications satellites that followed later, instantly linked people living thousands of miles apart.

The Race to Space

John Glenn describes his orbital flight to President Kennedy, 1962.

Beep ... beep ... beep ... beep.... The eerie signals beamed down to Earth from the heavens. The date was October 4, 1957. Orbiting overhead was the first human-made satellite, called Sputnik—and it was Russian. The United States' chief rival had taken the first step toward exploring outer space. The next month the Soviet Union tested the effects of space travel on living creatures by sending a dog, named Laika, into orbit.

Ashamed and alarmed at being outdone, America scrambled to catch up. Thus began the race to conquer space.

In January 1958 the U. S. sent into orbit a satellite of its own. In July the U. S. created a center for the exploration of space, called the National Aeronautics and Space Administration, or NASA. But for several years, America seemed to be always just a step behind.

In April 1961 the Soviet Union launched a man, Yuri Gagarin, into space. In May, Alan Shepard became the first American in space with his 15-minute flight in a capsule named *Freedom 7*. Then President John F. Kennedy gave the space program a clear mission. He declared that America would land a man on the moon before the end of the decade.

Within a year John Glenn circled the Earth tucked inside a Project Mercury capsule.

Still, the Soviet Union won the early glory. It had already sent the first man into orbit—and,

Watching the first launch of an American astronaut, Florida, 1961

A lunar rock on display

Apollo astronaut James Irwin salutes on the moon, 1971.

later, would send the first woman. Also, a Soviet spacecraft was the first to land intact on the moon.

But on July 20, 1969, an American—Neil Armstrong—put the first human shoeprint on the moon's surface. As he planted his foot, he said, "That's one small step for a man, one giant leap for mankind." President Kennedy's vow was kept. People the world over marveled and applauded.

The United States has continued since then to explore space. One vehicle, the shuttle *Columbia*, can be used over and over. As America's capabilities grow, one thing becomes clear: Our ventures into space have only begun.

First American "walk" in space, 1965

Shuttle Columbia *rockets into space, 1981.*

A snapping police dog rips a marcher's trousers during a civil rights demonstration held in Birmingham, Alabama, in May 1963. The blacks, including many children, had planned a peaceful protest, but the police attacked them with dogs, clubs, and fire hoses. The blacks' demands included the right to use any park, restaurant, or other public facility in Birmingham. Photographs such as this one aroused sympathy and support for the Civil Rights Movement across the nation.

Many white people helped the blacks in their struggle for equal rights. One white Southerner in Birmingham admitted, "If I were in their shoes I might do the same thing. I think maybe we've handled it wrong."

president. The MIA vowed not to ride on city buses until the city and the bus company agreed to let all people sit on a first come, first served basis. It set up carpools to carry people to and from their jobs. For more than a year the black people of Montgomery rode in cars or walked while the buses rolled along nearly empty.

In May 1956 the MIA went to federal court and asked that Montgomery's Jim Crow bus law be struck down. This case, just like *Brown* versus *Board of Education*, went all the way to the Supreme Court. In November the Court announced its judgment: A city cannot set people apart on its buses. Montgomery's black people had won. The buses again filled with passengers; blacks and whites sat side by side.

The Army Integrates Central High

In September 1957 nine black students tried to enroll at all-white Little Rock Central High School in Arkansas. But Orville Faubus, governor of Arkansas, ordered Arkansas National Guardsmen, armed with rifles and bayonets, to block the black children from entering the school. When 15-year-old Elizabeth Eckford came up to the school gate, a soldier barred the way. As she turned back, a jeering, howling mob gathered around her. The next day Americans saw the front page picture: Elizabeth, calmly and with great dignity, walking past the crowd of hate-filled faces. They didn't see her reach a bench at the bus stop, sink down upon it, and begin to sob. Three weeks later President Dwight D. Eisenhower sent U. S. Army troops to Little Rock to enforce the decree of the Supreme Court—that black students must be guaranteed their right to go to the same schools as white students.

Early in 1960 young blacks decided to take action to end Jim Crow laws. They began to defy segregation laws by "sitting-in" at restaurants, lunch counters, theaters, churches, libraries, hotels, and beaches. "Sitting-in" meant that they stood or sat in public places where state or local law forbade them to be. All across the South, police struck back against the sit-in movement. By April 1960 they had arrested more than 3,000 demonstrators. In jail the young people linked hands and sang a protest song that became an unofficial anthem of the Civil Rights Movement:

> *We shall overcome, We shall overcome,*
> *We shall overcome some day;*
> *Deep in my heart, I do believe,*
> *We shall overcome some day.*

On Easter weekend of 1960, more than 300 leaders of the sit-in campaign met at Shaw University in North Carolina to discuss setting up an organization to carry on the battle against Jim Crow laws. They called their new group the Student Nonviolent Coordinating Committee—or SNCC for short. For the next five years, SNCC took the lead throughout the South in a struggle that had two goals: One was to fight discrimination in public establishments.

Martin Luther King, Jr.
1929-1968

"**P**ut on your marching shoes. Walk with me into a new dignity," challenged a young minister in 1956. His powerful voice inspired black citizens of Montgomery, Alabama, to walk to their jobs until the city integrated the buses. And it inspired blacks and whites everywhere to join his crusade for equality.

Martin Luther King, Jr., was a man with a dream. He dreamed of help for the poor—on dirt farms in the South, in ghettos in the North. He dreamed of peace.

Big dreams, yes. But Martin King relished big ideas. As a boy in Atlanta, Georgia, he was known as a bold and persistent fellow. He worked hard and played hard. His drive won him honors at seminary and the hand of Coretta Scott, who had made up her mind to become a concert singer.

After the protest in Montgomery, Dr. King led a nationwide campaign to end unjust laws and practices. During the 1963 March on Washington, this great orator held a huge audience spellbound as he described his hopes for his country. In 1964 he won the Nobel Peace Prize for his practice of nonviolence in seeking social change.

News photos spotlighted Dr. King . . . jailed for peaceful demonstrations . . . conferring with the President . . . stabbed while autographing his first book . . . playing with his children. Then came the news flash that stunned the world: *Martin Luther King, Jr., killed by assassin's bullet.*

Dr. King had warned his followers: He would lead them close to the America he dreamed of. But others would finish the journey.

LILLIE G. PATTERSON

Martin Luther King, Jr., during the 1963 March on Washington

305

The other was to overcome the obstacles that kept most black Southerners from voting.

Ever since the failure of Reconstruction, blacks had been denied their constitutional right to vote. Laws requiring voters to pay a tax at the polls or to pass a difficult reading test or interpret some complicated passage in the state constitution all were designed to keep people who were poor or uneducated from voting, and in the South that meant most black people. Many brave people, both black and white, risked much—job, home, life itself—to register black citizens and help them vote.

In spring of 1963, Martin Luther King, Jr., led a new drive against Jim Crow laws in Birmingham, Alabama, the South's biggest industrial city. Thousands of young people marched downtown to picket the stores. Squads of police with dogs and fire hoses attacked the unresisting marchers and arrested them. Television cameras caught the terrifying scene for the whole country to see, and Americans everywhere condemned the brutality of the police. Finally, the city's business leaders were overwhelmed by the weight of public opinion. They agreed to end Jim Crow practices in the stores and to remedy other wrongs that blacks suffered.

Marching for Jobs and Freedom

That same year, 1963, was the 100th anniversary of the Emancipation Proclamation, which had declared the slaves free. Now, said black leaders, it was time to go to Washington and to ask for full and equal citizenship. Thus was born the March on Washington for Jobs and Freedom. On August 28, 1963, a quarter of a million people, both black and white, massed in Washington, D. C., to demonstrate peacefully for a new civil rights bill.

President Kennedy proposed new civil rights legislation, but Congress would have to enact it into law. Kennedy was wrestling with the problem of how to persuade a reluctant Congress when, on November 22, 1963, he was assassinated in Dallas, Texas. No event had so shocked the nation since the Japanese bombed Pearl Harbor. The country was plunged into deep mourning. Many people felt that the promising future Kennedy had represented died with him.

The new President, Lyndon B. Johnson, persuaded Congress to pass the Civil Rights Act of 1964. The law prohibited discrimination against blacks and other minorities in all the most important activities in American life. Congress also enacted a Voting Rights Act, as well as many proposals by President Johnson to help poor people, both black and white, train for better jobs. This package of programs was called the "War on Poverty." But another war—a shooting affair in faraway Vietnam— was beginning to capture Johnson's attention.

More than 200,000 people gathered near the Washington Monument during the 1963 March on Washington. Speakers such as Martin Luther King, Jr., challenged America to end all racial injustice. For black parents like the father below, some of King's words had special meaning: "I have a dream," King said, "that my four little children will one day . . . not be judged by the color of their skin but by the content of their character."

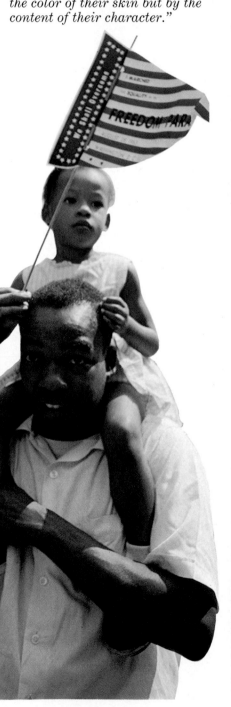

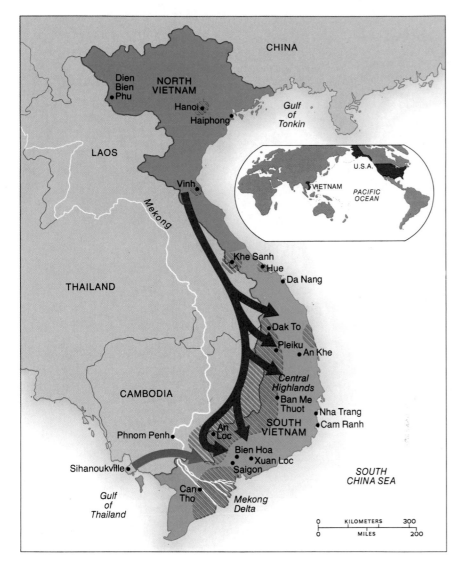

➡ Ho Chi Minh Trail
➡ Sihanouk Trail
▨ Major areas of fighting and/or bombing

Conflict between North and South Vietnam drew the United States into another costly Asian war (map left). As in Korea, Communists from the North tried to overthrow a U.S.-supported government in the South. During the late 1950s the U.S. sent several thousand military advisers to help the South Vietnamese forces. In the early 1960s, as the conflict grew worse, President John F. Kennedy sent 13,000 more advisers. In 1964, when Lyndon B. Johnson had become President, he reported the news that North Vietnam had fired on two U.S. warships in the Gulf of Tonkin. President Johnson responded by bombing North Vietnam and, in 1965, sent U.S. ground troops into battle. By 1968 more than half a million Americans were fighting in the cities and jungles of South Vietnam. Communist troops and supplies poured into the South along two major trails (map). Orange stripes indicate places where the fighting was heaviest. Combat raged along the delta of the Mekong River and along the Cambodian border. U.S. air raids stabbed far into the North, often targeting the capital city, Hanoi.

But years of bitter fighting failed to drive the North Vietnamese from the South. Many Americans at home became strongly opposed to U.S. participation in the war. Finally, in 1969, President Richard Nixon began bringing U.S. troops home. By 1973 most Americans were gone from South Vietnam. Two years later, the country fell to the Communists.

Vietnam had long been a part of the French Empire. In 1954 a nationalist-Communist government ousted the French and gained control of the northern half of the country. President Eisenhower had refused to send combat troops to help the French, despite the urgings of many of his advisers. In the South a proud but ineffectual anti-Communist leader took power. Many people turned against him, and by 1959 war had broken out between government forces and Communist guerrillas closely tied to North Vietnam. The U.S. sent advisers to help the South Vietnamese government. In the mid-1960s, as a Communist victory looked more and more likely, President Johnson decided to send combat troops. By 1968 more than half a million American soldiers were in Vietnam.

But even with so many American soldiers committed, the Americans and their South Vietnamese allies were not winning the war. Months of savage fighting turned into years. The American public watched as more and more young American men died in the jungles of South Vietnam.

People realized that the United States had been gradually drawn into a deadly war for reasons that were not entirely clear. Growing

U. S. Marines duck as enemy shells explode an ammunition dump in Khe Sanh, South Vietnam (left). Some 56,000 American troops died in the Vietnam War; more than 300,000 others were wounded. "How many of us won't be around tomorrow?" one marine wrote in his diary. Vietnamese civilians (below) also suffered terribly. Hundreds of thousands were killed. Survivors were often left homeless and hungry.

War in Vietnam brought conflict to Americans at home. Above, banner-carrying protesters parade past the Capitol Building in Washington, D. C. At right, a young demonstrator stuffs flowers into the guns of military policemen. Into the mid-1960s, most Americans supported the U. S. involvement in Vietnam. But as the fighting dragged on, public opinion became bitterly divided. Why, many people asked, were Americans spilling blood in a war in far-off Asia? Students taunted President Johnson with the chant, "Hey! Hey! LBJ! How many kids did you kill today?"

numbers of young people began to burn their draft cards. They organized anti-war marches, wore peace symbols, waved the North Vietnamese flag. Other Americans watched the protests with shock and often anger. Bitter arguments took place among family members. Not since the Civil War had Americans been so divided.

On April 4, 1968, an assassin shot and killed Martin Luther King, Jr., in Memphis, Tennessee. In cities across the country, black people rose up in outraged rioting, fighting police and burning whole neighborhoods to the ground. Then on June 5 another assassin struck. This time the victim was Senator Robert F. Kennedy, younger brother of the late President and himself a candidate for the Democratic presidential nomination. Few Americans could remember a more distressing time in our history.

Peace at Last

Richard M. Nixon, elected to succeed President Johnson, faced the task of ending the war. He began to pull out American troops while stepping up large-scale bombing raids. After four more years of death in Vietnam and divisive bitterness at home, peace accords were signed in January 1973. The U. S. withdrew, leaving Vietnam to the Communists.

The peace came just in time for Nixon: A struggle to save his Presidency now engulfed him. Seven months before, five employees of Nixon's reelection committee had been caught breaking into Democratic Party headquarters in the Watergate building in Washington, D. C. In spite of Nixon's frantic efforts to cover up the truth, the story of a fantastic conspiracy began to unfold—a conspiracy masterminded by the President's closest aides to illegally harass and weaken political opposition. After the affair was exposed in the press, many of Nixon's top assistants were sentenced to prison for their involvement, and the President was threatened with impeachment—a charge of misconduct brought by the House of Representatives. Rather than face the dishonor, Nixon resigned from office, the first President ever to do so.

As the seventies rolled on, Americans began to put Vietnam behind them and turn to new issues. One of the most far-reaching was a new civil rights movement, this time on behalf of a group that make up a majority of America's population—women. The "Feminist Movement," or "Women's Liberation," as the news media call it, had won a string of victories. These included laws that required giving women the same pay as men for the same work, the same opportunity as men to try for and get almost any kind of job or office, and, for married women, the same rights as their husbands to borrow money or sign contracts.

In the 1980s, Americans still faced some of the same problems they had worried about since the end of World War II—especially the dangerous rivalry with the Soviet Union and the terrifying threat of nuclear war. But the society that dealt with these problems had changed greatly. The American people enjoyed more genuine equality than ever before in the nation's history.

Gerald R. Ford (upper) takes the presidential oath on August 9, 1974. The man he replaced, Richard M. Nixon, is seen on television (lower) saying goodbye to his staff before departing that same day. Nixon's fall resulted from a series of events known as "Watergate." In June 1972 five men were caught ransacking the offices of the Democratic Party in a Washington, D. C., building called Watergate. The burglary was soon linked to Nixon's Republican reelection committee and later to the White House itself. Nixon denied knowledge of the burglary. Tape-recorded conversations showed that Nixon had known about it and had tried to hinder an FBI inquiry. Facing almost certain impeachment, Nixon chose to resign.

Epilogue

*It looked as if a night of
dark intent
Was coming, and not only a
night, an age.
Someone had better be prepared
for rage.*

When Robert Frost published these lines in 1926, his poet's eye looked ahead many years. He saw dark days. Perhaps he saw oil spills on the sea, the dying marshes, the piles of poisonous waste. Perhaps he saw Americans still denied their rightful opportunities. And over all of us he may have seen the threat of cataclysmic war.

Robert Frost also saw that anger would come. He saw that we would fight to save our land—and ourselves.

Our land is big and varied. We use more than half of it for growing crops and raising livestock. Unlike many other countries, we feed ourselves.

Much of the rest of the land also serves us. Mines and oil wells give us riches from the earth. Rushing rivers power factories that make everything from plows to giant airplanes.

All that work has been hard on the land. Stripped of trees and plowed too often, land loses its fertile topsoil. Invisible chemicals rise into the sky from factory smokestacks and fall as "acid rain." Smog drifts over our national parks.

In our society the struggle for equality persists. Exactly 20 years after Martin Luther King,

Inspecting oil at a Louisiana refinery

Boeing jets under construction, Everett, Washington

Harvesting wheat in Oklahoma

312

Jr., led the 1963 March on Washington for civil rights, people marched again. Blacks, women, the handicapped, the elderly carried signs that said, "We still have a dream: jobs, peace, freedom."

Peace? The world is bristling with missiles. "Sometimes these weapons make it all seem so worthless. . . . Sometimes I wonder why I should be doing my homework or why I should bother to get up in the morning," a

Tiny "chip," the computer's brain

teenager said at a peace rally.

Problems. Ever since people from many nations came together to make one nation, Americans have been solving problems.

The American solution is the same as ever: work together to change old ways. In New Jersey, people make a park out of a dump. In Pennsylvania, people mix waste sulphur with asphalt to fix roads. In West Virginia, people reclaim a surface coal mine as pastureland.

The Constitution makes change possible by giving us the right to speak out and to vote. Environmentalists persuaded Congress to pass laws to clean up our air and water. Blacks and Hispanics showed their power by electing many candidates to city and state

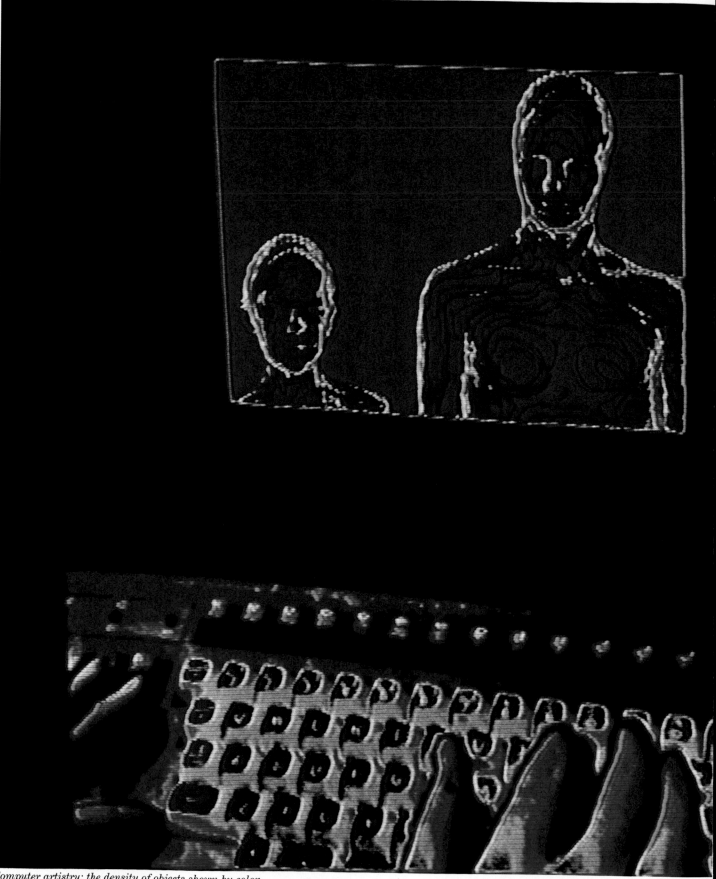

Computer artistry: the density of objects shown by color

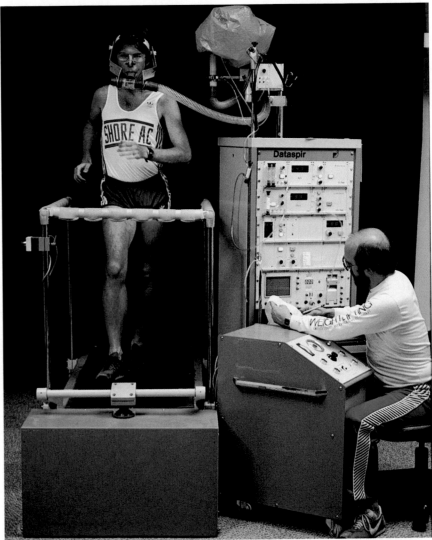

Computer measuring an athlete's lung capacity, Olympic Training Center, Colorado

A robot programmed to weld machinery, Danbury, Connecticut

315

offices. Women's groups helped persuade President Reagan to appoint a woman to the Supreme Court.

The nuclear freeze movement sparked debate and informed lawmakers and the President of many Americans' deep concern. Together we can diminish the threat of war if we insist that our leaders work hard to reduce world tensions.

Discoveries also change our society. We send a man to the moon, a spacecraft to Saturn. Soon people will live and work in space stations. Satellites—our eyes in the sky—watch the weather and warn of potential danger. They scan the earth for mineral deposits, thus helping us to plan for the future.

Part of that future arrived with the development of a magic "chip": the heart and brain of the computer. Suddenly, computers were leading us along new paths. In a hospital, a computer full of facts about diseases helps doctors treat patients. In an automobile factory, where 30 workers once welded 60 cars an hour, computers guide robots welding 100 cars an hour.

Computers will bring changes in the way we live, as did the car and the jet plane, the telephone and the TV set. How they change our society depends on how we use them. The time line, *America on Parade*, shows how long Americans have been making choices. Now, more than ever, our choices affect people the world over. Our fate is closely linked with theirs.

The poet Archibald MacLeish once said, "the future is America's to shape, not because we have many planes or great numbers of ships or rich industrial resources but because we have the power as a people to conceive so great a future . . . because we have behind us a tradition of imagination.

"But because we have the power we have also a responsibility to use the power. While there still is time."

Crowd at Kool Jazz Festival, St. Louis, Missouri, 1983

316

Good Reading

*An asterisk indicates fiction.

████████████████

Nomads, Explorers, and Settlers
Asimov, Isaac. *The Shaping of North America: From Earliest Times to 1763.* Houghton, 1973.
Bakeless, Katherine and John. *They Saw America First.* Lippincott, 1957.
Baker, Betty. *Settlers and Strangers: Native Americans of the Desert Southwest and History As They Saw It.* Macmillan, 1977.
Campbell, Elizabeth. *The Carving on the Tree.* Little, 1968.
Ceserani, Gian. *Christopher Columbus.* Random, 1979.
Coy, Harold. *Man Comes to America.* Little, 1973.
Golding, Morton. *The Mystery of the Vikings in America.* Harper, 1973.
Hays, Wilma and R. Vernon. *Foods the Indians Gave Us.* Washburn, 1973.
Irwin, Constance. *Strange Footprints on the Land: Vikings in America.* Harper, 1980.
Jacobs, W. J. *Samuel de Champlain: A Visual Biography.* Watts, 1974.
Lyttle, Richard. *People of the Dawn.* Atheneum, 1980.
Morison, Samuel. *The Story of the "Old Colony" of New Plymouth, 1620-1692.* Knopf, 1956.
Siegel, Beatrice. *A New Look at the Pilgrims: Why They Came to America.* Walker, 1977.
Steele, William. *Talking Bones: Secrets of Indian Mound Builders.* Harper, 1978.
Viereck, Phillip, editor. *The New Land: Discovery, Exploration, and Early Settlement of Northeastern United States.* John Day, 1967.
Williams, Barry. *The Struggle for North America.* McGraw, 1969.
*Baker, Betty. *Walk the World's Rim.* Harper, 1965.
*Bulla, Clyde. *John Billington, Friend of Squanto.* Crowell, 1956.
*Clapp, Patricia. *Constance: A Story of Early Plymouth.* Lothrop, 1968.
*O'Dell, Scott. *The King's Fifth.* Houghton, 1966.

Colonies in the Wilderness
Dickinson, Alice. *The Colony of Massachusetts.* Watts, 1975.
———. *Taken by the Indians: True Tales of Captivity.* Watts, 1976.
Earle, Alice. *Child Life in Colonial Days.* Darby, 1980.
———. *Customs and Fashions in Old New England.* Tuttle, 1973.
Gill, Harold, Jr., and Ann Finlayson. *Colonial Virginia.* Nelson, 1973.
Lawson, Don. *The Colonial Wars: Prelude to the American Revolution.* Abelard-Schuman, 1972.

Meltzer, Milton. *All Times, All Peoples: A World History of Slavery.* Harper, 1980.
Perl, Lila. *Slumps, Grunts, and Snickerdoodles: What Colonial America Ate and Why.* Seabury, 1975.
Raskin, Joseph and Edith. *Tales of Indentured Servants.* Lothrop, 1978.
Rich, Louise. *King Philip's War, 1675-76.* Watts, 1972.
Scott, John. *Settlers on the Eastern Shore, 1607-1750.* Knopf, 1967.
Tunis, Edwin. *Colonial Craftsmen: The Beginnings of American Industry.* Crowell, 1976.
———. *Colonial Living.* Crowell, 1976.
———. *Shaw's Fortune: The Picture Story of a Colonial Plantation.* Crowell, 1976.
———. *The Tavern at the Ferry.* Crowell, 1973.
Yates, Elizabeth. *Amos Fortune, Free Man.* Dutton, 1967.
*Petry, Ann. *Tituba of Salem Village.* Crowell, 1964.
*Speare, Elizabeth. *Calico Captive.* Houghton, 1957.
*———. *The Sign of the Beaver.* Houghton, 1983.

From Colonies to States
Bakeless, Katherine and John. *Signers of the Declaration.* Houghton, 1969.
Commager, Henry, and Richard Morris, editors. *The Spirit of 'Seventy-Six.* Harper, 1967.
DePauw, Linda. *Founding Mothers: Women in America in the Revolutionary Era.* Houghton, 1975.
Evans, R. E. *The War of American Independence.* Cambridge, 1976.
Fritz, Jean. *Traitor: The Case of Benedict Arnold.* Putnam, 1981.
Lomask, Milton. *The First American Revolution.* Farrar, 1974.
Mollo, John. *Uniforms of the American Revolution.* Macmillan, 1975.
Peterson, Harold. *The Book of the Continental Soldier.* Stackpole, 1968.
Sanderlin, George. *1776: Journals of American Independence.* Harper, 1968.
Scott, John. *Trumpet of a Prophecy: Revolutionary America, 1763-1783.* Knopf, 1969.
*Clapp, Patricia. *I'm Deborah Sampson: A Soldier in the War of the Revolution.* Lothrop, 1977.
*Collier, James and Christopher. *My Brother Sam Is Dead.* Four Winds, 1974.
*Finlayson, Ann. *Rebecca's War.* Warne, 1972.
*———. *Redcoat in Boston.* Warne, 1971.
*Forbes, Esther. *Johnny Tremain.* Houghton, 1943.
*Monjo, F. N. *A Namesake for Nathan: Being an Account of Captain Nathan Hale by His Twelve-Year-Old Sister Joanna.* Coward, 1977.
*Peck, Robert. *Fawn.* Little, 1975.
*Snow, Richard. *Freelon Starbird: Being a Narrative of the Extraordinary Hard-Ships Suffered by an Accidental Soldier in a Beaten Army During the Autumn

and Winter of 1776.* Houghton, 1976.
*Wibberley, Leonard. *John Treegate's Musket.* Farrar, 1959.

The Early Republic
Asimov, Isaac. *The Birth of the United States, 1763-1816.* Houghton, 1974.
Barry, James. *The Louisiana Purchase, April 30, 1803.* Watts, 1973.
Falkner, Leonard. *For Jefferson and Liberty: The United States in War and Peace, 1800-1815.* Knopf, 1972.
Loeper, John. *Going to School in 1776.* Atheneum, 1973.
Lomask, Milton. *The Spirit of 1787: The Making of Our Constitution.* Farrar, 1980.
Patterson, Lillie. *Benjamin Banneker: Genius of Early America.* Abingdon, 1978.
Starkey, Marion. *Lace Cuffs and Leather Aprons: Popular Struggles in the Federalist Era, 1783-1800.* Knopf, 1972.
Vaughan, Harold. *The Constitutional Convention, 1787.* Watts, 1976.
*Blos, Joan. *A Gathering of Days: A New England Girl's Journal, 1830-1832.* Scribner, 1979.
*Collier, James and Christopher. *The Winter Hero.* Four Winds, 1978.
*Finlayson, Ann. *Greenhorn on the Frontier.* Warne, 1974.
*Monjo, F. N. *Grand Papa and Ellen Aroon.* Holt, 1974.
*Wibberley, Leonard. *Leopard's Prey.* Farrar, 1971.
*Williamson, Joanne. *The Glorious Conspiracy.* Knopf, 1961.

Democracy on the Move
Bealer, Alex. *Only the Names Remain: The Cherokees and the Trail of Tears.* Little, 1972.
Fisher, Leonard. *The Factories.* Holiday, 1979.
Franchere, Ruth. *Westward by Canal.* Macmillan, 1972.
Jones, Kenneth. *War with the Seminoles.* Watts, 1975.
Laycock, George. *How the Settlers Lived.* McKay, 1980.
Macaulay, David. *Mill.* Houghton, 1983.
Meltzer, Milton. *Bound for the Rio Grande: The Mexican Struggle, 1845-1850.* Knopf, 1974.
Miller, Douglas. *Then was the Future: The North in the Age of Jackson, 1815-1850.* Knopf, 1973.
Nabokov, Peter, editor. *Native American Testimony.* Crowell, 1978.
Patterson, Lillie. *Frederick Douglass: Freedom Fighter.* Garrard, 1965.
Perl, Lila. *Hunter's Stew and Hangtown Fry: What Pioneer America Ate and Why.* Seabury, 1977.
Scott, John. *Hard Trials on My Way: Slavery and the Struggle Against It, 1800-1860.* Knopf, 1974.
Tunis, Edwin. *Frontier Living.* Crowell, 1976.
———. *The Young United States, 1783-1830.* Crowell, 1976.

*Hunt, Irene. *Trail of Apple Blossoms.* Follett, 1968.
*Lasky, Kathryn. *Beyond the Divide.* Macmillan, 1983.

Mid-Century Crisis
Asimov, Isaac. *Our Federal Union: The United States from 1816-1865.* Houghton, 1975.
Bacon, Margaret. *Rebellion at Christiana.* Crown, 1975.
Commager, Henry, editor. *The Blue and the Gray.* Irvington, 1980.
Commager, Henry, and Lynd Ward. *America's Robert E. Lee.* Houghton, 1951.
Fritz, Jean. *Stonewall.* Putnam, 1979.
Goldston, Robert. *The Coming of the Civil War.* Macmillan, 1972.
Graham, Lorenz. *John Brown: A Cry for Freedom.* Crowell, 1980.
Kemble, Frances. *Journal of a Residence on a Georgian Plantation in 1838-1839.* University of Georgia, 1984.
Lacy, Dan. *The Abolitionists.* McGraw, 1978.
Lawson, Don. *The United States in the Civil War.* Abelard-Schuman, 1977.
Lester, Julius. *To Be a Slave.* Dial, 1968.
Longsworth, Polly. *I, Charlotte Forten, Black and Free.* Crowell, 1970.
McPherson, James. *Marching Toward Freedom: The Negro in the Civil War, 1861-1865.* Knopf, 1968.
Petry, Ann. *Harriet Tubman: Conductor on the Underground Railroad.* Crowell, 1955.
Sandburg, Carl. *Abe Lincoln Grows Up.* Harcourt, 1940.
Scott, John. *Woman Against Slavery: The Story of Harriet Beecher Stowe.* Crowell, 1978.
Wellman, Paul. *Gold in California.* Houghton, 1958.
*Cummings, Betty. *Hew Against the Grain.* Atheneum, 1977.
*Fox, Paula. *The Slave Dancer.* Bradbury, 1973.
*Haynes, Betsy. *Cowslip.* Nelson, 1973.
*Hunt, Irene. *Across Five Aprils.* Follett, 1964.
*Meltzer, Milton. *Underground Man.* Bradbury, 1972.
*Vining, Elizabeth. *The Taken Girl.* Viking, 1972.

Rebuilding the South
Bontemps, Arna. *The Story of George Washington Carver.* Grosset, 1954.
Ingalls, Robert. *Hoods: The Story of the Ku Klux Klan.* Putnam, 1979.
Meltzer, Milton, editor. *In Their Own Words: A History of the American Negro.* 3 volumes. Crowell, 1964.
———. *Thaddeus Stevens and the Fight for Negro Rights.* Crowell, 1967.
Sterling, Dorothy, editor. *The Trouble They Seen: Black People Tell the Story of Reconstruction.* Doubleday, 1976.
Trelease, Allen. *Reconstruction: The Great Experiment.* Harper, 1971.
Washington, Booker. *Up From Slavery: An Autobiography.* Doubleday, 1963.

The Cowboy Saga

Adams, Andy. *The Log of a Cowboy.* University of Nebraska, 1970.

Baker, Donna. *Frederick Remington.* Children's, 1977.

Boesen, Victor, and Florence Graybill. *Edward S. Curtis, Photographer of the North American Indian.* Dodd, 1977.

Ehrlich, Amy. *Wounded Knee: An Indian History of the American West.* Adapted from *Bury My Heart at Wounded Knee* by Dee Brown. Holt, 1974.

Erdoes, Richard. *The Sun Dance People: The Plains Indians, Their Past and Present.* Knopf, 1972.

Freedman, Russell. *Children of the Wild West.* Houghton, 1983.

Goble, Paul and Dorothy. *Red Hawk's Account of Custer's Last Battle.* Pantheon, 1969.

Katz, William. *Black People Who Made the Old West.* Crowell, 1977.

Neihardt, John. *Black Elk Speaks: Being the Life Story of a Holy Man of the Oglala Sioux.* University of Nebraska, 1961.

Seidman, Laurence. *Once in the Saddle: The Cowboy's Frontier, 1866-1896.* Knopf, 1973.

Strait, Treva. *The Price of Free Land.* Lippincott, 1979.

Ward, Don. *Cowboys and Cattle Country.* American Heritage, 1961.

*Beatty, Patricia. *Wait for Me, Watch for Me, Eula Bee.* Morrow, 1978.

*Benchley, Nathaniel. *Only Earth and Sky Last Forever.* Harper, 1972.

*Brink, Carol. *Caddie Woodlawn.* Macmillan, 1973.

*O'Dell, Scott. *Sing Down the Moon.* Houghton, 1970.

*Wilder, Laura. *Little House on the Prairie.* Harper, 1953.

The American Colossus

Atkinson, Linda. *Mother Jones: The Most Dangerous Woman in America.* Crown, 1978.

Bales, Carol. *Tales of the Elders: A Memory Book of Men and Women who Came to America as Immigrants, 1900-1930.* Follett, 1977.

Blow, Michael. *Men of Science and Invention.* American Heritage, 1960.

Boardman, Fon, Jr. *America and the Gilded Age, 1876-1900.* Walck, 1972.

Faber, Doris. *Oh, Lizzie! The Life of Elizabeth Cady Stanton.* Lothrop, 1972.

Freedman, Russell. *Immigrant Kids.* Dutton, 1980.

Holland, Ruth. *Mill Child.* Macmillan, 1970.

Katz, William and Jacqueline. *Making Our Way: America at the Turn of the Century in the Words of the Poor and Powerless.* Dial, 1975.

Meigs, Cornelia. *Jane Addams: Pioneer of Social Justice.* Little, 1970.

Meltzer, Milton. *Bread—and Roses: The Struggle of American Labor, 1865-1915.* Knopf, 1967.

Novotny, Ann. *Strangers at the Door.* Chatham, 1983.

Sandler, Martin. *The Way We Lived: A Photographic Record of Work in a Vanished America.* Little, 1977.

Sung, Betty. *The Chinese in America.* Macmillan, 1972.

Weisberger, Bernard. *Captains of Industry.* American Heritage, 1966.

*Sachs, Marilyn. *Call Me Ruth.* Doubleday, 1982.

*Skurzynski, Gloria. *The Tempering.* Houghton, 1983.

*Yep, Laurence. *Dragonwings.* Harper, 1975.

Becoming a World Power

Bird, Caroline. *The Invisible Scar.* McKay, 1966.

Churchill, Allen. *Over Here! An Informal Re-Creation of the Home Front in World War I.* Dodd, 1968.

Davis, Daniel. *Behind Barbed Wires: The Imprisonment of Japanese Americans During World War II.* Dutton, 1982.

Goldston, Robert. *The Road Between the Wars: 1918-1941.* Dial, 1978.

Graff, Stewart. *The Story of World War II.* Dutton, 1978.

Greenfield, Eloise. *Mary McLeod Bethune.* Crowell, 1977.

Hamilton, Virginia. *W.E.B. Du Bois: A Biography.* Crowell, 1972.

Hoobler, Dorothy and Thomas. *An Album of World War I.* Watts, 1976.

Jantzen, Steven. *Hooray for Peace, Hurrah for War: The United States During World War I.* Knopf, 1971.

Katz, William. *An Album of the Great Depression.* Watts, 1978.

Lawson, Don. *An Album of World War II Home Fronts.* Watts, 1980.

———. *FDR's New Deal.* Crowell, 1979.

———. *The Secret World War II.* Watts, 1978.

Marrin, Albert. *Overlord: D-Day and the Invasion of Europe.* Atheneum, 1982.

McElvaine, Robert, editor. *Down and Out in the Great Depression.* University of North Carolina, 1983.

Meltzer, Milton. *Brother, Can You Spare a Dime? The Great Depression, 1929-1933.* Knopf, 1969.

———. *Never to Forget: The Jews of the Holocaust.* Harper, 1976.

Meltzer, Milton, and August Meier. *Time of Trial, Time of Hope: The Negro in America, 1919-1941.* Doubleday, 1966.

Roosevelt, Eleanor. *This I Remember.* Greenwood, 1975.

Stallings, Laurence. *The Story of the Doughboys.* Harper, 1966.

Terkel, Studs. *Hard Times: An Oral History of the Great Depression.* Pantheon, 1970.

*Hooks, William. *Circle of Fire.* Atheneum, 1982.

*Taylor, Mildred. *Let the Circle Be Unbroken.* Dial, 1981.

*Uchida, Yoshiko. *Journey to Topaz.* Scribner, 1971.

Americans in the Nuclear Age

Branley, Franklyn. *Feast or Famine? The Energy Future.* Harper, 1980.

Collins, Michael. *Flying to the Moon and Other Strange Places.* Farrar, 1976.

Englebardt, Stanley. *Miracle Chip: The Microelectronic Revolution.* Lothrop, 1979.

Greenfield, Eloise. *Rosa Parks.* Crowell, 1973.

Halacy, Dan. *Nuclear Energy.* Watts, 1978.

Haskins, James. *The Life and Death of Martin Luther King, Jr.* Lothrop, 1977.

Ingalls, Robert. *Point of Order: A Profile of Senator Joe McCarthy.* Putnam, 1981.

Lawson, Don. *The United States in the Vietnam War.* Crowell, 1981.

Patterson, Lillie. *Martin Luther King, Jr.* Garrard, 1969.

Pringle, Laurence. *Lives at Stake: The Science and Politics of Environmental Health.* Macmillan, 1980.

Sasek, Miroslav. *This is the United Nations.* Macmillan, 1968.

Siegel, Beatrice. *An Eye on the World: Margaret Bourke-White, Photographer.* Warne, 1980.

Sterling, Philip. *Sea and Earth: The Life of Rachel Carson.* Crowell, 1970.

Stevenson, Janet. *The School Segregation Cases: (Brown v. Board of Education of Topeka and Others).* Watts, 1973.

UPI and American Heritage Magazine. *Four Days: The Historical Record of the Death of President Kennedy.* American Heritage, 1964.

Overview

Caney, Steven. *Kids' America.* Workman, 1978.

Clements, John. *Chronology of the United States.* McGraw, 1975.

Hoople, Cheryl. *As I Saw It: Women Who Lived the American Adventure.* Dial, 1978.

Marzio, Peter, editor. *A Nation of Nations: The People Who Came to America as Seen Through Objects and Documents Exhibited at the Smithsonian Institution.* Harper, 1976.

Scott, John. *The Ballad of America.* Southern Illinois University, 1983.

Trager, James. *The People's Chronology.* Holt, 1979.

Urdang, Lawrence. *Timetables of American History.* Simon, 1983.

Weitzman, David. *My Backyard History Book.* Little, 1975.

Wolk, Allan. *The Naming of America.* Nelson, 1977.

We also recommend these books published by the National Geographic Society:

The American Cowboy in Life and Legend. 1972.

The Civil War. 1969.

In the Footsteps of Lewis and Clark. 1970.

Our Country's Presidents. 1981.

The Revolutionary War. 1967.

Visiting Our Past. 1977.

We Americans. 1975.

The Wild Shores: America's Beginnings. 1974.

The World of the American Indian. 1979.

Acknowledgments

We would like to thank the people and organizations who contributed their time and knowledge to this book. Special thanks go to Walter Bradford, U. S. Army Center of Military History, Washington, D. C.; Jay Luvaas, U. S. Army War College, Carlisle Barracks, Pa.; the staff of the National Geographic Library; Phyllis Gibbs Sidorsky, National Cathedral School; Nina K. Schwartz, St. Alban's School; the Smithsonian Institution's National Museum of American History for allowing us to photograph objects in their collection; and the historical societies and museums which sent us illustrations.

We are also indebted to Jim Baker, Plimouth Plantation; Charles Blockson, Temple University; Kathleen J. Bragdon, Dennis Stanford, and William C. Sturtevant, Smithsonian Institution; the Cheshire Cat Bookstore; Georgia B. Bumgardner, American Antiquarian Association; John E. Carter, Nebraska State Historical Society; Norman Miller Cary, Jr., and James W. Dunn, U. S. Army Center of Military History, Washington, D. C.; Robert Joseph Chandler, Wells Fargo Bank; David E. Collier and Mary Alice Quigley, Trenton Historical Society; Tom Cook, National Cattlemen's Association; David Dary, University of Kansas; Paul D. Escott, University of North Carolina at Charlotte; Richard D. Faust, National Park Service; Louise Fishbein; Charles Haberlein, Navy Memorial Museum, Washington, D. C.; and Michel Hardelay.

Also Rodney H. Hardinger, Hammermill Papers Group; Katharine W. Higgins, Ben Murch Elementary School, Washington, D. C.; Jack Hilliard, Air Force Museum, Dayton, Ohio; William Iseminger, Cahokia Mounds State Historical Site; Thomas Lackey, Terry Shaw, and Birgitta Wallace, Parks Canada; Henning Leidecker, American University; Jeff Meyerriecks; Don Montgomery, U. S. Navy; Robert M. Pennington, Bureau of Indian Affairs; John C. Reilly, Jr., Naval Historical Center, Washington, D. C.; Joseph P. Rivers, Normandy American Military Cemetery; Earl H. Robinson, Jr.; Samuel Stelle Smith; Kenneth L. Smith-Christmas, Marine Corps Historical Center, Washington, D. C.; George E. Stuart, National Geographic Society; Frank Taylor and the social studies specialists of Fairfax County Public Schools, Virginia; Maureen Taylor, Rhode Island Historical Society; and Richard Wilson, Montgomery County Schools, Maryland.

Illustrations Credits

The following abbreviations are used in this list: (t)-top; (c)-center; (b)-bottom; (r)-right; (l)-left; AR-Abby Aldrich Rockefeller Folk Art Center; AAS-American Antiquarian Society; AB-Anne S. K. Brown Military Collection, Brown University Library; Abbott-*National Museum of American History* by Shirley Abbott; BA-Bettman Archive; Barenholz-*American Antique Toys* by Bernard Barenholz and Inez McClintock; BB-Brown Brothers; BM-British Museum, London; CHS-Chicago Historical Society; CTHS-Connecticut Historical Society; EPD-E. P. Dutton, Inc.; GC-Granger Collection, NYC; HA-Harry N. Abrams, Inc.; HPW-Henry Francis du Pont Winterthur Museum; HSP-Historical Society of Pennsylvania; LC-Library of Congress; MCNY-Museum of the City of New York; MET-Metropolitan Museum of Art; MFA-Museum of Fine Arts, Boston; NA-National Archives; NGP-National Geographic Photographer; NGPA-National Geographic Publications Art; NGS-National Geographic Staff; NYHS-New-York Historical Society; NYPL-New York Public Library; PS-Pilgrim Society, Plymouth, Mass.; SI-Smithsonian Institution; TGI-Thomas Gilcrease Institute of American History and Art, Tulsa, Okla.; UPI-United Press International; WM-Woolaroc Museum, Bartlesville, Okla.; Yale-Yale University Art Gallery, Mabel Brady Garvan Collection.

Cover and 1-4, Gerard Huerta. 4-5, Medford Taylor. 6-7, Tim Thompson, Aperture Photo Bank. 9(t), Stephen J. Krasemann, DRK Photo. (b), SI: Breton Littlehales. 10, Michael A. Hampshire. 11, NGPA. 12-13, Tony Chen and NGPA. 13, NGPA. 14-15, Michael A. Hampshire. 15, David Brill. 16, Georg Gerster, Photo Researchers. (r), Milwaukee Public Mus. 16-17, John J. Egan, St. Louis Art Mus. 18-19, Charles Deas, TGI. 19, Paul Kane, 1845, Art Gal. of Ontario, Toronto. 20, W. Robert Moore. 21, Tony Chen and NGPA. 22-23, Michael A. Hampshire. 23, NGPA. 24-25, Percy Moran, 1892, U. S. Naval Acad. Mus. 25, Thomas Hart Benton, New York Power Auth. 26, Tony Chen and NGPA. 27(t), Steve Proehl, Photo Researchers. (b), NGPA. 28, John White, BM, Bridgeman Art Lib. 29(l), John White, BM, Fotomas Index. (r), John White, ca. 1585, BM. 30, William R. Leigh, WM. 31(t), Farrell Grehan. (b), Ira Block. 32-33, Richard Schlecht. 34, Percy Moran, PS. 34-35, Wayne McLoughlin. 36, NGPA. 36-37, GC. 38(t), Doris Lee, John Hancock Mutual Life Ins. Co. (bl), Alexander De

Batz, Peabody Mus., Harvard U. (br), Archaeological Survey of Canada, National Museums of Canada. 38-39, Utah Mus. of Natural Hist.: Victor R. Boswell, Jr., NGP. 39(tc and tr), PS. (cl), both, SI: Breton Littlehales. (c), "Historia Canadensis," François du Creux, 1664, British Lib. (cr), PS: Walter Meayers Edwards. (bl), New York State Mus. (br), Mus. of the American Indian, Heye Fdn., NY. 41(t), LC. (b), David Hiser. 42, NGPA. 43(t), Rufus Hathaway, 1795, Stephen Score Coll. (b), From Herman Moll's "Map of North America," ca. 1710, LC. 44-45, 1825, Garbisch Coll., MET. 45, Lowell Georgia. 46-47, John Berkey, Frank and Jeff Lavaty Assoc. 47, NGPA. 48-49, Edward Hicks, TGI. 49(t), HSP. (b), Arents Coll., NYPL. 50-51, I. N. Phelps Stokes Coll., NYPL. 51(l), John Lewis Stage. (r), John Dunsmore, 1928, NYHS. 52(t), William Birch, 1800, HSP. (b), Mariners' Mus., Newport News, Va. 53, Tony Chen and NGPA. 54(t), SI: Breton Littlehales. (b), AAS. 55, GC. 56-57, Robert Rakes for *Life*, Time, Inc.: Robert Crandall. 58(t), John Lewis Stage. (b), Ira Block. 59, CTHS. 60-61, Tony Chen and NGPA. 62, John Wollaston, ca. 1742, National Portrait Gal., London. 62-63, John Lewis Stage, Image Bank. 64(t), GC. (l), SI: Breton Littlehales. (c), Free Lib. of Phila. (r), Bucks Co. Hist. Soc., Mercer Mus. 64-65, NYHS. 65(tl), Wenham Mus., Wenham, Mass.: Breton Littlehales. (cl), HPW. (cr), SI: Breton Littlehales. (tr), AR. (br), Whaling Mus., New Bedford, Mass. 67(t), Benjamin West, 1770, National Gal. of Canada. (b), AB. 68(tl), NGPA. (tr), MET. (b), Massachusetts Hist. Soc. 69, George Cook, Virginia Hist. Soc. 70-71, GC. 72, Tony Chen and NGPA. 73, John Lewis Stage. 74-75, Winthrop Chandler, MFA. 76-77, John Lewis Stage. 77, Robert Edge Pine after Edward Savage, 1790, HSP. 78-79, Vladimir Kordic, Rumple, Inc. 80, Dir. of Army Education, England. 80-81, John Ward Dunsmore, 1915, NYHS. 82(t), LC: Victor R. Boswell, Jr., NGP. (b), AB. 83, NGPA. 84-85, Patricia A. Topper. 86-87, H. Charles McBarron, U. S. Army Center of Military History: Victor R. Boswell, Jr., NGP. 87, NGPA. 88, GC. 88-89, John Lewis Stage. 90(tl), John Carter Brown Lib., Brown U. (tr), Yale. (b), HPW. 91(l), NYHS. (r), NGPA. 92, U. of Michigan, William L. Clements Lib. 92-93, V. Zveg, 1969, U. S. Navy. 94-95, Louis-Nicholas Van Blarenberghe, 1786, Private coll. 95, NGPA. 96(t), GC. (l), AR. (c), John Lewis Stage. (r), Colonial Williamsburg Fdn. 97(tl), HSP: Victor R. Boswell, Jr., NGP. (tc), Yale. (tr), HPW. (bl), John Durand, ca. 1765, CTHS. (br), Ted Spiegel. 99(tl), Junius Brutus Sterns, Virginia Mus. of Fine Arts: Emory Kristoff, NGP. (b), Thomas L. Davies, National Park Serv. 100-101, NGS Lib. 101, AAS. 102, NGPA. 103(t), GC. (b), Atwater Kent Mus. 104(l), Mather Brown, 1785, New York Hist. Assoc., Cooperstown: Joseph H. Bailey and Larry

D. Kinney, both NGS. (r), Lisa Biganzoli, NGS. 105(t), LC: George F. Mobley, NGP. (b), NGPA. 106, Rembrandt Peale, NYHS. 106-107, Boqueto de Woieseri, CHS. 108, Tony Chen and NGPA. 109(t), Robert W. Madden, NGP. (b), Missouri Hist. Soc.: Dick Durrance II. 110, Acad. of Natural Sciences, Phila. 110-111, Royal Ontario Mus. 111, Jackson Co. (Mo.) Parks and Recreation: Breton Littlehales. 112, NGPA. 113, GC. 114-115, Thomas Birch, U. S. Naval Acad. Mus. 115, GC. 116, I. N. Phelps Stokes Coll., NYPL. 116-117, AB. 118(t), Johann Eckstein, 1788, MFA. (l), Isobel and Harvey Kahn Coll.: Breton Littlehales. (c), Friendship Firehouse, Alexandria, Va.: Victor R. Boswell, Jr., NGP. 118-119, HPW. 119(tl), Howard and Catherine Feldman Coll., EPD. (c and r), SI: Breton Littlehales. (b), MFA. 121(t), GC. (b), MET. 122(t), Herman Decker, Mus. of Art, R.I. School of Design. (b), HSP. 122-123, CTHS. 123, NGPA. 124, Henry Grosinsky. 124-125, Yale. 126-127, E. L. Henry, Albany Inst. of Hist. and Art. 127(tl), John William Hill, NYHS. (tr), Canal Mus. (b), Sam Abell. 128-129, MCNY. 129, Bostonian Soc.: Mark Sexton. 130-131, Alice R. H. Smith, Carolina Art Assoc., Gibbs Art Gal. 131(t), GC. (b), Lib. Co. of Phila. 132, NGPA. 132-133, GC. 134-135, Robert Lindneux, 1942, WM. 135, NGPA. 136, NYHS. 136-137(t), John Stobart, 1977, Wunderlich and Co. (b), Charles C. Nahl, 1856, Stanford U. Mus. of Art. 137, NGPA. 138, David Hiser. 138-139, William Henry Jackson, Scotts Bluff National Monument. 140, William Henry Huddle, Texas State Capitol. 141(t), Alamo Mus. (b), Texas State Capitol. 142, NGPA. 142-143, AB. 144(t), IBM Corp., Armonk, NY. (l), Daniel and Joanna Rose Coll., EPD. (c), Jimoxi Ostrowski Coll.: Steven Mays for Time-Life, Inc. 144-145, Bill Holland Coll. 145(tl), Cooper-Hewitt Mus., SI. (tc), MCNY. (tr), LC. (b), SI: Victor R. Boswell, Jr., NGP. 147(t), State Street Bank and Trust, Boston. (b), GC. 148, Noble, Missouri Hist. Soc. 148-149, Eyre Crowe, 1853, CHS. 149, NGPA. 150, Charles Blockson Coll. 151, Tony Chen and NGPA. 152-153, Patricia A. Topper. 154(l), NGPA. (r), Jodi Cobb, NGP. 154-155, John Steuart Curry, 1941, Kansas State Capitol. 156, NGPA. 157, AB. 158-159, Vladimir Kordic, Rumple, Inc. 160, LC. 161(t), West Point Mus. (c), CHS. (b), LC. 162-163, Patricia A. Topper. 164, CHS. 165(t), LC. (b), Union League Club, NY. 166, Edward D. Miner Lib., U. of Rochester School of Med. and Dent. 166-167(t), Kean Archives. (b), U. S. Military History Inst., Mollus-Mass Coll.: Joseph H. Bailey, NGP. 167(t), American Red Cross. (b), SI: Breton Littlehales. 168(t), LC. (b), GC. 169, AB. 170-171, AB. 171, Maryland Hist. Soc. 172, NGPA. 172-173, CHS. 174-175, Tom Lovell. 175(l), NGPA. (r), NGS Lib. 176-177, Morton Kunstler. 177, Farrell Grehan. 178(l), AR. (t), Winslow Homer, 1864; Art Inst. of Chicago. (b), Mariners' Mus., Newport

News, Va. 178-179, George H. Meyer Coll. 179(tl), SI: Bill Ray. (tr), SI: Breton Littlehales. (r), Dan Smith Coll.: Joseph D. Lavenburg, NGP. 181(t), GC. (b), Lib. Co. of Phila. 182-183, LC. 183, Tom Lea, 1939, Gen. Serv. Admin.: Breton Littlehales. 184, NYPL. 184-185, Virginia Hist. Soc. 186(t), William Wotherspoon, 1850, Hunter Mus. of Art. (b), Penn Community Services. 187, GC. 188(t), From *Budget of Fun: 1865-1866*, Frank Leslie. (b), SI: Breton Littlehales. 188-189, GC. 190, Hayes Presidential Center. 190-191, Patricia A. Topper. 192, GC. 193(t), BA. (b), Valentine Mus. 194(t), NAACP. (b), California Mus. of Photography. 194-195, LC. 196(t), Richard Norris Brooke, 1881; Corcoran Gal. of Art. (l), Abbott, HA: Michael Freeman and Robert Golden. (b), Mus. of the Confederacy. 196-197, Barenholz, HA: Bill Holland. 197(tl), Nancy and Gary Stass Coll., EPD. (tc), NYHS. (tr), Lester S. Levy Coll. (c), GC. (b), SI: Breton Littlehales. 199(t), James Walker, TGI. (b), Steven Fuller. 200(l), Huntington Lib., Calif. (c), Princeton U. Lib. 200-201, Clara McDonald Williamson, Wichita Art Mus. 202-203, Frederic Remington, 1911, TGI. 204, Tony Chen and NGPA. 205, CHS. 206-207, Vladimir Kordic, Rumple, Inc. 208-209(b), Huntington Lib., Calif. (t), LC: J.C.H. Grabill. 209, Santa Fe Railway. 210-211, California Hist. Soc. 211, Jo N. Mora. 212(tl), Glenbow-Alberta Inst. (r), NGPA. 212-213, GC. 214, NGPA. 214-215, William R. Leigh, WM. 216(l), NGPA. (r), SI. 217(t), Remington Art Mus., Ogdensburg, NY. (b), Eastern Washington State Hist. Soc. 218, NA. 219(t), SI. (b), NGPA. 220-221, W.H.D. Koerner, 1932, Buffalo Bill Hist. Soc., Cody, Wyo. 221, Nebraska State Hist. Soc. 222, Amon Carter Mus. 222-223, Nebraska State Hist. Soc. 223, NGPA. 224(t), David R. Phillips Coll. (l), H. J. Heinz Co. (c), Abbott, HA: Michael Freeman and Robert Golden. (r), SI: Breton Littlehales. 224-225, Bertrand Coll., U. S. Dept. of Interior, Breton Littlehales. 225(tl), Levi Strauss and Co. (cl), J. C. Allen and Son. (tr), Cooper-Hewitt Mus., SI. (c), CHS. (cr), Young Can Opener Coll.: Joseph D. Lavenburg, NGP. (br), Greeley Municipal Mus.: Ben Benschneider for Time-Life, Inc. 227(t), Yale U. (b), Montana Hist. Soc. 228(l), NGPA. (r), Oregon Hist. Soc. 229, LC. 230, LC. 230-231, National Steel Corp. 231(l), Lester S. Levy Coll. (r), LC. 232, LC. 233(t), GC. (c), SI: Breton Littlehales. (b), Abbott, HA: Michael Freeman and Robert Golden. 234-235(t), LC. (b), Free Lib. of Phila. 235(t), HSP. (b), SI: Breton Littlehales. 236, NYHS. 236-237, MCNY: Byron. 238, BA. 239(t), Wayne McLoughlin and NGPA. (b), NGS Lib. 240(t), NGPA. (b), LC. 240-241, LC. 241, George Eastman House. 242(t), LC. (b), George Eastman House: Lewis W. Hine. 243(l), BB. (r), LC. 244, GC. 245, BB. 246(t), CHS. (b), National Portrait Gal. 247(t), NGPA. (b), Culver Pictures, Inc.

Index

Illustrations are in **boldface type.** Map references are in *italic*. Text references are in lightface type.

Type composition by National Geographic's Photographic Services.
Color separations by Beck Engraving Co., Inc., Philadelphia, Pa.; Chanticleer Co., Inc., New York, N.Y.; The Lanman Progressive Companies, Washington, D. C. Printed and bound by R. R. Donnelley & Sons Co., Chicago, Ill. Paper by S. D. Warren, Boston, Mass.
Library of Congress CIP Data

Scott, John Anthony, 1916-
The story of America.

Bibliography: p.
Includes index.
1. United States—History—Juvenile literature.
[1. United States—History] I. National Geographic Book Service. II. Title.
E178.3.S35 1984   973   84-2018
ISBN 0-870-44-508-1
ISBN 0-870-44-535-9 (lib. bdg.)